Tin Pan

ASPIRATIONS

The Golly Goulding Story

as told to
Dave Lodge

Published in 2017 by GG Exports

ISBN: 978-1-5272-1135-3

INTRODUCTION

It would be impossible to tell Golly Goulding's life story in one book. He has packed so much in to his life so far that it would take a trilogy to even scratch the surface. Tin Pan Aspirations is telling some, but not all of Golly's fabulous story.

You will marvel, as I did, Golly's musical aspirations. He took his talent to London and to this day his abilities are recognised not just in the UK and Europe, but also in the USA. You will read how much even the great James Burton admires Golly's ability with the guitar.

But there is more to Golly than just musical talent, he is a very astute businessman. Follow his rise to the highest echelons of the antique business. This hard working man who has cleaned windows and reared pigs during his climb to the top of the tree is an example to us all.

Golly is a good husband and fine family man, there are not enough pages in this book to tell or describe the impact he has made on the people around him, there will never be another like him.

So don't be surprised if there are follow ups to this book, Tin Pan Aspirations. Because Golly Goulding is a man who dared to dream, then followed his dreams. Enjoy and share in his dreams and his achievements, you will be amazed.

But remember this book has only touched the surface of the life of an extraordinary man and his remarkable achievements.

Dave Lodge
Author

CONTENTS

To Mam and Dad and Carol
For the positivity they've always displayed
toward everything I've tried to do in life.

ACKNOWLEDGEMENTS

Mam and Dad, for all the right things they taught me when I was growing up.
Cousin Harold, for his skills as a craftsman.
Tommy Steele, for introducing me to Guitars and Rock n Roll Music.
Hank Marvin, for making it possible for me to play like him.
The Drovers, watching them rehearse at every opportunity.
Chuck Berry, for his obscure playing and paving the way for my own individual style.
Screaming Lord Sutch and The Savages, changing my musical direction completely.
Bill Parkinson. As I've said many times. "Without him there would never have been a Golly Goulding".
Mel Deane. The absolute best singer that ever lived and I was his Guitarist.
Alan Morrin, for persuading me to quit my day job at the age of 17.
Owen Williams, for teaching me how to go self-employed and be independant.
Carol my Wife / Girlfriend and Business partner, for believing in me and sticking by me through thick and thin.
Alexis Korner, for his pure passion and dedication to the British Blues Scene
Kevin Farmer, for introducing me to the Antique Business.
Jim Collins {Trade Antiques} for educating me and giving me a leg up in the early days.
Gordon Dyson. He knew every trick in the book and I learned much from him.
My three children, Jay, Rob and Carol-Anne who all turned out well.
Steve Searle. Brilliant Musician and an inspiration.
Jay Goulding, for helping to make us Worldwide Antique Dealers.
All our American friends and loyal customers - Dan Pond, Rob Steeves, Larry and Maria Dobos and many many more.
James Burton. As well as my Guitar Hero, now my personal friend.
Dave Lodge. Who has become our friend and inspired me to tell this story.
Russ Holden. For his expertise, experience and making this book possible.

CHAPTER 1

THE BEGINNING OF IT ALL

Stephen James (Golly) Goulding was born on the 2nd of August 1947, in Whitehead Street, Barrow in Furness. Back then it was still in Lancashire, now of course a change in boundaries means that it is now   part of Cumbria. Stephen was Christened at the local Church, St. Marks, on Rawlinson Street. His mother loved the name Steve after the famous radio star, Steve Conway. Incidentally the author also thinks that Steve Conway was wonderful, one of my favourite songs, "Take Care My Foolish Heart" was a hit for him. Sadly he had a heart condition and died at a young age. Anyway when the Vicar asked his Father Jack "Is it Stephen spelt with a PH"? Jack mistakenly said "Yes" Of course his Mother wanted it spelt with a V so his name could be shortened to Steve.

Whitehead Street   *St Marks Church*

It wasn't long after the end of the war and because Stephen's Dad worked as a labourer for Stephens Uncle Bert who was a 'Slater'. Steve's first months of life were spent living in Barrow.

1947 being one of the hottest summers on record, then the winter was one the coldest. Maybe that is why Golly has the varied abilities that you will read about as we tell his story.

Successful business man, brilliant and innovative Guitarist, these are just two of the amazing abilities that Golly Goulding has displayed throughout his life. Golly possesses a speed of thought and movement that would have guaranteed success in any field he had chosen to enter. I for one as the author am very glad he chose to play the guitar.

Mam and Dad's wedding photo

During that very severe winter in 1947, Golly's Dad and his Uncle Bert went out 'Snow Shifting'. Because there were such heavy snow falls houses were blocked by the height of the drifting snow. This snow shifting involved Golly's Dad and Uncle Bert taking their shovels and clearing all the snow from pathways and drives in the area. Golly thinks they charged about half a crown, (twelve and half pence in today's money).

During the spring of 1948, Golly's Mam and Dad and Golly of course returned to Lancaster. They had nowhere to live so they moved into Golly's Nana and Granddad's house on Lune Street. The three of them in one room, they were a desperate to find a flat or rooms anywhere. Luckily they heard about a house on Derby Road, No 48, two streets away that was empty. A couple had decided to take it and in order to cut costs they were willing to rent out a couple of rooms. Well of course Golly's Mam and Dad jumped at the opportunity, they immediately took it on, moved in and they thought they were in heaven.

Derby road, Lancaster

Not so for the couple who had taken on the house in the first place. They wanted to get away because the house was too rough. There was no electricity for starters. As a consequence of this Golly's Mam and Dad ended up having the whole house to them-selves. It has to be said that the rent was a burden, but they somehow managed to afford it.

Golly's Mam and Dad had an insurance man called Mr Briggs, employed by "Royal Liver" he, as was the way in those days, called at the house to collect the premiums. On one of his visits he told them "I can get you a mortgage on this house for a fixed interest and it will work out at the same price as the rent". A mortgage, for a young working class couple? Almost unheard of in those days. Golly's Mam was for it, but his dad understandably was scared. He said, "I don't want a rope around my neck for the next 25 years". Nevertheless, Golly's Mam persuaded his Dad to take it on. The price £500...... a lot of money in those days.

Well now the young family really were in Heaven, home owners in 1948, that was pretty uncommon in Golly's area. The bought some utility furniture etc and after a few years they got electricity installed. The house became their little palace. Having said that, there was the downside of an outside toilet and no bathroom, still the family spent a very happy 17 years there.

King George VI inspecting troops in Lancaster (including Golly's dad, Jack. See arrow)

Golly's Dad was an ex soldier who had served in the 2nd World War. This left him with a sense of duty so he was enlisted into 'The Territorial Army', they were sometimes referred to as 'The Terriers'. In spite of working shifts Golly's Dad would go down to the Drill Hall between those shifts. His rank was Sergeant Major and he was paid a few bob a week, plus he was paid to go away to camp for two weeks every summer, which was a real bonus for the family. Golly remembers that when his Dad came home he always brought him a good present.

Ireland 1950.
L to R Uncle Vincent, Dad, Mam, Steve

Golly remembers his best ever present a pair of light blue jeans and a flashy shirt, a bit like Tommy Steele used to wear. When Golly went out in that outfit, he was "Tommy Steele".

In 1950 Golly's Dad, who was from Galway in Southern Ireland, had not been back home since joining The British Army in 1939, so he decided to take the family over for a visit. Although they didn't have

much money Golly's Mam and Dad saved up as best they could so that the family could have their first holiday in Galway. Golly was only three and as he says he remembers next to nothing about it.

He does remember being told that they sailed from Heysham to Belfast and that the crossing was as smooth as silk. The return journey was horrendous, the Irish sea is notorious for being rough. On this occasion

Mam & Steve in Ireland

it was it was extremely rough!! Everybody

on board was being violently seasick. With the exception of Golly, he slept through the whole crossing, obviously as he says he doesn't remember but it was something that the family talked about for many years. Apparently when his Mam and Dad went to bed the whole room was still spinning. They were often heard to say, "Never again"! They never did get on the boat again, but many years later they did go back to Galway, but this time by plane.

Golly's, earliest memories are of being 18 months old and living on Derby Road Lancaster. Cold mornings with Jack Frost practising his artistic talents on the windows of the houses in the street, hoary breath in the air outside. Breakfast of bread porridge (Pobs) washed down with cod liver oil and a teaspoon of Baby orange juice.

Then what turned out to be the joy of Ryelands Nursery School and walking across 'Johnny's Field' with his Mam through the cold air. This first day was an important day Golly believes and possible shaping his future life. As he says he got a good dinner, still very important and then he would go to sleep on a small camp bed during the afternoon. He also got a new playmate, Billy Elliot. His Mam would tell him in later times that she cried every day when she left him.

As the days went by Steve would have different people who would pick him up and take him home. These people included their neighbour Jacky and sometimes his Dad who would come for Steve on his bike and let him ride home on the cross bar.

There was one very important day in Steve's young life and he remembers it very well, because he was exactly four and a half years old. This day was the 6th of February 1952. Steve's Dad pointed out to him that the flag on Lancaster Castle was being flown at half mast. This was done to recognise the sad passing of King George VI. The day was remembered for another reason, their bicycle skidded on the ice and both Dad and Steve fell off.

Steve & cousin Stan

The name that Steve is known by is Golly and it would appropriate to explain how he got the name at this point in the narrative. It was probably around mid 1952 as Steve recalls it, just before he started school when he and his cousin Stan were learning to draw and spell very basic simple words.

Stan learned to spell Steve's name, because he thought it was two words, STEP HEN. Having mastered that, he attempted to spell his surname. This was more difficult as it is Goulding, pronounced Golding. Stan got as far as G O L, then before Steve could correct him, "That's Gollywog" he said, or "Golly", "Stephen Golly" he called him.

Golly's and Gollywogs were in those days very popular items. For example there was the famous Robertson's Golly being used to advertise their products, Jam, Marmalade, Jelly etc. You could even collect paper ones from the jars and send away for a metal badge Also there were Books, Jigsaws and a soft toy known as a "Golly". It has to be said that "Golly" was a pretty common word back then.

As soon as Stan started calling him Golly all Steve's friends and cousins and playmates heard him and of course that became his name. Amazingly the name stuck and he is known as "Golly" Worldwide. Even the business, (Started in 1967) is known as G.G. There is only his Mam and a couple of old relatives that still call him Steve.

Time moved on and at the age of five, in September 1952 Golly started to attend Skerton Infants School. On his first day Steve's (Golly's) little playmate Billy Elliot, who together had gone through nursery school, sat next to him in class. The teacher Miss Mothersill had a great way of teaching them the alphabet, Steve remembers it to this day. She told the class A is for Apple, B is for Ball, C is for Cat, etcetera. It seems Steve (Golly) was a good student and when it came round to the first test, he came second out of the whole class. This early success made his Mam think that Steve was really clever when it came to his school work. Steve thought so too and continued to do well until he was older, when as he put it, he suddenly realised that he just could not figure out what was going on. More of that problem later.

First school test showing little Steve came second in the class!

One thing Steve had at the age of six and still has now was the ability to make friends, he gets on well with people, this meant that he had lots of playmates at school and enjoyed all the games that they played.

In 1953 Steve moved up to Miss Dyson's class and Steve continued to impress the school and his Mam with his learning ability. Although it may be surprising to know that lessons were still being taught at old oak desks with the benches attached. Teaching aids were chalk with slates for the pupils to write on. People may think that such implements were obsolete at this time having been used in Victorian and Edwardian times, but at Skerton Infants School in Miss Dyson's class circa 1953 these were the only teaching aids available.

1953 was a very significant year because the 2nd of June was the Queen's Coronation Day and Golly remembers it vividly. The reason being that all the houses on Derby Road were decorated with bunting (triangular flags) coloured, red, white and blue.

Another reason why Golly remembers that date was the fact that in the local newsagents shop window was a model of the Golden Coronation Coach and Horses, made from die-cast lead and gilded over, it was priced at seven shillings and sixpence. Unbeknown to everyone, Golly's Mam, Anne, had been paying sixpence a week in advance, so that she could buy it as a souvenir for her son. Golly still treasures the souvenir to this day. That Coronation Coach and a small Prayer Book are two of the very few things that Golly has from his childhood.

Golly's treasured Coronation coach

There was to be a fancy dress competition held in the next street, Earl Street and young Golly was keen to take part in it. His Mam made him a pirate suit from 'Blackout material'. This is what had been used during the war to hang in the windows of the houses at night. It prevented any light escaping and being seen by the enemy bombers as they flew over.

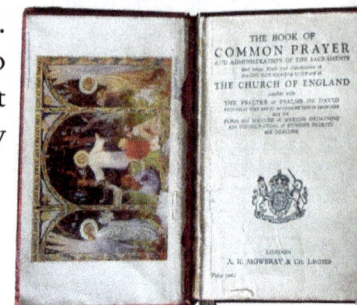

Golly's childhood Prayer book

He had a plastic cutlass tucked down his belt and an eye patch to complete the look, he really did look the part. Now Golly had seen a few pirate films and was excited about being a pirate, that was until it came to the day of the competition. He went shy and refused to take part. His Mam was having none of it and when the parade was passing the house she pushed him into the line. The procession proceeded on to Earl Street and guess who won second prize? Yes, lile Golly. Afterwards there was a huge street party, with jelly, ice-cream all for free. Then in the evening there was a magnificent firework display In Ryeland's Park. A very memorable day in Golly's life and one he will never forget.

Golly in his Cubs uniform

We find ourselves in 1954 and Golly used to see a neighbour of his Ian Kidd in a very smart and impressive uniform, he was in the Cubs One day he asked Golly, "Would you like to join? You are old enough now".

Golly wanted to join, so he asked his Mam and she agreed. So he joined the 32nd Lancaster, St Luke's Cubs. As Golly says, he really enjoyed going to Cubs and he found a lot of good mates there. He thinks he had a couple of years in the Cubs, but as various people left so did he.

Golly never wanted to progress to the Scouts. He didn't like the idea of being with the big lads and men in shorts scared him a bit. They just didn't look right!

In September 1954 aged seven, Golly started at Skerton Junior School, in Miss Monk's class, Form 1B. Golly was still achieving good marks in class. In fact he was one of the best pupils in his year. Everything was coming naturally to him and he clearly understood all the things that Miss Monks had taught him. The staff were so pleased with his progress it was decided, after discussions with the Head Mistress, Miss Ochiltree, (who later became a magistrate) that Golly would move up to Form 2A, which was Miss Shaw's class in September of 1955.

This was a terrible decision from Golly's point of view, it just wasn't for him and he was very unhappy in this class. As he puts it, he was with the Class A snobs, who he did not like. He simply could not grasp the lessons and worse still from his point of view, he really missed his mates.

Steve can clearly remember Miss Ochiltree and Miss Shaw discussing the situation, Miss Olchiltree saying, "Stephen clearly isn't happy here". So they shifted him to 2B, what a difference. 2B had a brilliant teacher Mr Rigby who had just finished his National Service in the Army.

Apart from the other lessons Mr Rigby entertained them with great stories about his time serving with the Army. One of the stories he told them was about a time when the Army left the camp where they had been bivouacked, as they moved out the Arabs moved in. The camp was well set out with wooden billets, which were only a few years old and had been built with no little effort and skill. As soon as the Arabs moved in they started pulling the billets down, for firewood! As Mr Rigby explained wood is in very short supply in the desert and it is very cold at night and firewood was more use to them than billets. Within days the whole camp had disappeared. Golly and his mates thought that was a great story.

When Golly went into 2B he was seated next to a girl called Sheila Frankland. Incidentally Sheila had a sister whose name was Rosemary and she a lovely girl was a beauty queen. In fact Rosemary Frankland later went on to become Miss World.

Well Sheila was great, a real pal, she let Golly copy all her work. This meant that he never had to think for himself. Better still he was back with his old mates Stan Parrot, his cousin, and the one and only Mally Lord, we will hear more of him in the coming pages.

Of course like most families in the 1950's Golly's family could not afford holidays. But Golly did have one big annual treat a week in

Barrow at his cousin's house. Not that much to do but nevertheless to Golly it was his summer holiday.

Even the car journey was exciting, Golly's Uncle Bert would drive through from Barrow to Lancaster to pick him up. Golly getting excited as he waited with his little suitcase containing his summer clothes and Ten bob, (50p) spending money. Golly would arrive in Barrow, then be straight out playing n the street.

On the next street to where Golly's cousin Derek lived there were a row of shops. In that row was a coffee bar called 'The Pussyfoot', all painted up in Pink and Candy Striped. Inside was a Juke Box and all the local 'Ted's' used to sit around in their Drape Suits. Of course Golly never went in there, but he could see it all through the large windows.

There was a similar place in Lancaster called 'Macari's' and Golly will tell us more of that later.

However as the family progressed through the fifties Golly's Mam and Dad were starting to get on their feet a bit. Golly's Dad had learned to drive with the TA (Territorial Army) and when he was competent enough he passed the official Driving Test. Golly thinks that probably in 1959/60, his Dad got a little car. It was a 1950's Ford Popular. It was a little beauty, they used to go for days out, pure luxury!!

Ford Popular – Dad's first car

This would be a good time to mention another thing that helped improve the lives of Golly and his family. After not being able to have much in the way of holidays, a stroke of good fortune earned by his Uncle Reg, benefited the whole family. Uncle Reg used to work for The Lancaster Bus Company, he was a Transport Manager and he was offered and took the position of Transport Manager in Middlesbrough, a much bigger area.

Uncle Reg and his wife Aunty Cath moved across to the North East. Every summer, sometimes Easter and Christmas, Golly and his Mam and Dad would go across to the Yorkshire Coast for their holidays. Great times, they would go to a different resort every day. Scarborough, Whitby, Robin Hoods Bay, Redcar, Saltburn and many more. These were beautiful places back then, some still are, Golly has very happy memories of them all.

American jeans advert

Another thing that pleased Golly was the fact that from a young age he always wore jeans and round his way he was probably the only boy who did. Or so he thought until one afternoon a neighbour came knocking on the door. Mam went to the door and the neighbour started shouting straight away, "Your Steve has been giving me cheek". "When was this"? Mam asked her, "This afternoon" the neighbour replied. "Can't have been our Steve" said Golly's Mam, "Because he hasn't left the house". "Well" said the neighbour, "The lad I saw was wearing jeans and your Steve is the only lad I've ever seen round here wearing jeans". Golly says "I can tell you now after all these years it wasn't me and we never heard any more about it".

Golly's Mam used to buy his jeans from 'The Army & Navy Stores', but a lot of the time the legs would be too baggy, so she would get the sewing machine out and take them in. Golly of course would be delighted he had another pair of drainpipes.

The thing was Golly hated short pants, who wears short pants? Only English kids. All the American kids on the pictures and the telly go to school in jeans.

Any way back to the misery of school because as with all things in life the time came for change and in September 1956, after the summer holidays, Golly's joy in his lessons came to an abrupt end. He moved up a year into 3B, Mr Dilly's class and he could not have known how bad his school life would become.

Mr Dilly had come to Golly's attention before he went into his class because his wedding photo had been in the Lancaster Guardian, so if nothing else he knew what he looked like.

Another piece of information Golly knew about Mr Dilly was that he was a great musician. He had a piano in the classroom and he was always playing it, he never seemed to be off it. Music was his big thing and because of this, he got the whole class singing every day.

That said there was a very nasty side to his nature. He was a bully very quick with his hands, always slapping the children around the face and head. They were not light slaps either, the children's heads would rock on their shoulders when he struck them. It should be remembered that these children were only nine years old!

One day he hit Golly so hard that he perforated his eardrum. To this day Golly is partially deaf as the result of this vicious assault. Golly recalls the incident as if it were yesterday. He had turned round to speak to the person who was sitting at the desk behind him and Dilly hit him so hard round the side of his face and head that he nearly knocked Golly out.

This man Dilly should have been sacked and prosecuted for his violent conduct, in Golly's opinion the only place for men like him is prison. He was a mean, cruel man, who should never have been a teacher. Golly believes that Dilly hated him for the following reason. Dilly used to set the class mental arithmetic tests. Now many of the children in the class would make notes to help them work out the problems, Golly didn't need to do that he could always get the answer quickly in his head, it is called mental arithmetic after all. Dilly could not accept that Golly had this ability, so he accused him of copying by looking at what his classmates had put on their paper. This clearly upset Golly, because, nobody likes to be falsely accused.

One day he gave them all the mental arithmetic tests that he had set. Golly did them very quickly and got them all right. For some reason this enraged Dilly who dragged Golly out to the front of the class, once again accusing him of cheating. Not satisfied with that he set another test, shouting, "Try this one Goulding without copying"! Well Golly did the test and knew that he had got the answers right. Wrong again roared Dilly, this upset Golly because he knew the answer was right, if it hadn't been, Dilly would have taken great delight in putting the right answer up on the board. Dilly never did offer what was supposed to be the right answer, because as Golly says, he was a liar!! What's more he was a coward as well, always hitting kids who couldn't fight back.

As Golly said to me when he was giving me the information for this book. He would still like to say to this dreadful man, "Sorry Dilly, you were a mean cowardly bullying bastard and you gave me a long and very unhappy year of my young life"!

Thank the Lord, September 1957 finally arrived and aged ten Golly moved to 4B, Miss Mitton's class. Miss Mitton was a great teacher!! She use to read them stories such as "Just William" by Richard Crompton and "Treasure Island" by Robert Louis Stephenson. These were all interesting and exciting stories, right up Golly's street.

One thing Golly wasn't too keen on was sport, his Dad tried all sorts of ways in the early days to try and get him interested in football. Golly just couldn't take to it, he knew he was in the minority, but that never really bothered him. Football was a weekly lesson at Skerton School and if you didn't have boots, the teacher Mr Adams would make you hang around the goalposts as a fullback. As you might guess, Golly always made it his business never to have a pair of football boots.

Golly recalls one Friday afternoon when they were lined up in the school yard waiting to be taken to the football field. This field just happened to be 'Johnny's Field', Golly's own personal playground. So

Golly and his mate Brian Edmondson, bored as usual, climbed up and sat on top of the school wall as Mr Adams, the teacher approached. "Right you two" he said, "You two are not going to football, you know it's forbidden to climb". Naturally Mr Adams saw this as a punishment. Not to Golly or Brian, he hated football too, almost as much as Golly did.

Mr Adams pondered for a few seconds while he thought of a chore that he might get these lads to do. "Follow me", he said. Taking them to the school veranda where there was a lawn. "Right you two, get on there and pick off all the daisies". Punishment, eh? It was a lovely summers day and Golly and Brian messed about on the lawn all afternoon. As Golly says, "A real treat"!

1957 was the year Golly and his class-mates were approaching the 11 plus, it was voluntary in those days, needless to say Golly did not attempt it. As he said, "As a Skerton boy the idea of going to Grammar School, scared the life out of him".

Skerton Senior School

So in September 1958 Golly started at Skerton Boys Senior School. The first morning his little gang nicknamed the Teddy Boy Union met up in the junior school yard due to their reluctance to enter the senior yard. They heard the whistle blow so they were forced to make the move into the senior boy's yard.

Bill Boundy *Charlie Emmett*

Teaching staff at Skerton Senior School

15

They were instructed to line up and walk to morning assembly, then after assembly they were led their new classroom where they met their new form teacher. To their surprise it was a lady, Mrs Elliott, she was an Australian, a tough old bird, who took no nonsense, she knew how to whack and cane them if they stepped out of line. There was a rumour that Mrs Elliott was having an affair with Mr Boak the Choir Master, who knows? He was another tough old teacher who once set about Golly for what they used to term as "Dumb Insolence"

Golly around age 13

To be fair most of the teachers were OK, very strict but OK. There were two exceptions, Charlie Emmett and Bill Boundy. There will be more of them later.

Skerton School was always overcrowded, 45-50 pupils to every class, the other problem was that there were not enough classrooms. Science Labs, Woodwork Room, Metalwork Room, Storerooms etc. were all used as classrooms

There was another classroom, this was in "The Scout Hut". "The Scout Hut" was an old wooden building set in the Local Church (St Luke's) grounds.

Golly dreaded every Monday afternoon, because Charlie Emmett would march them down to the Scout Hut for a triple period maths lesson. Triple period, for Golly that was one and a half hours of misery and despair.

Once they got down there Charlie Emmett would lock and bolt the door, then the maths lesson would start. Woe betide the pupil who couldn't just grasp what he was on about. Of course that unfortunate boy was always Golly. Charlie Emmett would beat Golly unmercifully around his head and face, just because Golly didn't get it. He would never try to explain or help Golly or any other unfortunate child who fell foul of his temper.

Basically he just enjoyed hurting kids. Charlie Emmett tried his best to break him and make him cry but he never succeeded. That annoyed this vicious bully even more. Golly has actually seen that bastard, as he calls Charlie Emmett, throw kids out of the classroom on to the lawn, followed by a chair and a desk.

The man was a pure sadist, who delighted in mental and physical cruelty. Unless of course you were good at football, which Golly wasn't. If you were, then you would be OK, no matter how you struggled to understand his maths lessons. In those cases he would just turn a blind eye to any failings a kid might have academically, because football was important to him. If ever a man should have been jailed it was Charlie Emmett.

School to Golly was pure Hell! Somehow he got through the first year, don't ask him to explain how. The second year might have been a touch better, well some of it at least.

The new Form Room was actually the Woodwork room, the new Form Master, Mr Wilson turned out to be quite a decent bloke really, although he was very strict. Nobody minds teachers being strict as long as they are fair. Golly says he was OK at woodwork, in fact he really enjoyed it.

The Metalwork Room was next door and the teacher Mr Birkett was a "grumpy old sod" But Golly ever fair minded says, "He probably had reason to be, putting up with us lot".

If any of the kids stepped out of line, as Golly says, "Me of course", Mr Birkett would nip them by the hair at the side of their ears and lead them around the class room.

In those days the pupils had their dinner in the Form Room and Mr Birkett had his meal with them. They had a little salt pot on each desk and one day when he thought no one was looking Golly unscrewed the top, placing it back on the pot loosely so that it appeared to be intact. The lad sitting next to him, Olly Alston decided that he would have a sprinkle of salt on his food and the lot came out all over his plate. Olly shouted out, "You did that Goulding" of course old Birkett heard him. Everyone in the class was laughing, except Alston and Birkett.

"See me in the library Goulding"! shouted Birkett. So at 1pm Golly went into the library. Actually it was the Medical Room, all it had to make it a library were a couple of shelves containing books.

Mr Birkett picked out a big heavy encyclopedia and turned to the salt section. Well, there were pages and pages on the subject. "Right Goulding you will stay in every dinner time until you have copied this lot out."

It took Golly weeks to copy it all out and when he had finished it he presented it Mr Birkett. He didn't even look at it, he just tore it up in front of him and dropped it in the bin. Looking back Golly thinks the punishment was deserved.

This meant that Golly's lunch time breaks, (dinner hours as they called them in those days), were free again. Once again Golly and his pals could go back to nipping into Main Street, which was being demolished at the time. They would play in the old houses and the cellars. Golly recalls these places being full of 'old junk', good antiques he would call it now.

One day Golly and his mates were playing in an old back yard and cut down an old washing line. They used it to tie Roland Timmis to the clothes post, well they called it a "Totem Pole".

Old Main street, Skerton

Then they lit a fire around Roland and the post and set about doing a war dance. That would have been bad enough but then they started picking out bits of burning wood from the fire and singeing his legs. This would be really painful and frightening for Roland, remember all the boys wore short pants in those days.

As it was approaching 1.30 pm. Golly and his mates went back to school, they just left Roland there, tied up.

Well all was fine until about half an hour later, at that point Golly and his mates were summoned to the headmaster, Mr Weavers Office. Golly says that Mr Weaver was a decent sort, but of course there was a limit to how much leeway he could give his pupils.

It seems that someone had heard Roland's cries for help and gone to see what the problem was and then set him free. Then this person had brought him back to school and reported the incident to the headmaster. Naturally, Roland named all his tormentors.

So there they were, Mally Lord, Kev Barratt, Bill Waddell, Brian Edmondson and of course Golly Goulding, aka 'The Teddy Boy Union' all lined up for the cane. Needless to say they all got a good caning, but as Golly said he got the cane frequently, so he kind of got used to it.

During the second year, 1959/1960 Golly's Maths teacher was Bill Boundy. Bill Boundy had been a public schoolboy and was a real snob. To make matters worse, he had taught Golly's mother at the same school in the 1930's.

Golly has to say that when he was in Junior School he wasn't too bad at maths, (Arithmetic) but when he got to Senior School he just couldn't get what they were on about, X = Y and all that stuff. As he says, "Come on, I thought Maths were about numbers"!

Bill Boundy really had it in for Golly, just because his maths book was gibberish. Once again in disbelief at the treatment he received Golly says. "I swear to God I did try my best but I just couldn't grasp it. What they were saying to me made no sense at all". Bill Boundy used to beat and cane him all the time and one day he said in front of the class, "I would gladly pay the cost of repair, to have the pleasure of throwing you through the glass window". As Golly thinks back he says, "What a thing to say to a twelve year old boy who was basically a good lad just trying his best. Bill Boundy was a horrible, bitter, evil old man! May he rot in hell".

During that year, Golly's lot joined the school choir and to be fair they were all pretty decent singers.

School choir

The other aspect of being in the choir was that there were perks to be had. For example every now and then you would be allowed to skip lessons so that you could attend choir practice. Even better than that you would have the opportunity to go to the 'Winter Gardens Theatre' in Morecambe for the Summer Festivals and they did get that opportunity, they went. But it got even better because at the Winter Gardens was access to the Fairground and oh boy did Golly and his mates take advantage of that!

1960 saw Golly moving up into third year at Skerton Boys Senior School both Golly and his mates were getting a bit bigger and a bit tougher. The handful of Bully teachers were easing off at bit, Golly wonders why?

Things seemed a bit better and the atmosphere in school had changed. The lads only had a couple more years of school left to go before they would be leaving.

The big news was that National Service had been abolished, so Golly and his mates were talking about careers and jobs, plus girls of course.

In Golly's case he was hoping his artwork would prove the key to his future career. He always came high in the exams, annual tests, he had the talent and his ambition was to be a sign writer when he left school.

It looked as though he would succeed in this ambition as he knew somebody in the trade.

The lads were maturing and Golly thinks the teachers acknowledged that. Golly would take his guitar into school and impress all the lads with his playing. Surprise, surprise, the teachers were not impressed.

Golly was now an official teenager which meant something back then. He joined the Red Rose Boys Club. The club was located on the other side of the river from his house at Lancaster Quay. This was a great club and Golly would attend every week night.

Mr Toole was the man in charge, he was a great guy, a pure gentleman. Of course some of the lads saw him as a soft touch and took advantage of him. They would take drinks and biscuits, even going behind the canteen counter to steal. Golly never did that and he never would. There used to be a Saturday dance every now and again in the main hall which had a stage.

There was a group called "The Drovers" who practised at the club and Golly would go and watch them, never miss. The group had a singer called 'Johnny Dark' but mainly the group played "The Shadows" instrumentals. The guys in the group would all have been in their mid to late teens at the time and Golly knew all the tunes they played. He was only thirteen, he knew what they were playing. Golly could play this music too. He did, but not in a group that would come later in 1962.

The other good thing about being thirteen for Golly was the fact that he could get a job, and he did. He started work as an errand boy at the local Co-op. His hours were 4.30pm to 5.30pm Thursday and Friday and 8am-12noon on a Saturday. Ten Bob (10/-) (.50p in today's money) a week, and just about another 10 bob in tips. Wow!! A quid a week, Bloody good money for a schoolboy, then.

Co-op errand boy's bike

Having this money meant that Golly could take a girl to the pictures on a Saturday night, buy his Fags, he smoked 'Bristol Tipped' and have a coffee in "Macaris" when he wanted. Golly Goulding was well off and life was good.

So school days were passing by but Golly was still finding ways to get himself into trouble. One such incident came about due to his fascination with weapons. Normally he made them and other things himself, but the weapon of choice this time was a small pen knife that he had acquired from somewhere, maybe in a swap, he just can't remember.

Anyway one dinnertime Golly was out of school hiding behind a fence, hoping for a suitable victim to come past and be taken by surprise. He was not disappointed along came Wirey Webster a classmate of his. Wirey Webster was the sort of kid we all knew in our school days, always jumping at the slightest thing, which made him good for a laugh. Anyway Golly jumped out from behind the fence, he took him by surprise all right, because the bloody pen knife seemed to have a mind of it's own it cut the inside of Wirey's wrist. He cried out in pain and surprise, "I'm going to report you to the headmaster, Goulding", he said.

Well Golly panicked and couldn't apologise enough, he knew about the vein on the inside of the wrist, how you could bleed to death if it was cut. He thought he had bloody killed him, luckily it soon stopped bleeding when it was dressed, he was OK. But not Golly, he got a good caning, but as he says, "I was really glad that was all that happened".

Diana air pistols

Another time when Golly gave himself a great scare it involved the use of the Pellet Pistol he got in a swap from Brian Edmondson one of Golly's gang, 'The Teddy Boy Union' As pistols went it wasn't very powerful or even very accurate. On the day in question the lads were playing in 'The Paddy Fields'. Just fields really, Golly guesses they were so called because they were prone to flooding on a regular basis.

Well there was this cheeky kid called Barry who was a bloody nuisance, so as he was fed up with him, Golly shot him in the arse at close range. Well Barry immediately dropped to the ground and pretended to be dead. Golly panicked because he thought he really had killed him and after a minute or so Barry jumped up squealing and ran off the field, over the bridge to his house, shouting, " I'm going to bring my Dad to you Goulding". Well Golly says, "I ran like hell, with his dad running after me, but he never caught me". "Plus he didn't know who I was as I was a Skerton boy and he was from The Vale Estate. A lucky escape.

September 1961 and Golly could feel the excitement building, only a year until he could leave school. He was impatient for the day and the teachers knew it. They knew the lad's hearts weren't really in schooling and neither was theirs. A lot of the time Golly and his mates used to "nick off" he doesn't think anyone really cared.

1961 was the year that Golly joined the Army Cadets. The idea behind joining the cadets was to get young people interested in joining the army as a career. That was the last thing Golly wanted to do.

But the lads did get to Camp Lydd in Kent. Great! A long train journey that also took them right through London, carrying rifles, pointing them at people as they passed through all the stations. Golly and the others thought they were real soldiers, a few of the lasses who saw them thought so too. They had a great time down at camp, they shared the NAFFI with the real soldiers.

All young lads can't wait to grow up and start shaving, soon as they saw facial hair growing apart from being able to shave they could grow sideburns, sideboards we used to call them. As Golly says, "How cool was that"? They were just lads wanting to be men.

The other thing Golly and all the other lads his age all seemed to want was a tattoo, as Golly says now, "bloody stupid" but back then it seemed a pretty cool idea. Golly had seen lads who had been to approved school or Borstal as it was known, with tattoos, they were not very professionally done but they were real tattoos. One of Golly's mates, Ronnie Bateson, known as "Basher Bateson" as Golly and his other mates used to call him, tattooed himself, God knows where he learned to do it, but he did.

So having seen Basher with his tattoo Golly, Mally Lord and a few others learned the method, wait until you read this!!! You need a tin of "Zebo Black Lead Grate Polish" (Deadly Poisonous) and a sewing needle, that's all, nothing more. All you had to do was dip the needle in the Zebo and proceed to puncture your skin hundreds of times.

Golly's first attempt was an Anchor on his left arm. As with all self made tattoos, think about it, there was blood everywhere and his arm swelled up, all you could see was black lead and blood for a week or more. Golly's arm was a right mess, his parents never saw it and even if they had it was too late anyway.

After a few weeks it settled down and Golly had his first tattoo. Then he decided that he wanted to make the anchor bigger so he made a few patterns round it and put his initials S.J. G. to the side. Again after a few weeks the arm settled down and Golly had a bit of an armful. That wasn't enough for Golly so he tattooed his knuckles with four crosses. More than fifty years later these crosses have faded and you would have to look hard to see them. Back then they were very prominent, people used to say to Golly, "Oh you are that guitarist with the crosses on your knuckles, I've heard of you".

Of course Golly's Mam and Dad did eventually see his tattoos and they called him silly and stupid saying, "Don't you realise that that black lead stuff is deadly poison and that it will stay in your bloodstream forever". Well, no, Golly didn't realise, it was a crazy mad thing to do but as he says, "He has done a lot of crazy mad things". Some of these things will be revealed in this book and some will never be revealed. As Golly says, "Nothing that bad, but better left unmentioned".

As we have mentioned Golly liked a Fag and in those days there were plenty of shops willing to sell them to anybody. All Golly's mates liked to smoke so they would club together and buy a packet of ten. On a Friday night a few of them would go to the Pictures. Right next door to "The Palace Cinema" there was a tobacconist, in there you could buy 4 Domino Cigarettes in a paper packet for about 6d (two and a half pence today) or a large cigarette called a "Joy Stick" for 4d (2 pence today) This was great because back then you could  smoke in the cinema, no one could see if you were just a kid in the dark. So of course Golly and his mates always smoked in the cinema.

Another good place to go to buy their fags was a shop near their school called Camms. They sold everything, to everybody, including

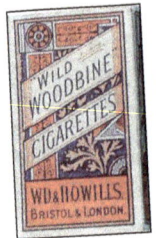

kids. Schoolboys could buy a single cigarette, usually a Woodbine, even half a Woodbine. In between the two O's was exactly half a cigarette, they would slice it with a razor blade, then charge a penny, (1d) for half a fag. Happy days.

The last few months at school felt magic, not much work to do and everybody was buzzing about leaving school. Golly was looking forward to his apprenticeship as a Sign-writer. Morecambe was the ideal place for such a career, owing to its abundance of arcades, gift shops and of course two fairgrounds. All of these places were elaborately painted with beautiful artwork.

Traditionally at Skerton School all the leavers, or most of them took part in a concert, which was held during the last week of school, some would sing a song or do at bit of poetry etc. other small groups would do a short play, you know the sort of thing.

Now a few months previous to the concert, Golly and Mally Lord had bought themselves a harmonica apiece and they were able to play them pretty good, they were a pair of naturals when it came to musical ability. So they formed a little band with Mel Woods on Piano Accordion, and Steve Boyd, on a drum that he borrowed from the Boys Brigade. Golly named the band, "Archimedes and The Principles". He picked the name because there was a local group called 'Pythagoras and The Squares' who were enjoying a lot of success. Golly thought the names had a similar ring to them. The band performed for 15/20 minutes at the concert and they stole the show. As Golly said, "Everyone enjoyed their performance, but he is not too sure about the teachers though".

Like most schools back then, they held the annual 'Speech Day'. Skerton held theirs at Lancaster Town Hall and always in the evening. Golly hated these boring events but every pupil was forced to attend All the smart kids and ' Goodie Goodie' types being awarded a prize, always a bloody boring book.

Golly and his mates couldn't wait to get it over with and this being the last one they would ever attend, they planned to go for a pint afterwards. Co-incidentally the nearest pub was 'Marton Street Vaults' which was the only place they knew of where they could get served.

A small part of this pub had a room with an outside door called 'The Jug and Bottle'. Most people know these places as being called 'The Snug'

The place was usually pretty empty and especially mid-week, so young lads used to enter from the street, via the outside door.

Nine 0 Clock arrived and Golly and his mates rushed out of the Town Hall, straight into 'The Jug and Bottle and ordered a pint of bitter each. An old lady used to run the bar and she really knew that they were under age but never let on. She always served them.

The lads stood at the bar enjoying their pints with fags in their mouths, when into the main bar, which backed on to the small bar, appeared a couple of teachers......F......Hell. One of them was 'Charlie Emmett' and of course spotted Golly's lot boozing and smoking. They quickly supped up and scarpered. They knew what to expect next morning at school and they weren't too bothered as they only had a matter of days to go before leaving. But do you know? Nothing was ever mentioned, so they knew they'd got away with it.

It finally came, 20th July 1962, Golly left school. As he said earlier, he thought he was going to walk straight into a Sign-writing Apprentice-ship. The problem with that was, when the bloke who Golly thought was going to teach him the trade realised that Golly was serious, he got cold feet, because the idea of having to pay a small wage, scared him and he withdrew the offer. Golly found out later, that although the bloke was a very skilled artist, he was also a boozer and as soon as he got a few quid in his hand, he stopped work and went to the pub. So that was the end of that.

Eager to find work Golly heard that they were looking for lads to work at Storeys Cotton Mill in Lancaster. So he went for an interview and got a job. He couldn't start work straight away because he was already committed to go to Army Camp with The Cadets, from Saturday the 4th of August until Sunday the 12th of August . So on Monday the 13th of August Golly started work at Storeys Mill. The hours were 7.30am until 5pm, 5 days a week, his wages were £3-1 shilling and 6 pence, less tax and insurance, Golly lasted nearly six weeks.

Storeys Mill - Golly's first job

So, school-days are at an end but we need to catch up with some other things.

CHAPTER 2

OTHER THINGS

W̶e are fast approaching a point in the story where other things would start to fill Golly's life. School had its place but a boy like Golly was quickly finding other interests.

A programme had started on the TV would change Golly's life, '6.5 Special', bringing Rock and Roll into people's homes, and Golly was blown away by it.

Golly's introduction to rock n roll

Golly's Mam and Dad didn't have a TV at this time, but Auntie Doris next door did. Golly had heard about the show and he knew about Bill Haley and Elvis Presley. However he was totally unprepared for what came on the screen the first time he saw the show, 'Tommy Steele'. As he said, he was smitten to say the least. Up to this time he hardly knew what a guitar was, not to mention the great looking guy with the Teddy boy hair cut.

As Golly says Tommy Steele was such an influence on him, without Tommy Steele there would not have been the Golly Goulding we know today. Tommy Steele was a massive name during the 1950's, so in 1957 his management team decided to make a film based on his rise to fame. They called it "The Tommy Steele Story" and it was a smash hit at the box office.

Naturally Golly went to see the film at "The Palace" and he was glued to the screen. Guitars, great clothes, great hairstyle! Golly wanted to be like Tommy Steele, the whole thing, the music, the look, the excitement, was an inspiration to a young lad. Golly went to see the film later in the week, he simply couldn't get enough of it, When the film came to the end of its run, it had been so popular the cinema brought it back again the next year. Naturally Golly went back to see it twice, in the same week.

Another film that had a great effect on Golly was, "These Dangerous Years". The film starred Frankie Vaughan as the leader of a Liverpool Teddyboy gang, once again that great format, the clothes the hair and Rock and Roll songs. Frankie's character Dave, was called up to do National Service and he wasn't best pleased by this.

This was a recurring theme in the 1950's because as a lad at that time you knew that you were going in the "Services". The constant cry from adults of the day was, "Wait till you get in the Army, they will make a man of you". Golly thinks he was looking forward to it but, by late 1960 it was all finished, although it would be 1963 before all the lads came home.

But of course it was Tommy Steele who kicked off Golly's and many other people's interest in playing guitar. Golly went home after seeing 6.5 Special for the first time, desperate to have an instrument he got a pan lid, stuck a wooden spoon down the handle and put four elastic bands on it. It didn't make any sense, but Golly had his first guitar, he was up and running.

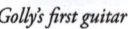

There were other things that were taking Golly's attention. Ever since he had been a small boy his Mam and Dad had taken him to 'The Pictures'. He recalls that he fell asleep while watching most of them. Golly remembers doing that while watching Gene Kelly in "Singing in the Rain". The ones he really loved were the ones that

Golly's first guitar

featured Cavalry Soldiers and Indians. Young Golly wanted to be a Cavalry Soldier because his Dad had told him that there were still Cavalry Soldiers in the Army. As he looks back today he thinks that there probably were, but not like the ones on the Pictures.

Golly as a cowboy

The War had only been over for a few years at this time, but they kept on bringing out War films. Golly thinks it was to inspire the young lads to go and do their National Service, although it was compulsory. These films (mostly American) were always in black and white, unlike the Westerns which always seemed to be Technicolour. Dad always used to take Golly to see them, because they both enjoyed them. Now and again a real treat was 'Butterkist' popcorn and of course there was always an ice cream tub during the interval.

On one memorable occasion Dad took Golly to 'The Palace' in Lancaster to see a War film then took him to 'The Odeon' to see another one. Two pictures in one night, unheard of!

You see, there were five picture houses, as we called them in Lancaster, 'The County', 'The Palladium,' 'The Palace', 'The Odeon' and 'The Rex' also known as the 'Bug Hut'. This meant that as you would normally only go and see one film a week, you had to make your choice and this could be difficult. Someone at work might say to Golly's Dad, "Go and see so and so, at The Palladium, it is brilliant". Then someone else would say, "The Odeon has a good film on this week you need to go and see it". But in those days, most people only went to the pictures once a week, so deciding which film to see could be a problem.

Speaking of National Service brings Golly to another of his favourite films, "Idle On Parade". Based on the lives of squaddies doing their National Service. This film starred Anthony Newley, he portrayed the role of one 'Jeep Jackson'. In the film 'Jeep Jackson' was a 'Rock and Roll Idol' who had been called up to do his National Service in the Army. From his point of view the film gave Golly the chance to hear loads of great songs that the soundtrack provided.

The way he looked at it someone had got the title wrong, he just wasn't impressed by the play on words, Golly thought it should have been 'Idol On Parade', anyway 'Idle' it was. He loved it and like the 'Tommy Steele Story', he went to see it four times.

Strange as it may seem for a young lad who was really excited by "Rock and Roll", Golly never saw any Elvis films back in the day but now "Jailhouse Rock" is a real favourite of his.

Golly just thinks when it came to films, it was really the English stuff that attracted him, he could better relate to that. When he saw the film trailers for the American stuff it just seemed too fantastic, after all teenagers with Cadillacs etc, that was way beyond his comprehension. Teenagers in Britain travelled by bus! Teenagers with a car? Never!! It just couldn't happen.

In the 1950's on Golly's street, there were only two people who had a car, how could he take these American films seriously?

Of course even now the old British films are his favourite, 'Bridge On The River Kwai', 'Mutiny On The Bounty' and 'The League Of Gentlemen' to name but three.

Electric train at Green Ayre station

Other big treats were visits to Morecambe, Golly felt lucky to live in Lancaster only five miles from Morecambe. He could get the bus or electric train from Green Ayre Station which was directly across Skerton Bridge, over the River Lune. That makes Golly think of the old steam trains, Golly used to love them. More about Morecambe later!

Mainly in the summer, Golly says, "we would go to Hest Bank", this was just a small place situated on the outskirts of Morecambe, you had the sea and a bit of sand. (Not much, mostly shingle) but, the attraction of the place was, that there were no attractions, meaning that there was nothing to spend money on. "We as kids, never had any anyway and Mam and Dad had next to nowt. So we would take a ball or a cricket bat and ball and just have family fun"!!

When they went to Hest Bank they used to meet up with Golly's aunties, uncles and cousins. A big day out, and it cost next to nothing, just 6d for a jug of hot water. Mam would make a brew, and they would eat sandwiches and home- made cakes.

At Hest Bank with cousins Gordon & Elsie   *Cousin Kevin & Golly sat under a deckchair*

Other summer treats may be an afternoon boating, they lived right next to The River Lune and you could hire a rowing boat for a shilling. You could get eight people in the boat so Golly thinks the price was OK. Now and again Golly and family would be invited out for Sunday tea, usually to Golly's Uncle Harold's house on the other side of town. The family always walked there and back. Uncle Harold always used to cut Golly's hair! He did it with the old hand clippers and as Golly says "It nipped like Hell"! His dad always insisted he had an Army haircut, short back and sides.

Golly hated it, more on Golly's hair later.

The real treat for Golly at his uncle's house was the 'Lyon's Family Brick' This was an ice cream block cut in equal portions as Golly says, "Beautiful".

Every year the Circus would come to town, it was always set up in Ryelands Park. This was also close to Golly's house, as he thinks back from a boy's point of view they were well situated. Anyway his Mam always took him there. Golly loved a circus, still does to this day.

Also once a year the fairground would visit Lancaster, held at Quay Meadow which was further up the river from them on the opposite side.

Golly and his family never went to that one but, in the mid 1950's

'Scott's Travelling Fairground', would come to Ryelands Park. Golly was there every day and in the early evening. He didn't have any money to go on the rides, but they were playing all the great Rock and Roll records, Golly was in Heaven.

CHAPTER 3

CHRISTMAS

Just taking a step back into early childhood, Golly like all children, truly believed in Father Christmas and everything about Christmas time. Christmas was something to look forward to! The first one Golly really remembers was 1950 going into New Year 1951, he got a Red Pedal Car, what a beauty!! As he says, if he still had it today it would be worth £100s. The year after he got a Red 3 Wheeled Bike, this was also a great present, because he could ride it round the streets.

The following year things got really good, he got a Black Two Wheeled Kids Bike. Unbeknown to Golly it was second hand, his Mam taught him to ride and he soon mastered it. It was fine for a while but one day while giving his cousin a "Crossie" (sat on the crossbar) the bike just snapped in half. Golly thinks it must have been some rusty old thing that was half rotten and painted up to sell.

Steve on his first bike

No worries, because luckily Mam and Dad bought Golly a brand new "Coventry Eagle" child's' bike, (Bottle Green) It was like a small version of policeman's bike. Golly had that bike for years and even when he had out grown it, the condition of it was still like new, well almost.

One of the really good Christmas presents Golly's Mam would get him was a Rupert Bear Annual, then, she would repeatedly read the story's to him. Rupert was a little bear who had the most fantastic adventures.

They were great stories, a couple he remembers were 'Rupert and the Cannibals' and one story that really frightened him, 'Rupert on The Pirate Ship' Golly can still picture in his mind's eye, the face of the pirate that frightened him so much. When he learned to read himself, Golly spent many happy hours reading these books over and over again.

One of Golly's favourite stories

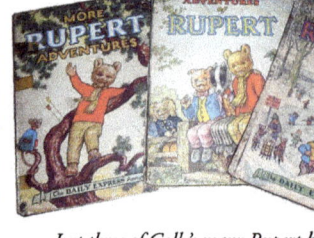

Just three of Golly's many Rupert books

The scary pirate

When Golly was Seven he got an enormous farmyard for Christmas. It was huge, hundreds of lead animals, haystacks, fencing and everything you could possibly need for the perfect toy farm. It really was a gift of love. Golly's Mam's friends son, he was about eight years older than Golly, had been collecting and cherishing the pieces for donkeys years.

Incidentally Golly used to take piano lessons from this boys Grandma, we will hear more about that as we read on.

Christmas 1958 was a milestone Christmas in Golly's life his present was his first guitar, a small plastic four string Ukulele type thing. It was called 'The Tommy Steele Gitar' (Note the Spelling) It was never out of Golly's hands. The guitar had a paper transfer of Tommy Steele on the front. Golly scraped that off after a year or so to make look more like a real guitar rather than a toy. He even learned to play little tunes on it. Amazing really, Mam and Dad thought this 'guitar thing' was just a novelty and a phase that he would grow out of. No Chance! "Aspiration".

Tommy Steele 'Gitar'

Christmas 1959 Golly got another 'Tommy Steele Guitar', this was a much bigger more realistic toy, it sounded like a real instrument. Still only four strings but they were real wire guitar strings and they sounded 'right'. It was Cream Coloured with a Black Scratch Plate, plus it had a cut-away body.

Now at this point Golly thinks he is a real guitarist, as he says "No chance, not yet anyway".

Golly thinks Christmas 1960 is coming up and Rock and Roll is still very much in vogue and he really needs a genuine six string wooden guitar, well he did! His Mam bought him one for 30 bob, (£1.50p in todays money).

As Golly told me in the time between 1956 to 1960 every kid wanted to learn how to play a guitar, 99% couldn't understand the skill required or make sense of the technique, so they just abandoned their instruments. Golly believes that even now more than fifty six years later there will be some really good guitars, (Hidden Gems) that haven't seen the light of day in all that time, lying under beds, in attics or at the back of sheds.

It has to be said, what a time this was, Teddyboys, Rock and Roll Music, Guitars. Golly was taking no interest in school and being chased by the coppers, more of that later. Exciting times indeed!!

Going back to Golly and the guitar he was part of that 1% that would

have the ability to learn how to play the instrument. With his 30 bob Spanish type guitar he was, as he puts it, "doing pretty good". He had learned to play The Shadows great hit, "Apache" and as they continued to release records, Golly was quick to learn them, his theory was what Hank Marvin can do, I can do. But as he says he was using a cheap Spanish type guitar, he really needed to upgrade to a better instrument.

Rosetti Lucky 7

This happened quite quickly. Christmas 1961, saw Golly being taken by his Mam and Dad to Simmons Music Shop in Lancaster. Once there, Golly picked out a Rossetti, Red/ Sunburst guitar at the cost of seven a half guineas. (A guinea was 21 shillings in real money). This 'flash in the pan' interest in playing the guitar was here to stay!

As Golly says now the Rossetti wasn't a good instrument but he loved it and it was miles better than his previous guitar and it brought him on as a player no end. He can remember all his mates being very impressed by what he could do musically. As he looks back Golly says it was next to nothing, but at the time it seemed magic. He could knock up almost any tune on that guitar, especially the instrumentals. Golly used that guitar until he started work.

We need to take a step back in time here as in the excitement of the progress with the Rossetti guitar we are ahead of the story.

Back to Christmas treats and Christmas 1954 brought Golly a present that he still loves today, a big Red Sledge that his cousin Harold made him. Harold was Golly's hero, he could make anything. This ability seemed to be a bit of a family talent. Golly's Granddad could make something out of next to nothing, and his Uncle Leo could make furniture out of scrap wood.

Anyway Harold made Golly this magnificent Red Sledge, which he still cherishes to this very day. He used to pray for snow so that he could take it out. It seemed to Golly that it snowed more in the 1950's

Golly's red sledge

than it does now, but that could be his imagination. That said, Golly's sledge was definitely the best sledge in the area. It was big enough to carry two riders, it had iron runners, it used to shift like hell!

No wonder that Golly looked forward to Christmas every year. The presents he received must have made his home seem like Aladdin's Cave.

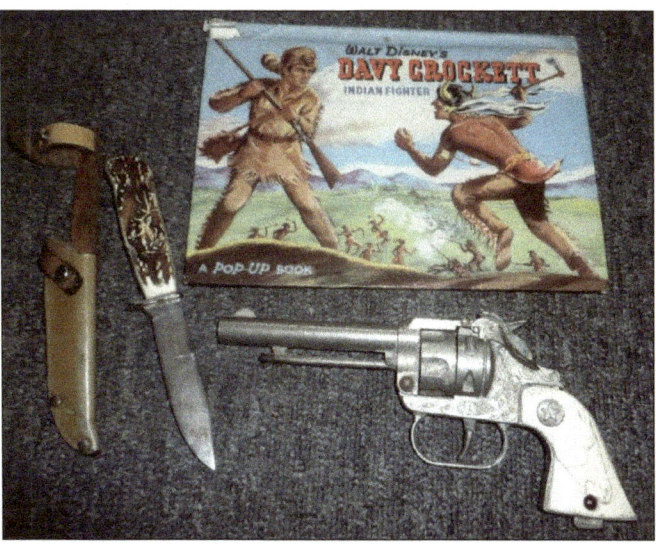

A few of young Golly's favourite toys

It is clear that we have not covered all the marvellous presents Golly received. I am sure he will want to mention other things he remembers as we continue the narrative.

CHAPTER 4

PASTIMES, HOBBIES, AND HEROES

As kids Golly and his mates never had any money so they had to create their own pastimes and hobbies. It has to be said that Golly appears to have more ability and invention in the pursuit of these things than the rest of us. He really knew how to have a good time. As Golly told us earlier, he and his family lived right next to the river, this meant that Golly did a lot of fishing, he did this just using a hand line. Always inventive, Golly made his own sinkers, the material he used to make these was old lead piping that he found in the cellar of their house. He would chop up bits of piping with an axe then put the pieces in a tin can on the gas stove. When the lead melted he would then pour it into a matchbox, then slip in a bit of wire for a loop. Of course this meant the kitchen would fill with smoke and Golly got into trouble for wasting gas, which cost money, and making a mess.

Of course as time went on Golly would be making many other useful items, including Catapults, Bows and Arrows, Tomahawks, Guns, Crossbows and Daggers etc.

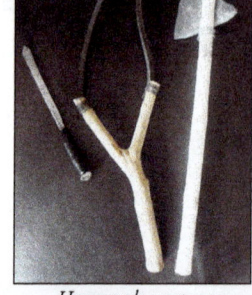

The making of Bows and Arrows of course involved mooching around the trees and bushes, looking for the right 'bits'. The Bow was the easy bit. The arrows required no small amount of skill, in order to make a decent job. Golly would find a piece of twig, it had to be as straight as possible. Then he would split one end of the twig and insert a bit of strong cardboard for the flight, he would seal the flight by wrapping copper wire round the twig above and below the flight.

Homemade weapons

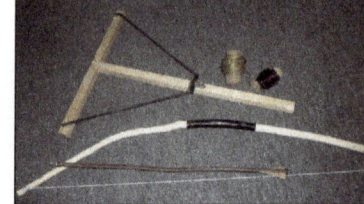

Golly had found a reel of copper wire while walking down by the side of the railway track near their house. He treasured this because he could bend it in to any shape he wanted, without the use of a pair of pliers.

Getting back to the arrow, He'd done the fight, so now he had to sharpen the end like a pencil. Once again using copper wire wrapped round the pointed end, for balance. He later invented the Mark II model. This was a pointed piece of metal cut out from a tin lid. When it was complete he would fire it, the arrow would fly the full width of Johnny's Field, it flew pretty straight too.

Golly never aimed the bow and arrow at anyone, but if he had there is no doubt it would have stuck in them, it was a proper piece of kit. He doesn't remember much more about bows and arrows

Tomahawks were a very necessary piece of kit for an aspiring warrior and Golly made great ones. He would root around the old houses that were being demolished for the right shaped piece of slate (Triangular). When he had found the right piece Golly would take a short length of wood and split it, the insert the piece of slate, then bind both ends of the wood with wire. Golly said to me, "What a great a great weapon that was"!!

Then there was Golly's personally designed dagger. (see photo opposite) He had a great idea for the blade, he would take a 6 inch nail then put it on the railway line, when the train came it would run over the nail and flatten it. The result was a long pointed blade. Then having got the blade Golly would wrap the top half of it with Black tape and that would be the handle.

One of Golly's other specially designed weapons was his gun. For this he required a piece of pipe which he would then bend the end of it over insert a penny banger, lit, followed by a stone for the bullet. Bang, flash and the bullet would fly.

At this time there was a programme on TV called 'William Tell' the hero played I think, by Conrad Phillips was very skilful with a crossbow. Golly was intrigued by crossbows, so of course he had to invent one. Two bits of wood nailed together in the form of a letter T, then catapult elastic pinned to each end and when it was pulled back gripped with a bulldog clip. A home made arrow and a couple of nails for sights, the perfect weapon. Photo.

Going onto another useful piece of kit that Golly aspired to, a 'Fishing Rod'. One of the older lads who used to fish nearby had one, the rest of the boys including Golly just used string. Well Golly dreamed of having one but he didn't get a bought one until he was thirteen. But being Golly he made one.

The bottom half of the rod was a billiard cue that his dad brought home from a club, the top half was a golf club that his Uncle Reg gave him. Golly bought a brass ferrule from Atkinson's Ironmongers, cut and shaved the end of the cue and the golf club, then joined them together with the ferrule. Lo and behold, he had built a great fishing rod!

Golly was then able to buy a wooden reel from someone at school, so now he was almost ready to hit the water. But yet, he just needed a line, he would have to buy that. Even though it probably only cost half a crown, (twelve and a half pence) it took a bit of getting together, saving those pennies. So eventually Golly reached the point where he was a proper fisherman. He used that rod for years catching mostly Eels and Fluke.

But one memorable summer, probably 1957/8 there were loads of Salmon in the river. Illegal to take, but that didn't mean much to Golly at that time. As the river was tidal, when the tide went out you could see the Salmon coming to the shallow water and if you could beat the seagulls, you could pull the Salmon out. One week Golly got nine decent sized Salmon. Golly and his family ate like royalty that week.

Golly was never in the house, he spent all his time outdoors, day and night. Every chance he got, weekends, school holidays, Golly spent his time building all sorts of great things. Things like Tree Houses, Swings and Dens, Golly could make and build anything, he was just having fun and enjoying life.

Another of Golly's hobbies was making Rafts. This idea had come about after he saw the lad who lived in the house at the back of Golly's, David Ham with his canoe. This would be a good time to tell you about David, he was ten years older than Golly and a real hero to him. David had all the things Golly aspired to, a pellet gun with a telescopic sight, the afore mentioned canoe, a camera and later a Motor Bike, he was Golly's idol.

David Ham's canoe   *Pellet gun with telescopic sight*

The way David dressed, tight black jeans, flashy shirt, that great fifties look, David even had a "Tony Curtis" hairstyle. When he got married, he was the talk of the town, David and his best man had full light blue 'Teddyboy' suits, Drape jackets, Velvet collars and cuffs, Drainpipe pants, 'The lot'!!

The neighbours thought it was scandalous and a disgrace! It really was shocking at the time. So much so that one of the National News papers offered him a fridge as a wedding present, if he gave them permission to print his wedding photo.

Golly thought he looked fabulous! David was the man!

Photo of David Ham's wedding that
shocked the neighbourhood

Returning to the rafts, because he was fascinated by anything that floated, Golly decided he must build a raft.

Captain's Row

Golly and his family lived in a terraced house, these houses had been built around 1880, which in their area was considered modern. The reason for this was that all around there were properties that had been built in the 17th century, Captains Row----- Main Street etc. In the late 1950's these older properties were all being demolished so there was tons of old wood lying around, this wood was ideal for raft making.

With this old wood attached to oil drums that had been nicked from the demolition men, Golly started building. When the rafts were completed they would hang around 'Old Bridge' waiting for the tide to come up. Then Golly and his mates would set sail. They really only sailed out a few yards because as soon the tide turned the current would come into force and if you were caught in that you would be out to sea in no time.

Old Bridge

On one occasion Golly's raft got caught in the tide and he had to jump off and swim to shore, fully clothed! The raft carried on with the tide and he never saw it again.

One of Golly's quieter hobbies was collecting cigarette packets, he loved doing this, in fact he still has a passion for it. There were dozens of different brands and some of them are very rare. 'Passing Clouds', 'Black Russian', 'Craven A', 'Kensitas', 'Sweet Afton' '3 Castles' etc. etc.

Golly and his mates used to go to the tip and root around, Golly loved the tip and still does today, the only downside being that you can't just take things away any more. As Golly himself has said he is a Steptoe at heart.

This would be a good time to look at just what was being demolished at that time in Golly's area because being an astute business man that he is now, has a completely different view of what was happening then. Now he would collect, not break. There was a row of old shops, near where he lived, (Owen Road) being pulled down. As soon as the shops were vacated Golly and his mates were in. They smashed up beautiful advertising mirrors, good Victorian shop fittings loads and loads of stuff that had no value then. If Golly could turn the clock back he would happily give £100,000 (today's money) for  the clearance rights. That stuff was magnificent! From memory, on the corner of the street was an old pub, 'The Red Cross', then 'Davis's Garage',' Shoe Repairs', 'Bake House', 'Grocers', 'Fish and Chip Shop', 'Toffee Shop', 'A Dairy', all fitted out with the best stuff and just left there to be flattened. But you see sixty years ago it was all worthless.

Across the road was Main Street where the Potters (Gypsy origin) lived. This was a really ancient street that lead right to Golly's school. They also flattened that. Today it wouldn't and couldn't happen, it would all be listed and preserved. Those properties were built in the 1600's, quaint interesting places, but back in the 1950's, slums.

Today that road is known as 'Mainway' all high rise flats.

• CHAPTER 5 •

BONFIRES

O ne thing Golly remembers is that where ever he went he would build a fire, sometimes his fires got out of control. Like setting fire to the railway embankment, when this happened Golly and his mates would scarper and the Fire Brigade would turn up.

Of course Bonfire night was a great event! Golly and his mates would start their bonfire weeks, sometimes months beforehand. They would collect all sorts of stuff from local houses.

Golly remembers being out with his mates collecting all sorts of 'junk' that he now realises would be worth good money today if he still had it.

Golly and his gang would build a massive stack of stuff, but they always had a den in the middle of it.

More often than not a gang from over the road would sneak up during the night and set fire to it. The next morning the lads in Golly's gang would see that their bonfire and den had been burnt to the ground. Golly thinks that sort of thing used to happen to peoples bonfires everywhere.

The gang across the road who were responsible for burning down Golly's bonfires were known locally as the 'Potters'. These people were, as told in the previous chapter, families of gypsy origin, they made their living as Scrap Metal Dealers and during the war they made a fortune.

They didn't have to serve in the Armed Forces during the war because Scrap Metal Dealing was classed as a 'Reserved Occupation'. To explain this description simply, this term meant that they were involved in work of National importance, essential to the country. What a job Eh ?!!

The Potters were a tough bunch but pretty much OK. Golly was bought up amongst them, all the kids in the same classes at school. Some of these lads are still Golly's friends to this very day. Golly has always been a very loyal person. Golly learned a lot from them for example how to live off his wits, something he still does right up to the present day.

• CHAPTER 6 •

WORK, MUSIC AND MORE HEROES

It will come as no surprise that the first thing that Golly did when he picked up his first weeks wage from Storeys Mill, he went with his Mam and Dad to Simmons Music shop and picked out an electric solid guitar, it was a 'Futurama II' for 26 Guineas, (A guinea was 21 Shillings, in those days a shilling was what we term 5p now, 20 shillings was a £1 so £.05p in today's money) Golly also got a an Elpico Amplifier for around 24 Guineas. As he says, "I might be slightly out on the price, but I know it was about £50 for the two."

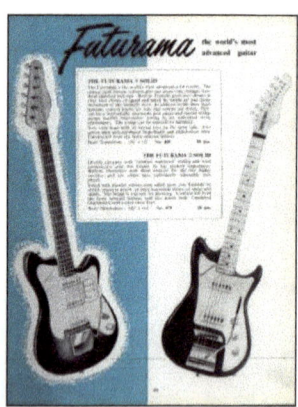

Golly's first electric guitar

Golly's first amplifier

Of course his Mam and Dad had to sign the HP (hire purchase) agreement on Golly's behalf. He thinks the payments were 30 bob, £1.50 in today's money. A real mill stone round his neck, but Golly knew he would be OK. He was, because he had a plan, he had already lined up some of his mates to form a group.

Bill Robinson, who Golly had met in The Cadets was a good singer, in fact he used to get up and sing with a group, 'The Defenders', who played at his local youth club in Lancaster. Mally Lord, Golly's oldest school mate had bought a mixed up set of drums from a local lad, Jim Livesey, Golly thinks his name was. To be fair he was a pretty good drummer, he never had lessons, but he had natural talent. A lad called Tony Dixon bought a red solid guitar and came in on Rhythm Guitar but he couldn't play so he faded out after a couple of days.

Anyhow they were making a pretty decent sound that made sense with just the three of them. They were playing mainly Buddy Holly stuff although Golly remembers learning 'Sheila', a Tommy Roe hit and 'Don't You think it's Time' by Mike Berry. But of special interest to Dave who is writing the book, the lads used to do 'Buttons and Bows' which had been recorded by Tommy Bruce. Dave of course was Tommy Bruce's friend and manager.

All this took place in late summer/early autumn 1962 and around that time a lad that Golly knew slightly called Dave Graham, came knocking on his door. He knew that Golly could play a bit and he invited him to join his group, well the one he was about to form. It is stretching it a bit to call them a group, in reality apart from Dave who could play, they were just a few lads, slightly older than Golly who had bought instruments that they couldn't play. They couldn't play anything, as Golly says, "basically they hadn't got a clue."

The line up would be, Dave Graham (Lead Guitar), Mick Whitfield (Drums), John Redfern (Bass),Golly Goulding Rhythm Guitar), and Albert Hogg singing through a tape recorder. Dave was really quite a talented musician who could play a few instruments. This was good for Golly because Dave taught him a few more chords. Albert had a very good voice but the other two, John and Mick, were completely and utterly out of it.

Golly had joined up with them for a couple of months and to be fair they had managed to get a few bookings at a place called 'Davy Jones Locker'. This was a pub in a cellar on Morecambe Sea Front. The place was full of drunks who didn't know the difference between music and none music, which as Golly said, "Was what they were playing." Anyway Golly got out of the group as quickly as he could.

Davy Jones locker

49

Having escaped from "That lot" as he put it Golly went back with Bill and Mally, they had met up with a lad called Adrian Elleray who could play a few chords, the lads did few rehearsals but it came to nothing. In the mean time Golly got back in touch with Dave Graham and asked him to join up with as he put it "Our lot". Dave did and a new group was formed. "Jet Black and The Dakotas". The group sounded OK and they did a few bookings. But Golly's playing was improving and he says about himself, "He was restless, very restless."

Jet Black & the Dakotas

Music was always going to be important but Golly still needed to work for a living so he was still working at Storey's Mill, moving around large bales of cotton and being treated like a Victorian street urchin. He was not happy with the situation but was unsure how to change it.

One day you might say fate took a hand, because a notice appeared in the window of the local Co-op, 'Youths required for shop work'. The pay was £4 – 4 shillings and six pence. If he got the job it would mean Golly working until 4-30pm on Saturdays, 5.30 pm the rest of the week, but he would get Wednesday afternoon off because that was half day closing.

Well Golly knew Mr Parkinson, the manager from his time as an errand boy. Golly had done that job for two years and he'd only finished a couple of months earlier. So he went to see Mr Parkinson. It seems he was pleased to see Golly and got straight on the phone to head office, he gave Golly a glowing reference which resulted in Golly being hired right away.

Golly started work there at 8 o'clock the following Monday. He loved working at the Lune Street branch it was only 5 minutes from home and he knew the lay-out of the shop. Also he got on great with all the staff.

Unfortunately Golly didn't realise, in fact he didn't know, that it was common practice for the youths employed by the Co-op to be shifted around from branch to branch and after a few weeks in Lune Street, that is exactly what happened to Golly.

The furthest branch he had to travel to was Bentham, a small town/village, it was about 20 miles away and he had to make his own way there. Golly's Dad was on shift work and he was able to take him some mornings. On the days he couldn't, Golly had to get an early bus to get him there for 8O' clock. Getting home was a nightmare.

Luckily a lad called Stuart who worked at a branch, in the same direction but even further away at High Bentham, had a motor-bike and he used to pick Golly up from the shop and drop him off at Halton where he lived. This meant Golly only had to endure a five mile walk home to Lancaster, great!

Anyway this was situation which couldn't last, moving around from shop to shop was doing Golly's head in. Winter was drawing in and the weather was horrendous, no wonder the winter of 1962/63 was dubbed 'The Big Freeze'. Golly was struggling

The big freeze 1962/1963

51

round from shop to shop on his push-bike. There must have been 25-30 branches of The Lancaster and District C.W.S. And Golly would bet that he worked almost every one. In fact he can't think of the one that he did not work at! Sometimes Golly was only at a store for a day. It was not unusual for him to do two three shops a week.

Of course there was no let up from Golly in pursuit of his musical dream. So he is still with his group, 'Jet Black and The Dakotas', rehearsing and doing the odd booking. Rehearsals at the infamous Scout Hut. In winter The Scout Hut was freezing, like being in an Igloo, no that's not right, an Igloo would have been warmer!

Golly was still popping over to the Red Rose Club now and again to see and hear what was going on. One night Golly heard this sound, it was music coming from a few lads having a practice in one of the small rooms. Well he knew one of them Adrian, from a previous get together rehearsal, he had improved a bit. But what really struck Golly was the way the lad playing drums, Mick Elliott was laying down a real heavy driving beat. Ideas came quickly to Golly, he thought "I will pull these two for my next group."

So the thing was 'The Dakotas' a name they had pulled from a current Western TV series was about to fold. In case anybody was wondering Golly had the perfect reason, he'd just seen a group called 'Billy J Kramer And The Dakotas', how could his current line up continue to call themselves 'The Dakotas'? they couldn't. Without hesitation, Golly had his new line up, Bill Robinson, Mick and Adrian and they became 'The Fontaines'.

So once again Golly was back in rehearsals, this time at his old Boys club, which had Central Heating, lovely and warm. So there was a decision to be made, what would be the new groups sound? All the local groups were playing 'The Shadows' numbers, not very well. By now 1962, Golly had been introduced to 'Chuck Berry', while he admits to never having heard of him before, he wanted to play like Chuck.

Tony and the Fontaines

Almost all guitarists were just playing single strings, but Chuck Berry was much different. When he played a solo he was hitting two or three strings at a time. This to Golly was the way forward, so he set about learning to play this style, of course he hadn't allowed for the size of Chuck Berry's hands. Compared to Golly's, they were massive. However in spite of that difference Golly mastered the skill.

By 1963 Rhythm and Blues was coming in so 'The Fontaines' became an R&B Group. They desperately needed a Bass Player but had been unable to find one. Then they heard about a lad called Terry Aitcheson who lived in Carnforth, a village about six miles from Lancaster. The lads met up with him and tried him out, enough said. Terry looked OK and he said he would buy a Hofner Violin Bass and a suit. Well they took him on, he made up the numbers but musically he added little to the groups sound.

Nevertheless 'The Fontaines' were becoming extremely popular , the sound they were putting out must have been OK because they started to get busy, plenty of gigs were coming in. They looked the part too, Brown Stage Suits with velvet half collars and their hair was getting longer. 'The

Fontaines' were playing gigs in Barrow-in-Furness and the surrounding area quite a lot by this time and becoming well known. They had a load of supporters, followers, and how amazing is this? A Fan Club, which was run by two girls, Pat and Jackie. Where ever the group played they packed the place out.

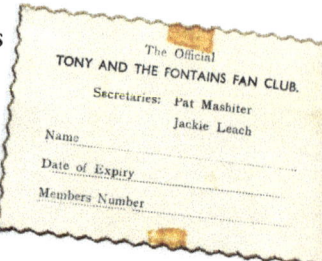

At that time the best group performing in the Barrow area were 'Frankie and The Trendsetters'. They had previously been known as 'The Tornados' and they had changed their name for obvious reasons. They saw 'The Fontaines' as rivals, a real threat. Musically these lads were way ahead of Golly's band. But, 'The Fontaines' were current and had the right look, plus they were playing R&B as were 'The Rolling Stones' and such like.

Articles about the group were beginning to appear in the local newspapers they were drawing a lot of attention. This led to 'The Fontaines' being approached by a man called John Trevorton, with a view to him becoming their manager. This man was the manager of the local cinema, a really nice bloke, he did become the groups manager and got them loads of work. More than that, he got them very good money and he would also arrange free accommodation as they would often be over in Barrow three or four nights at a time.

After a few months things were going so good, John drew up a contract for the group to sign. But they never did sign the contract, this was due to the reluctance of their singer Bill Robby. "Sign nothing" he said. Golly wanted to sign because he knew that they could have benefited highly from it.

John was an honest, straight man. Agreed, he was looking for commission, so what? He was entitled to it, because he'd put a lot of work into

54

getting them established. Golly says "We treated John badly" and after a while they just drifted apart.

It would seem that Golly in his early musical influences was obviously obsessed by guitars and guitar players. Clearly 'The Shadows' were his group of choice. He loved instrumentals and he possessed the natural talent, ability and work ethic to be able to learn and play them.

However late 1962 Golly saw a group who changed his whole musical direction. That group 'Screaming Lord Sutch and The Savages' appeared at 'The Floral Hall' Morecambe and what an impact they made, not just on Golly but the whole audience.

'Screaming Lord Sutch' always came on stage at Midnight 'The Witching Hour' as it was announced by the Dance Hall. 'The Floral' as Golly and the others called it, was one of the few Dance Halls in the country with a revolving stage. 'Screaming Lord Sutch' and his group used the revolving stage to great effect.

At midnight all the lights in the Dance Hall went out and the revolving stage came round. On stage were the Piano, Drum Kit and Amplifiers. The Guitars were leaning against the amps. But there were no Players.

For a few seconds everything was deadly quiet, suddenly there was loud shouting and yelling from the back of the room and then five figures came hurtling through from the back of the room through the audience, still shouting and yelling like Banshees. As they passed, Golly could see they were five blokes dressed in Leopard skin Loincloths and Moccasins. Everyone thinking, "What the hell is going on"? Girls were screaming with fear, even the lads looking scared, although they probably wouldn't admit it. What a shock!!

The group leapt on stage grabbed their instruments and proceeded to play. What a surprise, they opened up with 'Lucille' played as an instrumental. The guitarist's were holding their guitars almost vertical and jumping from side to side, "Pure showmanship"!

Golly says, "As a guitarist myself I can tell you what they were doing is not easy while making an excellent job of playing your instrument, I know I tried it!"

. The Savages were by far the best group that Golly has ever seen in his life. The Savages line up in 1962/63 was the best they ever had. Richie Blackmore (Guitar), Bernie Watson (Guitar), Ricky Brown, Stage name Ricky Fenson (Bass Guitar), Carlo Little, (Drums) and Andy Wren (Piano).

Screamin' Lord Sutch and the Savages

Of course 'Screaming Lord Sutch' had nicknames for a lot of his musicians. He called Richie Blackmore, 'Tulip', Bernie Watson was 'Strawberry' because he dyed his hair strawberry blonde and Andy Wren was known as 'Freddy The Flea'. Sutch called a lot of his piano players 'Freddy Lee' after 'Jerry Lee Lewis'. Incidentally 'Freddy Fingers Lee' kept the name throughout his career.

For two years previous to seeing 'Screaming Lord Sutch and The Savages' perform Golly had always dreamed of owning a solid guitar with a tremelo arm and playing 'The Shadows' music which he still loves today. But what he had started to notice was that all the hard driving gutsy groups were playing semi-acoustic guitars, no tremelo arms, instead, 'Pushing Strings', 'String Bending' as it is known today. The other thing was that none of these groups were playing Shadow's music.

Just after seeing 'The Savages' Golly heard about a local guy Bill Parkinson, (Parky) who lived quite close to where Golly lived in Lancaster. Parky had the reputation of being a good guitar player and he had a group 'Mel Dean and the Leaders'. The group used to rehearse at the local Scout Hut, (The same Scout Hut that Charlie Emmett used to lock Golly and his mates in and beat them up).

One night Golly's old group mate Dave Graham, who knew Bill, took him down to listen to the group rehearse. Well they were just about as good as it gets, they came very close to 'The Savages'.

Mel Deane -the best singer Golly ever worked with

Bill Parkinson with his Harmony Rocket Guitar, pushing strings all over the place. He was and still is one of the best guitarists in England. Golly was definitely smitten by Bill's playing, he quite simply changed Golly's life and became his lifelong hero, (One of them at least) Golly has a few more as he will tell us as we go through the book.

Best of all Bill Parkinson was a Skerton boy like Golly, something he hadn't known until that night. The whole group was amazing, Mel Deane was by far the best singer ever to come out of Golly's area, Golly can't praise him highly enough. John Boardman, JB to his friends, a quite brilliant Bass Guitarist, Sam Woods, another Skerton boy and an absolutely excellent drummer.

THE LEADERS WITH MEL DEAN

"This is it!" Thought Golly, he would now model himself and his group, 'The Fontaines' on 'The Leaders'. Golly didn't just want, he needed a semi-acoustic guitar, also he wanted to start to learn Bar Chords and String Bending and he did quickly!! Golly practised night and day and because of his determination and natural ability he became very good.

The 'Futurama' guitar went and Golly took himself off to Simmons Music Shop in Lancaster and ordered a 'Harmony Rocket'. Golly's whole outlook and musical style was about to change.

Harmony Rocket guitar

At Christmas 1963 Golly was still working at the Co-op although he wasn't doing shop work. He had applied for and got a transfer to the warehouse, harder work, but no Saturdays, that was important to Golly as he was out playing with his group every Friday night. As we say, it was Christmas and traditionally the staff from the warehouse went to the local pub at lunch time, (always called dinner time in those days).

Golly was only sixteen at the time but he was quite used to going into pubs. On this occasion Golly remembers having two or three pints which made him a bit merry. After lunch everybody went back to work and Golly remembers that he made a bit of a nuisance of himself and got told to go home by his boss. This prompted Golly to bravely announce, "I'm not bothered, I'm quitting anyway." He did and that meant that at the start of 1964 he was jobless.

Golly with his Harmony Rocket guitar which he still has to this day

When he heard about a job that was going at a firm called Lancaster Metal Spinners. So Golly went for an interview and they took him on. It was just a small family firm but Golly enjoyed working there. Unfortunately after six weeks the firm made him redundant, genuinely redundant, not sacked. The company closed down not long after they let him go. Golly thinks that they were probably unable to compete in a very competitive market.

So there he was February 1964 out of work again. This time it was two of the lad's who were in 'The Fontaines' with him who came up with a suggestion for a job. They were working at 'The Tan Yard' in Lancaster and they suggested that Golly join them. There were always jobs going at that place. Proper hard graft and awful conditions. But a young lad would be very highly paid compared to other jobs, about £7.50 a week. That was twice as much as Golly had been paid at the Metal Spinners.

So Golly went for an interview and got a job. What a dump that place was. The workers were treated like slaves, some people only lasted a day, Golly was there for about fourteen months.

While he was working in 'The Tan Yard' Golly was having his lunch and a youngish bloke wandered into the canteen, "I'm looking for Golly" he said. "Over here" said Golly. The Bloke walked over and introduced himself, "The name's Arnold, I'm Bud Bennet's son." Bud Bennet was an old time comedian who had done quite a bit of radio work during the war and post war. He had also appeared on T.V. doing programmes like,' The Good Old Days' etc. Bud had heard of 'The Fontaines' and thought it would be a good idea to manage them and also be their Agent. He certainly looked the part, he always wore a Crombie Overcoat and a Homburg Hat, he bore a strong resemblance to a famous entertainer, 'Jimmy James'. Added to that, he drove around in a big black Rover.

All that's best in modern entertainment
* * *

F.A.B. Entertainments

Direction : BUD BENNETT, B.B.C. Radio & T.V.
A.B.C. T.V. & Granada T.V. *(Artiste)*

All communications to —
36, GREAVES ROAD
LANCASTER
Lancs.

Telephone 2716

A meeting was set up and everyone agreed that he would handle the group. (Nothing on paper). Golly remembers that the first thing Bud said to him was, "Where do you go for your haircut? Lancaster Sawmills?"

Because of the generation gap and Bud being in his Sixties, he really had no idea what was going on in the music business. This meant that he relied on Golly to guide him. Golly did probably a little too much guidance really. Giving Bud all his contacts for venues, in no time at all Bud was putting other groups in the venues that Golly's group should have been appearing in. As Golly said he was extremely naive back then, after all he was still only 17 years old. As he looks back Golly doesn't think he was too bothered at the time because as he put it, the group was busy enough anyway.

At this point we need to think back a few pages to where Golly mentioned Bill Parkinson, 'Parky' and said what an exceptional guitar player he was. Something big was about to happen in Parky's career. Mike Millward from 'The Fourmost' had been taken ill and had to go into hospital for a few weeks. It was in all the Music Magazines at the time that in order for the group to fulfil their bookings, they needed someone to step in for Mike.

As the group were appearing at the 'The Pier' Morecambe on the next Friday, Parky went along and offered the group his services. He was as Golly said a really talented Lead Guitarist, he knew all the parts that he needed to play, so he impressed the other members and got the job as a temporary replacement for Mike. The other plus point was that Mike Millward was a well built guy and luckily so was Parky, and he was able to wear Mike's stage suits. Parky had the job for around eight weeks, even adopting the stage name of Wayne Lowe.

Of course this meant that the group he normally played with, 'Mel Deane and the Leaders' could not perform, in fact Golly thinks that was the end of the line for the group.

After Parky's stint with 'The Fourmost', he and Mel headed down to London. This meant that 'The Leaders' had now officially broken up. This being now, John Boardman, Bass Player, and Eric Broadbent , in Golly's opinion probably the best drummer around, were left without a group. It is worth mentioning that Bill Parkinson went on to be a guitarist of great renown playing with such luminaries of the music world as 'The Squires', 'PJ Proby', 'Screaming Lord Sutch' and 'Tom Jones'. He also wrote some great songs, including 'The Lost Soul' and 'Mother of Mine' which was a massive hit for Neil Reid. (Authors Note) What this means is that two great guitarist's came from the Lancaster area. Bill Parkinson and Golly Goulding!

As Golly says, this was his best ever break and he arranged to meet John in 'Sportsman's Coffee Bar' Morecambe, then they agreed that they should get together. Unfortunately for Golly, Eric had been offered and accepted a three night a week job drumming at 'The Jubilee Club'.

The Fontaines - Golly, Bill, Mick and JB

So with the line up of Bill Robby, J.B., Mick Elliott and Golly, 'The Fontaines' upgraded to the next stage of their career. It was Spring 1964 and the group were asked to play at 'The Tivoli' Morecambe Promenade, 7 nights a week. They were a brilliant group, their sound was spot on.

With Bill Parkinson (Parky) leaving town, all the doors were open for Golly, he jumped straight into Parky's shoes. Golly was now regarded, with good reason as the best guitarist in the area. The group had broadened their repertoire and were playing a lot of numbers previously played by 'The Leaders', for example 'Tossin' and Turnin' by Bobby Lewis and 'Bony Maronie' by Larry Williams. Stuff that none of the other groups in the area were playing.

There was another good group in the area, they were called 'The Doodlebugs'. This group were made up from past members of 'The Falcons' who used to play in France at the American Military Bases. Golly said, "I guess we were rivals in a way, but they got better work than 'The Fontaines'. This was down to a couple of reasons. A. they were older and had better equipment and B. they had a good manager, Mike Wilcox and lastly they played all the hits from the charts". 'The Fontaines' wouldn't touch that stuff, they considered it too simple and poppy. Nevertheless is was true that in those days any group who made a half decent job of playing pop stuff always seemed to be busy.

'The Fontaines' spent the summer of 1964 playing 7 nights a week at 'The Tivoli'. Suddenly J.B. Decided to leave the group, the reason being that he had got himself a girlfriend. She was a pushy little thing, who had made a 'B' line for him because he was a musician. They got married, which didn't last long. So with J.B. going and Mick Elliott courting strong 'The Fontaines' split up again.

But Golly didn't have the time to be concerned about things because Mel Deane, who had gone to London with Bill Parkinson, was back in Morecambe. Parky had joined up with PJ Proby as his Lead Guitarist. The thing was Parky was always looking out for himself and putting it bluntly, he dumped Mel. That's just the way Parky was. That said he had to let his talent take him as far as it could, anything less would have been a waste.

As Golly has said before Mel Deane was the best singer ever to have come from his area and he was looking for musicians to form a new group. Mel knew about Golly and Golly got the job as his guitarist. Mike Heap who had been in France, came in on Bass Guitar, Jim Mace a local drummer made up the group and they took over the name 'Mel Deane and The Leaders'.

Mel Deane and the Leaders - Glen, Golly, Jim and Mel

Who would have thought it, Golly taking over as the guitarist with 'Mel Deane And The Leaders', certainly not Golly. The very idea taking the place of Bill Parky as Golly says, "What an honour." It may well have been an honour but it is one that Golly deserved.

Because the original 'Leaders' had such a great reputation the new line up began to get work very easily especially with Mel Deane still being the front man. Plus the fact in Golly Goulding they had a very special guitarist indeed. Golly to this very day, while he knows his worth, does not realise just how talented a player he is. If he had been older he may have had similar opportunities to those that came Bill Parkinson's way.

So the group continued to work around the North West of England. At the time Golly was still working at The Tan Yard, but in the

Mel Deane and the Leaders - with new bass player Mike Heap

63

Spring of 1965 he walked out. This sudden departure came about because of his good friend and workmate, Alan Morrin persuaded him to leave. "Let's get out" said Alan, Golly said "OK I'll give them a weeks notice." Alan said, "You don't have to." "OK I'll leave on Friday," replied Golly. "No, Sod that, do it today!" said Alan. "Right" Golly said "we'll leave at 5 o'clock." "No" said Alan, "let's go now!" So they both walked out, 10.30am on a Tuesday morning, unheard of in those days.

They got their stuff together and walked through and out of the yard. People were shouting, "Where are you two going?" We've quit!" The two lads replied. "You can't do that, you have to work your notice," people shouted. Well they didn't and that was that. They did go back on the following Friday to collect their cards and a bit of holiday pay. From that very day Golly was on his own and he had to start to learn how to live off his wits.

He was doing OK with gigs for the group so he always had a few quid with which to pay the HP for his Vox AC 30 amp and his beloved Epiphone Casino Guitar.

In the meantime Golly took a trip to Manchester with his mates. They went to see Chuck Berry. Chuck Berry was playing through this massive square cabinet with an Amp sat on top. Golly was using a Vox AC30 the best thing around at the time, but Chuck Berry's was something different. Golly thought "What the hell is that? What a brilliant sound!" He just couldn't figure out what he was playing through.

'The Nashville Teens' were also on the bill and as well as doing their own set they were also the backing group for Chuck Berry and that would prove significant. A few months later the 'Nashville Teens' were playing at 'The

Golly with new Epiphone Casino Guitar

Floral Hall' Morecambe. They must have stayed over, at least one of them anyway, John Hawkden the Piano Player came into 'The Tivoli Bar' where 'Mel Deane and The Leaders' were appearing. Golly recognised him immediately and asked him, "What was that big thing Chuck Berry was playing through?" "It's called a Marshall," said John, "This bloke Jim Marshall makes them in this workshop down London, you can get them if you know where to look."

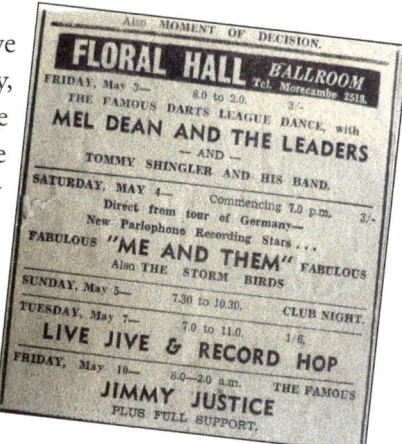

The next day Golly went into Stan Milston's Music shop in Lancaster and asked him about Marshall's. "Never come across that one" said Stan, "But I will make some enquiries". This he did and a few weeks later he told Golly that he knew how to get one, going on to say it will cost £160. Golly had no hesitation, "I want it" he said. Sure enough a month later it arrived. Golly was delighted but the HP payments had now increased to £3 ten shillings a week. Golly also remembers telling his Auntie Cath about his new amplifier and Guitar, which totalled around £350. "You must be crackers" she said "You could buy a nice car for that kind of money" "Ah, but I don't want a nice car" replied Golly. "These are my working tools" he added.

When Mick Heap, the group's bass player saw Golly's new Marshall, he asked Stan, "Do they do a Bass Amp?" Stan replied, "They do." So Mick ordered one too.

"Golly thinks we are up to Christmas 1964 or early 1965. As Golly said, 'Mel Deane And The Leaders' were doing pretty well in and around the North West, but you have to remember Mick had been a pro player in France and Mel had been a pro. singer in London. Golly was desperate to turn pro. So the group decided to go to London.

A. Because Mel had contacts there and

B. That was where they held the auditions for groups contracted to play in France and Germany.

Golly and Mel

Mick knew all about the American Military Bases in France, He filled Golly's head with great thoughts and ambition. He told Golly, "You can get £30 quid a week but you have to pay for your own hotel, which is fairly cheap so you end up with about £20 quid." Golly wanted some of that. So around springtime 1965, one Saturday morning, the group headed off to London. At this time the group had a Road Manager called Sib, he was a Rhythm Guitar player who had been playing with

Sib's J2 van

a local group called 'The Milestones'. He fancied doing something a bit different. So he did, by driving the band around in his Morris J2 Van and hanging out with 'Mel Deane and The Leaders' certainly was a bit different, that's for sure. So Sib's van was now fully loaded with musical equipment and suitcases. The lads had no idea where the hell they were going to, beyond the fact that it was London and that was the place to be discovered. They had very little money between them, but they did have one thing in their favour they knew that they looked and sounded great!! Remember this was the mid sixties and the whole music scene was alive and really buzzing.

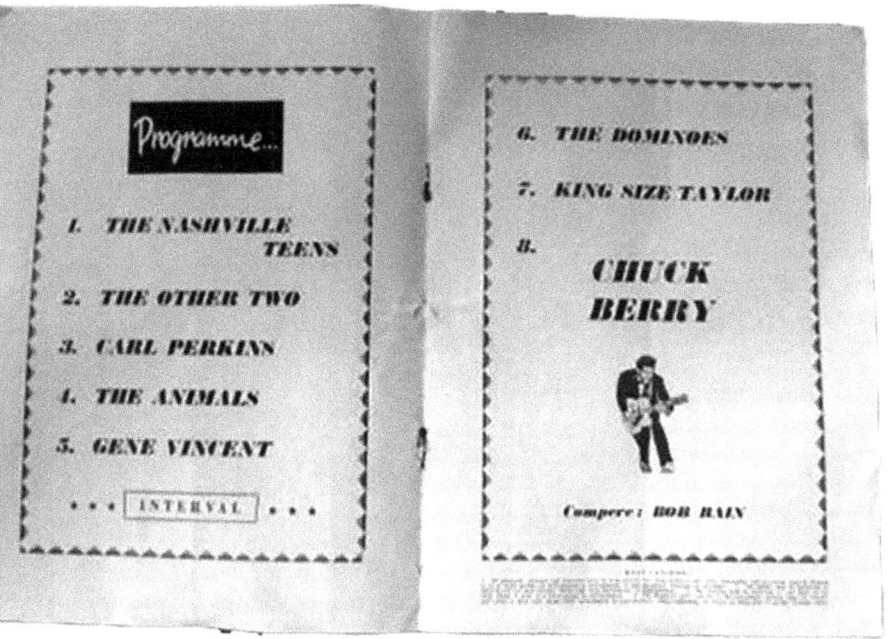

• CHAPTER 7 •

LONDON

They arrived in London and found their way to the West End. Mel took them to a club on Tottenham Court Road called 'The Plughole' because he knew the owner, Jimmy James. He was pleased to see Mel and he offered them a few bookings in the club. What a great start to their first day in the West End of London.

Happy and excited the lads went back to the van to start unloading all the gear. They saw a label/ticket thing on the windscreen, obviously a parking ticket. The lads had never known such things up north. So they asked Jimmy about it, "What's this?" they asked. "Where are you parked?" he asked, "Outside they replied." "Bloody hell, you can't park there, no wonder you got a ticket, go and park round the corner," Jimmy said. So Sib went and parked up and the rest of them went back into the club. When they came out again later, they had another parking ticket.

They couldn't understand it, but they soon learnt, they picked up five parking tickets during their first weekend in London. Parking Meters, Yellow Lines, restrictions and all that stuff. The lads had never seen or heard of these things before.

The lads could not afford accommodation in London so, as they had planned on doing when they set off on this adventure, they slept in the van. At least they had a base... Their base was 'The Plughole' That was where they could store their gear and rehearse, plus they could play there more or less any time.

Open six nights and six lunchtimes a week 'The Plughole' on Tottenham Court Road was a trendy club. At lunchtime you got all the office workers popping in for a bite to eat and maybe do a bit of dancing. The club had a resident DJ, his name was Errol Bruce, he had just left Radio Caroline to do 'The Plughole'. Errol was a Canadian, more importantly for the club, he was a great DJ and well connected. His job was to plug all the new pop records, hence the name.

'The Plughole' had a Janitor, a bloke called Arthur Brown. Arthur used to sweep the floor and clean the club in return for his efforts, Jimmy let him use the club in the afternoons for rehearsals with his group. 'The Arthur Brown Union'. Occasionally Arthur's band would share the bill with, 'Mel Deane and The Leaders'.

Arthur Brown

'The Arthur Brown Union' used to go down better with the audience than 'Mel Deane and The Leaders'. There was a good reason for this Arthur's group were playing Soul Music, 'Mel Deane and The Leaders' were doing R&B and American Rock and Roll. The problem with that was that 'The Mod' thing was just starting to hit the scene and the stuff Golly and the lads were playing (unbeknown to them) was or seemed a bit dated. Especially for 'Swinging London' in the 'Swinging Sixties' as they are now called.

Just as a matter of record there is a footnote to the Arthur Brown story. About 3 years later when 'The Plughole', Tottenham Court Road, London was just a memory for Golly, he and Carol were watching a TV music programme, 'Top of the Pops', Golly, to his amazement spotted Arthur Brown on the screen. Arthur was singing 'Fire'. Golly remembers saying to Carol, "That's a good song it will do well". It did do very well eventually making it the number one spot in the charts. Golly was really happy for Arthur because he always thought that Arthur was special, striking and a different kind of performer. Especially to a group of lads from the North. Having said that Arthur was from Yorkshire, but his style and music wasn't.

Sib's J2 Van was home for the boys throughout the Spring and Summer of 1965. Every night they would park up on The Tower of London Car Park. They had to get off there in the daytime otherwise they would have had to pay a charge. The Tower car park was the ideal spot for the lads, they had the benefit of great toilet and wash room facilities, kept spotlessly clean by a bloke who worked there all day. Also there was a snack bar/breakfast trailer where they could get tea or coffee, a bacon roll, or whatever they wanted.

There was a draw back with living in the van and parking where they did though. On one particular evening the lads came back and parked up the van. Sib and Golly were thirsty so went to look for a shop and get a bottle of pop. They were walking for some time and distance and found no sign of a shop. No surprise really as they were in the City of London there were no corner shops there. Of course Golly and Sib were from the North, they had no way of knowing that.

They kept walking and as they walked down one street they saw two bottles of milk on a door step. As Golly says, "You can guess what's coming." It is worth mentioning that in those days in The City of London milk was delivered the night before maybe it is still the same today, we don't know. Anyway they picked up a bottle each and started drinking it as they walked along. Walking towards them were two blokes, they asked the question, "Where did you get the milk?" Golly and Sib replied, "We just found it." "You just nicked them off a step." One of them said. Then the other said "You are coming to the station with us." Unbeknown to Sib and Golly the two blokes were CID policeman.

They were marched to the police station and charged, which the lads admitted to. Then they were asked, "What are you doing wandering round the city late at night?" Golly and Sib replied "Looking for a shop." The police officers were amused when they heard that. After that they treated the two lads with a more friendlier attitude. Several of the officers were talking to Golly and Sib asking them about why they had come down south. When the lads said they were in group and that they were living in their van and parking on The Tower of London Car Park, one of the officers said. "Oh I've seen that van, I know who you are."

The officers kindly brought Sib and Golly pints of orange juice and supper and of course gave them a cell for the night. The two lads were treated like celebrities

The next morning they were put in a police van, a 'Black Maria' as they were called in those days and taken to 'Bow Street Magistrates Court' where they were locked in another cell. After a while they were called and escorted through into the courtroom. The magistrates said, "You can be tried here and now if you choose, or you will be remanded in custody to be tried at the 'Old Bailey' on whatever date?" Well thought Golly, we have all heard of 'The Old Bailey' from news of Murder Trials etc. it was always popping up on Telly. Golly's response to the question was, "What for nicking a bottle of milk??" He couldn't hold back because he was clearly shocked and concerned. The magistrate replied, "If I hear another outburst like that I'll hold you in contempt of court." Unbelievable this. Golly Goulding in the notorious 'Bow Street Magistrates Court'.

Bow Street Magistrates

The lads were advised to be tried there and then. They had already pleaded guilty anyway and were then bound over. As Golly, said, "Whatever that means." and ordered to pay 15 shillings each Court Costs. But as Golly put it, "They had had the best night's sleep that they had had for ages and had been well catered for. Bloody Hell, what an Experience."

'Mel Deane and The Leaders' were a novelty to the people who worked around the area. Even the police, as mentioned in a previous paragraph, would come and chat with them late at night, asking them about their progress etc. Everyone knew why the lads were there and would say things like "We might see you on the telly sometime." As Golly said, "Bloody Hell, if only !!"

The lads found out through reading 'Melody Maker' magazine where all the auditions were being held for groups wanted for work on the Continent. They had a routine worked out for the auditions, starting with an instrumental called, 'Follow The Leaders', a great number written by Bill Parkinson the former guitarist with the group. Then Mick would introduce Mel and they would go straight into Ronnie Hawkins 'Southern Love', followed by Bobby Lewis's 'Tossin' and Turnin', finishing their set with Bobby Vee's 'More Than I Can Say'. The lads performed trimmed down versions of the numbers so as not to overdo it. They felt that this sequence of songs would show off their talent.

You see the people holding the auditions were agents who really only cared about money, just sitting there all day long listening to all the hopefuls who wanted to get ahead. A lot of the time they would stop the group mid song and say, "That's enough, we'll let you know." When 'Mel Deane and The Leaders' played the agents listened and the group sailed through every stage of the audition.

Golly says; "There were some very mediocre groups there, but we did see some really good ones who were signed up right away." After we passed our audition Mick would go up to the table but he always came back with the same answer. " Can't go till August because of Golly." You see Golly was still only 17 and you had to be 18 to work abroad. Golly wouldn't be 18 until the 2nd of August 1965, as he says. "I knew I was holding the others back, but they didn't hold it against me."

It was the same story every time. One agent said, "I thought you were already out there, Oh no, he's too young isn't he." Golly and the rest of the lads were probably too naive to lie about his age. As Golly said, "it would never cross my mind to lie about a thing like my age." Going on to say, "I've since learned that many a young lad lied about his date of birth and got away with it."

So the lads were still hanging around London waiting to go abroad, but Mel was not wasting time, he introduced the rest of the group to various agents and managers, some of whom took a shine to the lads and their music. One name Golly remembers was Brian Somerville apparently he had been a publicity agent, something like that for 'The Beatles'. Brian had seen the group perform and really thought they had potential. A meeting with Brian and the group was set up but the lads did not turn up.

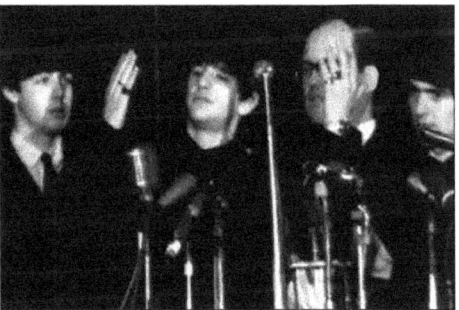

Brian Sommerville with the Beatles

As Golly puts it, "We couldn't be bothered to leave the pub." He goes on to say, "This sort of thing was normal for us, any chance or opportunity that came along we would blow it big style. Yes we knew we were good, better than most, as did a lot of other people who had seen and heard us perform, but not as good as we would need to be to ignore any opportunities that would come our way."

The thing was as Golly says "We treated our elders like shit, we wouldn't listen to any advice of any kind, from anyone, we thought we were it." Golly and the lads were heading for problems and as he says,

"We got a real blow one night." They were doing a gig in 'The Plughole' and some important agent or manager came to watch us. After the show he came up to Golly and said, "That was the biggest bastardisation of 'Walk On By' I have ever heard." Golly was stunned as he says, "To be honest I had put together a great arrangement of Dionne Warwick's 'Walk On By' and it was one of our best numbers, but not to this bloke, I was gutted. This was the first time in my life I'd ever been criticized, I came down to earth with a real hard landing, I just didn't know how to handle it."

Bill Parkinson was in the club that night, he was playing with PJ Proby at that time. Golly says, "I went and spoke to Bill and told him what the bloke had said." Bill replied "Don't let it bother you, it's happened to me many a time, this is how it is, you just haven't clicked with him."

Be that as it may, the four lads, Golly, Mel and the other 'Leaders' had big egos, like Golly would guess a lot of teenagers have, especially when they have talent and as 'The Leaders' were at that time, appearing regularly on stage. Golly says, "Back in the north we were 'big shots' but in London we meant nothing."

In the end hanging about living in a van and waiting for August got the better of the lads. They were falling out among themselves and generally fed up. So Golly joined up with London group 'The Rippers' and Mick also started playing with another group. Of course this was only meant to be on a temporary basis, the group just didn't know it. This turned out to be a good thing because it kept the lads apart for a bit. Just something different to do.

'The Mojos'? Mick Heap the group's bass player responded to an ad in Melody Maker 'Guitarist and Bass Player required for recording group'. Mick and Golly went on to meet with a bloke called 'Bob' who said he had been the singer with 'The Mojos' at some stage. He also said that he still had a recording contract. Well they had a rehearsal which went OK but nothing went any further than that.

Many, Many years later Golly asked Nicky Crouch an original member of 'The Mojos' about this 'Bob'. Nicky told him that when the original group split up in the 60's there were different line-ups, but he didn't recognise this bloke 'Bob'.

Anyway, things were not going well then Golly got a telegram from a lad the name of Will, this is the one and only telegram that he has ever received, he still has it. Will was a very good drummer, who had played with 'The Milestones' he wanted Golly to phone him. Golly made the call, it turned out that Will had a line-up of musicians and asked Golly if he wanted to come back to Morecambe and complete the group. If Golly would do this they would be guaranteed seven nights a week playing at 'The Tivoli Bar'.

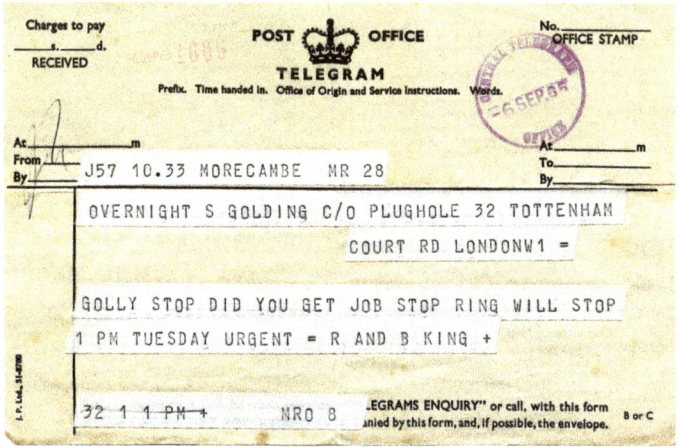

At first Golly was undecided but after thinking about it for a few days he made the decision to go back to Morecambe and play in the new line-up. With hindsight probably a good decision in the circumstances. In fact, as Golly has been known to reflect it might have lead to more success if they had gone to Liverpool in 1964 instead of going to London. If you think about it there was a lot more happening on Merseyside in the Sixties.

CHAPTER 8

HOME AGAIN

There were good things about the new group, Golly was back with his old singer Bill Robby, Will who sent the telegram and former member of 'The Milestones' also Sib who had been Road Manager with 'The Leaders' and Glen Knowles on Bass. The other lads wanted to use the name 'The Fontaines' once again. Golly had no objection to this, so 'The Fontaines' were back in business and they still had the best guitarist in the area.

The Fontaines in the Tivoli

So a few rehearsals later the group was playing at 'The Tivoli' seven nights a week, what's more they packed the place every night. Back then Morecambe, like all the seaside towns was very busy, people wanted to be entertained. This meant that 'The Fontaines' were in high demand and it was not unusual for them to appear at 'The Floral Hall' after they had already done a night on stage at 'The Tivoli'.

The Fontaines in the Tivoli

This was made possible by the fact that licensing laws in Morecambe and in most other places were very strict in those days, so at 10.30 pm on a Friday and 11 O'clock on a Saturday the lads would get their gear in the van and be on stage at 'The Floral' by midnight, As Golly says,

"Double Your Money, very nice."

Alan Birdsall 'The Floral Hall Manager' had a real knack when it came to booking Groups. He got great results. His success came from recognising which Groups were up and coming and booking them months in advance, so by the time they came to perform at 'The Floral Hall' they would be riding high in the charts. He achieved this many times.

Alan told Golly himself that he had been able to book the 'The Beatles' for 60 quid and Golly heard from another source that he got 'The Rolling Stones' for less than £100. The best night Alan ever had was when he had 'Acker Bilk' appearing. 'Stranger On the Shore' was at the top of the charts. Alan said that was his busiest night that 'The Floral Hall' ever had. That must have been some night because Golly has seen some busy nights there in his time.

Strangely enough Golly can't remember much about 1965, just that 'The Fontaines' were playing 7 nights a week and that situation went right through until the end of the year. Of course if any special events came along, The Tivoli management would allow them to bring in a dep. group, (a stand in).

The lads had been booked to appear at the Christmas Dance at Morecambe Football Club and that is where Golly met an absolutely stunning girl, Carol Bonnell for the first time. Carol was there with her mates and they were all knocked out by the music that 'The Fontaines' were playing. Carol had never heard Blues stuff played authentically. Probably the closest to it that she had heard was the stuff being played in the charts by 'The Rolling Stones' and 'The Pretty Things' etc. which was of course R&B. 'The Fontaines' were trying to knock it out in the way that the real Blues Players were doing it, And yes, they were, and that's a fact, what's more they were making a bloody good job of it.

The Tivoli

Anyway Carol and her mates got talking to the lads and they told them that they were playing at 'The Tivoli' every night. Well the following night they all came in to 'The Tiv'. From then onwards they carried on visiting at every opportunity to watch and listen to this fantastic Group. Carol loved 'The Floral Hall' as we all did, but a lot of her mates preferred 'The Pier'. 'The Pier' also a Ballroom, didn't have the atmosphere that 'The Floral Hall' had. "It couldn't come close," as Golly puts it.

The Floral Hall

'The Floral Hall' being a tough old joint was still frequented by the last remnants of 'The Teddy Boys'. The real plus factor was they always had the best music being played by groups who were by far the best musicians around. For example imagine having 'Screaming Lord Sutch and his Savages' on at 'The Pier', not that he would have appeared there, but if he had, the audience would have been too terrified to watch them.

So 'The Fontaines' carried on doing the 'The Tivoli' right up until New Years Eve 1965. Golly had got to know Carol a

The Pier

little bit better and liked her qualities. She was a decent local lass with a good education and impeccable manners. Dead working class but well brought up, she was also a bit of a 'MOD' and she could make her own clothes. She was very pretty as well, Golly was getting interested.

After 'The Fontaines' had finished playing for the night at 'The Tivoli' more often than not they would all walk across the road to 'The Sportsman's Bar'. This was a coffee bar that opened late, they didn't serve alcohol, but they did do great toasted sandwiches, a novelty then. They used to do a 'Sportsman's Special' for 'half a crown', expensive to most people but not for the lads out of the group, because they had just been paid £10 each by 'The Tivoli'.

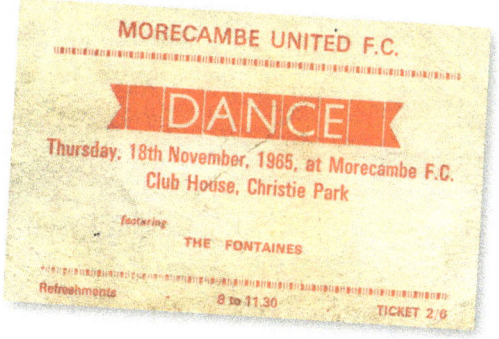

New Years Eve 1965 was an important night for Golly, because he took Carol home to her house in Lancaster, it was a couple of miles away from where he lived. From that night on Golly and Carol were officially dating. For the first time in years Golly had a steady girlfriend.

Now going back to Golly's school days we will remember the incident with a lad called Roland Timmis. He was the lad that Golly and his gang tied to the clothes post, then built a fire round him. Certainly not something Roland could forget anyway. Well like a lot of Golly's old school mates Roland used to come and watch the group play at 'The Tivoli'. Well he really fancied Carol's mate so now and then they would all go out to the pictures as a foursome. Roland's romance didn't last long, Golly doesn't think they were really suited, but Golly and Carol were!!

Golly's story has now reached January 1966 and as always things on the entertainment scene were quietening off. 'The Tivoli' put the group on two nights a week. All the other lads had day jobs but not Golly, he was too scared to even think about getting one.

Carol on the other hand had a good job in the drawing office of 'Morecambe Electric'. She was a good hearted girl so she always paid for the pictures. Golly now thought it was time she met his Mam so he took Carol home and introduced her. Golly's Mam was very impressed, saying later that she thought to herself, "Just the kind of girl our Steve, (Golly) needs". Carol's Mum and Dad on the other had were at bit curious about this bloke their daughter was going out with. "What does he do for a living?" they asked. "Well", said Carol, "He plays guitar in a pub." "What does he do in the day?" They asked. "Nothing" said Carol. Well that was it they tried everything to put her off Golly. Which Golly says now that this was a decision he understood, as parents they wanted the best for their daughter.

He can still hear what they had to say in his mind now. "This lad with long hair, no job, plays music in pubs and to make it worse he has no intention of getting a proper job. What do you see in him?"

The Fontaines having a few beers

On top of this Golly was getting plenty of earache from his own parents, on the same subject. But as he says, "a regular job just wasn't for me."

But salvation was just round the corner. Glen the Bass Player in the group used to have a pint in 'The Morecambe Hotel'. This place was very close to the Fire Station and all the firemen and auxiliary firemen used to drink in there. Well Glen knew this bloke, named Owen who was a part time fireman (auxiliary). He also had a window cleaning round, he said to Glen, "If your mate Golly wants a bit of work tell him to be at 'The George Hotel' on Monday morning at 9 0'clock. Glen passed on the message saying, "You will like Owen, all the lads do, he is a good laugh."

So 9 0'clock on the Monday morning, Golly was at 'The George Hotel', Golly found out that all the window cleaning lads met up there every second Monday. Golly introduced himself to the bunch of blokes there, which included Owen. He remembers that it must have been around Spring time because it was a nice sunny day. Golly was

Torrisholme Wagonette George Hotel

given a few instructions and a ladder. He picked the job up very quickly and enjoyed the work. Plus he was getting 5 bob, (Shillings) an hour, not a bad wage in those days.

Golly was actually enjoying going to work because it just didn't seem like a proper job. The way they worked was that 5 or 6 of the lads would start on a street. Some cleaning the front windows and others cleaning the back windows. They would not see much of each other for a few hours, then they'd meet up and go to the nearest café for tea and toast or something similar.

These were 'Happy Days', every day Owen would take Golly back to his house for dinner, his wife Hazel always had a good hot meal ready for them at 12.30pm. They really took Golly under their wing, he tried to pay them for his meals but they would never accept. Hazel was a great cook. The other thing Owen helped Golly with was transport. Owen realised that living in Lancaster getting to work in Morecambe every day was a problem for Golly. Sometimes Golly's Dad would run him down to work or pick him up it just depended what shift he was on. More often than not Golly had to get the bus. So Owen told Golly that he knew where there was a scooter for sale, it was a Lambretta and Golly bought it for £8 and he loved it. Golly had the scooter but he had no Insurance, Licence, L Plates or Crash helmet. He rode it right up to the day he got caught by a copper. He was fined for the lot, no Licence, no Insurance and no L plates plus driving without due care and attention. It wasn't compulsory to wear a crash helmet back then. Golly says, "That was the end of that, although maybe it wasn't, I think I still rode it."

Lambretta Scooter

Golly really loved working with Owen and the lads, he was saving money and was still able to pay off his HP. Yes it was still going. He had a steady girlfriend and playing music. Golly had it all.

There was a problem for Owen though as winter was drawing in and they were experiencing a lot of rain. Sometimes it rained all week, this meant that no windows could be cleaned so Owen wasn't earning anything, he was getting very depressed. The situation wasn't so bad for Golly he didn't need that much.

One day Owen said to Golly, "If I could sell up I'd do it tomorrow." Well, Golly just happened to know someone who wanted to buy a window cleaning round, not Golly it was out of his league. Anyway Golly set up a meeting and Owen sold the round. The buyer was none other than Jim Mace who had been Golly's drummer in 'The Leaders'. What a surprise.

Jim had stayed in London after Golly came back., while he was down there Jim did OK. So he came home with a few quid and like Golly fancied a Window Cleaning Round, working when it suited him and answering to no one. Anyway Jim bought the round there and then.

Golly also had plans. Because Owen had packed up he went in search of another job. He had the Lambretta Scooter that he had bought for £8 thanks to Owen. So being mobile he went down to the West End of Morecambe to look for a lead. The first window cleaner Golly saw was a bloke called Tom. He took Golly on immediately 6/- an hour good money for a good reason.

All the work was Hotels, Boarding houses, three and four stories high. As Golly says, "you needed to be more like a rock climber than a window cleaner for those jobs." Going on to say, "You see the way the properties were built, first or ground floor  windows were cleaned while standing on a small ladder, then second and third etc. would be cleaned by climbing up at one end and walking round the bay window while holding on with one hand and cleaning the windows with the other. There was always a drain pipe in between the houses, so when cleaning the windows you could climb across to the next house. I could clean the fronts of between eight and ten houses and never use a ladder. I'd be up there all day, it was like a circus act, I used to get an audience. Bloody Mad."

The West End of Morecambe had loads of window cleaners, all very busy, hundreds' of small hotels all spotlessly clean with hanging baskets outside. The hoteliers had great pride in their properties. There were also hundreds of shops and the older window cleaners had a monopoly on cleaning shop windows. Having shops on their books gave them security. Because shop windows were cleaned two to three times a week, raining or not. Plus you only needed a small pointed ladder to do the job. One of the window cleaners, Sid, had hardly used a ladder in years. If Golly could even get to that level, he would have cracked it.

The thing was, window cleaners were making three or four times the wage of the average working man. Golly wanted some of that. He had got to know a bloke called Frank Brooks, he had the best round in the West End. Frank advised Golly to start on his own. He told Golly about a block of Hotels that he didn't really want to do. He said, "I'll take £20 at £5 a week and you can have them." "I'll have them" said Golly. So he quit working for the other bloke and started on his own. He was getting six shilling per property and he could do two or three an hour, or just over. This equated to about 15 shillings and hour. Mega money. Imagine that!!

Golly quickly increased his round and within a few months he had men working for him. He was getting about £30 per week at a time when his dad was working shifts for about £17. Golly was really well off and business was growing so fast that he had six men working for him. As he said "Lile Golly Eh? Not bad!"

Golly was ambitious and he knew he was going places. Also he was getting serious with Carol and they would talk about work and the future. Carols Parents were getting to understand Golly a bit and his own Mam and Dad were proud of what he was achieving. As Golly says, "Of course it was all down to hard work , you don't get owt for nowt".

One night on the way home from 'The Tivoli', Golly said to Carol, "Shall we get engaged?" Golly thinks it was possibly a surprise to Carol, he doesn't know, but he thinks she said yes. Anyway they agreed to talk the following dinner time. With Golly working in the West End and Carol working a couple of miles down the road they were able to meet up every lunch time and he would treat her to chips and beans, or similar at Reddy's Café on Yorkshire Street. So they met up the following day, it was a yes and they went to look for a ring.

Golly and Carol

Carol fancied a Diamond Solitaire and they found one at a jewellers on The Promenade. She tried it on and they bought it there and then. So now Golly is really feeling like an adult, still only eighteen but he was engaged and a self employed 'Window Cleaning Contractor'. Golly says 'Contractor' because it always looked good on his Bill Heads. S J Goulding, Window Cleaning Contractor, Fully Insured ETC. ETC. Golly had some good jobs on his books he and Carol were saving up and collecting stuff for their bottom drawer, exiting times indeed!

Golly and Carol

Golly was still playing guitar but Bill, the group's singer was also engaged to be married and he was looking for a bit of security. But it still came as a bit of a shock to all the lads when he joined The Police Force. Bill said he joined because when you went in the police you automatically got a house with the job. He needed the house because they had a baby on the way. So faced with the loss of their singer 'The Fontaines' disbanded.

Golly thought that this might be a good time to put an idea he had into practice. His idea was to put together a group similar to 'The Graham Bond Organisation'. He had seen them perform a few times at 'The Marquee' down in London.

They were doing Blues/Jazz stuff which he loves. Graham Bond on Organ, Alto Sax, and vocals and playing Bass Pedals with his feet. Ginger Baker on Drums and Dick Heckstall-Smith on Tenor Sax, what a sound!!

John Boardman (JB) formally of 'The Leaders' and 'The Fontaines' approached Golly to say that after playing with 'The Doodlebugs' he was getting fed up and left the group along with Terry Norman (Organist), so they were looking for something different.

So this now brings Golly to the true story of 'The MBQ', there have been other versions but this is how it was. JB, Terry and Golly formed a group but they didn't have a singer. Luckily Mel Deane was back in town and at first he agreed to join them. Well that only lasted a week or two, Mel never could get on with J.B. Going right back to the early days of 'The Leaders' so

Will, JB & Golly. The start of the MBQ

Mel cleared off and another singer was required. Bill Robby, as said previously, had joined the police force and was stationed in Morecambe. So he came along to a couple of rehearsals but his heart just wasn't in it. Plus the fact that he had been told, "Policemen mustn't have a second job or mix with people from their past." Basically although Bill hadn't been perfect in his past he was now a 'Copper'.

This left the group still needing a singer. A bloke called Barry Griffin had just come back from a stint in France singing with a group called 'The Agents'. Griff as he was known came along to see the lads in the group and he immediately joined them. The group had a pretty good sound, especially with Terry on Organ, he was a proper trained musician, not like the rest of the group. Golly's old mate Will was on Drums.

Another musician joined them, Stan Vernon. Stan was a reasonable guitarist but he put his guitar away and took up playing the Tenor Sax. Many years later Golly heard that Stan had told people, "I can't compete with Golly on guitar so I am going to change instruments." Well Golly says that he and Stan were never in competition, but that's what Stan said and that's what he did. Back then Stan was an average Sax player so the lads took him in to the group. That said, Stan did improve quite a lot. As Golly says that he guesses, "This also went for all of them."

So they had a five piece group and they were rehearsing up in a scout hut in Heysham Village, which was pretty close to the church. Not ideal, the vicar was always telling them to turn down the volume, or as the used to say in those days , "Tone it down.. Golly doesn't think that they ever did.

The group were doing numbers by, 'Graham Bond', 'Chris Farlowe', and 'Cliff Bennett', you know the kind of stuff not 'Poppy', a fully gutsy sound! They were still in the rehearsal stage, but they needed a name. Well as usual it was down to Golly to find one, he knew of a group who were called 'The Modern Jazz Quartet' So Golly nicked the idea and called their group, 'The Modern Blues Quintet'. After all that is what they were playing, Bluesy stuff with a bit of a modern feel to it.

The group and the music clicked straight away and they became extremely busy and Golly was really enjoying playing this music. The problem was that by now Soul Music was getting very popular, Golly didn't care for it at all. As Golly says, "There is very little for a guitarist to play in Soul Music, jingling a few chords and that's about it, no wild riffs or string bending solo's.

Golly was getting bored because the other group members wanted to do more soul. He was getting restless, again, plus he was listening to a lot of music by 'Alexis Korner'. Alexis used to on TV every week with his band 'Blues Incorporated'. Golly was passionate about the stuff they were playing. Although Alexis wasn't a brilliant guitarist, he was a piano player really, nor was he a brilliant vocalist. What he did have was 'great feel' and you could tell he gave it everything. Golly loved the bloke, he idolised the bloke as he says, "Anyone who has ever seen him or had the pleasure of meeting him would agree". You have only got to listen to 'The Rolling Stones' talk about him. They were in the audience, watching him at every opportunity during the early sixties.

Back to 'MBQ'. Soul Music was taking over and Golly was ready for quitting. Things all came to head one night when they were playing 'The Mayfair Hotel' Morecambe. The trouble started when Griff announced that 'The Pier' wanted them to start playing there on a regular basis. Now as Golly has stated earlier, he wasn't keen on playing there, although he would have done. 'The Pier' had a resident old time dance band led by Alvin Atkins. The music they played was old fashioned and in Golly's opinion, a bit crappy. 'The Pier' also had a resident Organist, Harold Graham. Harold was a great player but it was still that old fashioned sound.

Alvin Atkins Band

Alvin hated modern groups like 'MBQ' and he wasn't afraid to shout his opinion from the rooftops. Alvin and his band were all members of The Musicians Union and if Golly's group wanted to play at 'The Pier' they would have to become members. Well Golly had joined the union in 1962, a waste of his bloody time and money. They never did anything for him. Anyway he owed about three years back subscriptions, he can't remember the total amount he owed, but it was a few quid, which he wasn't for paying. So, with Soul Music, 'The Pier' and back union fees that was Golly's moment to quit. Which he did after a heated argument!

'The MBQ' got a replacement guitarist, Trevor Read and he was also a trained musician, he made them all learn or at least brush up on written music. He took the group on to great success as a soul band. Golly certainly had no regrets and joined a fantastic little band called 'Mark 4'.

Golly feels we must be around late Summer/Autumn of 1966 and he was earning good money from his window cleaning and the business was going from strength to strength. He had a proper hand cart and a set of different sized ladders, all painted in the same colour, Turquoise Blue and he had men working for him. Back then Golly thinks that window cleaning was a semi-skilled trade. And window cleaners were treated with great respect. There are always the 'Knocking People' who'd have a dig for the sake of it . Things like "I saw you pushing your barrow, up Westgate yesterday," sniggering really but deep down they knew who was the better off and that didn't have the guts to do the job. They also knew that Golly was earning three or four times what they were and answering to no-one. Totally independent, that's our Golly.

• CHAPTER 9 •

MARRIAGE, PARTNERSHIP
AND MUSICAL DIRECTION

Golly wanted to share his good fortune with Alan Morrin, remember Alan? He was the bloke who persuaded Golly to walk out of the 'The Tan Yard' 18 months earlier. Golly offered Alan a full partnership, it took him a while to think about it but finally took Golly up on the offer, it was a giant step for Alan because he had job at Redifusion putting cables into houses.

Golly and Alan Morrin

So they gave the business a new title, "Goulding and Morrin Window Cleaning Contractors" and they started doing more commercial work.

Carol and Golly had arranged their wedding for Saturday 1st of April 1967. (Photo). It had to be the first Saturday in April to meet a Tax Year deadline. Although Golly wasn't paying any tax he knew there was a bill around the corner. Golly was 19 and Carol was 22 obviously the big question was where were they going to make their home. In those days you had to be 21 to get a mortgage so Golly's idea was to get a flat, he knew where there were some nice ones around the West End plus others that were being modernised. When Golly discussed his idea with his Mam she suggested a caravan. This was interesting because Carol had previously mentioned buying a caravan, but Golly had kind of dismissed the idea and never gave it any more thought. But after a proper investigation it became a great idea.

Golly and Carol on their wedding day

Directly opposite where Carol worked there was a nice Residential Caravan Site, ENCEE. It was owned by Mr and Mrs Purslow. So Golly and Carol went to see them one day, to ask about a vacancy on the site. They had a vacancy coming up around Spring Time, perfect for them.

You see the idea of getting a caravan was to buy it on HP, Golly's Mam and Dad would sign. Then they would sell it when Golly was 21 and in a position to get a mortgage on a house. So with these things in mind they went along and got Mr Purslow to show them a brand new

'Pemberton Six Berth Caravan' with a price of £650. It was beautiful, with a separate bedroom, kitchen, and lounge etc. Well Carol and Golly naturally fell in love with it and ordered one, right away. Golly had to put down a deposit, he can't remember exactly how much, but thinks it was probably £100 or £150 in cash. This was no problem to this happy young couple because they both had healthy bank accounts. In those days caravans weren't equipped with electricity, but Mr Purslow had it wired up for them for about £20, again no problem.

Their new caravan arrived about a month before they got married. As Golly said, "absolutely pure luxury." They had carpets fitted and brought in all their bottom drawer stuff. They had almost everything. In those days most people rented a television, Golly and Carol were no different, (More of that later). So now it was March 1967, Golly is very happy, the business is doing great and he is enjoying his music with 'Mark 4'. Golly and Carol are about to get married, they have their brand new home, times were so exciting. Carol and Golly also had a decent amount of money between them, but as always they thought that they could use a bit more. Golly decided to sell his beloved Epiphone Casino Guitar. Remember it cost 165 guineas in 1964. Jeff Normington from 'B.A. Fox' Music shop in Morecambe found Golly a buyer for it at a price of

£105, he kept the £5 as his commission. We will hear more about Jeff as we go on. Golly also sold his 'Marshall speaker cabinet' for an extra £60 to put towards the wedding. As it turned out they didn't even need the money anyway, so they just kept it in the bank.

These sales did not leave Golly without an instrument. That would never happen. He still had his 'Harmony Rocket Guitar' and his 'Marshall Amplifier'. His group 'Mark 4' had a spare speaker cabinet and that was Golly's to use indefinitely. So no problem about gear. This would probably be a good time to talk about 'Mark 4'.

The line up of 'Mark 4' had Paul Woodruff, (Woodie) on vocals, but his real talent was comedy. Previously Woodie had been the singer with 'The Midnights' around 1962 and then later joined 'The Chessmen', both good groups at the time. Tommy Lamb, guitarist with 'The Midnights' fancied going on Bass, so he was Bass Guitarist. Ronnie Jones on Drums had also previously been with 'The Chessmen'. With Golly on Lead Guitar 'Mark 4' were a bloody good group. As Golly says "Every night with 'Mark 4' was a big hit."

Everything going great, it was time for Carol and Golly's wedding. 1st April 1967 and there is no doubt that for Golly this would the transition from good times to great. Golly at this time was a young man with drive and ambition. Marrying Carol, a smart, intelligent, lovely girl would elevate his life to another level.

The happy day began at St Joseph's Catholic Church in Skerton Lancaster. This was because Carol had been brought up in the Catholic faith, Golly was C of E . Golly loved, indeed still loves Carol and he knew that her religion was more important to her than his was to him. In order for them to get married in The Catholic Church, he agreed to take religious instruction from the priest. This involved him going to the priest's house once a week in the evening, for three or four weeks. This was fine by Golly and at the end of that time he was accepted into the Catholic faith. As Golly says now and thought then, from his point of view there doesn't seem to be a great difference between the two religions. So the wedding took place, Carol, as we have said a very pretty girl, looked so lovely as she walked down the aisle towards Golly, that she took every ones breath away.

Their reception was held at 'The Castle Hotel' Lancaster. The happy couple had 70/80 guests. Golly's Best man was his old Bass Player Mick Heap and Alan Morrin was his Groomsman. Carol's bridesmaids were her cousin Gill and Golly's sister Ann. (Photo). After the reception, Carol and Golly took the London-Euston train from Castle Station to begin their Honeymoon.

They arrived in London and got to their Hotel at 10/11pm, dropped off their cases in the room and went straight out into the West End. Golly had loved being in London even though his time there had been spent living in a van and he, like Carol was fascinated by all of the many aspects of the city.

They knew where they were going, they were heading for a Blues Club called 'Les Cousins'. Alexis Korner was playing what they called 'The Allnighter'. This involved Alexis starting at midnight and playing through til dawn. As Carol and Golly were queuing outside the club a Busker was dropped off by car, he sang a few numbers then he was whisked away. Golly remembers that he was very good, a lot of London Buskers are. In the case of this one Golly saw him on T.V. a few weeks later singing, which led to him having No1 hits with 'Rosie' and 'Blue Eyes'. It was

none other than 'Don Partridge', he wore the same Snakeskin Jacket on T.V. that Carol and Golly had admired when they first saw him working to the crowd outside the club.

Once Carol and Golly got inside the club they got front row seats right by the stage. They watched Alexis for two or three hours by which time they were both falling asleep, it had been a long day. Incidentally Alexis had the 'Great' Danny Thompson, backing him on Double Bass, Golly remembered Danny being with Humphrey Lyttleton in 'The Tommy Steele Story'.

The rest of the Honeymoon was spent wandering round London, with Golly showing Carol all the places he had hung out during his time down there with 'Mel Deane and The Leaders' two years previously. Golly also bought a few rare Blues L P's which he still has of course. He thinks that they are pretty valuable today. Golly remembers showing Carol the 2 I's Coffee Bar in Old Compton Street, as he says, he used to go there with the lads from the group in 1964/65. Some of you who are reading this book will know about this famous place it was a coffee bar that was run by two Iranian's which opened in the 1950's .

This was the birthplace of the British Rock and Roll Scene and was home to Cliff, Marty, Tommy Steele, Wee Willie Harris, the list is endless. Indeed Wee Willie cut the single 'Rockin at The 2 I's' as a tribute to the venue. This was a legend of a place which is long gone and Carol and Golly were lucky enough to go there.

CHAPTER 10

FIRST HOME AND
FIRST STEPS INTO THE ANTIQUE GAME

So the honeymoon was over and Carol and Golly made the journey back and went straight into their new home. The one thing they hadn't got was a telly, as Golly mentioned before most people rented one. Carol and Golly weren't any different, they also rented one. The company they rented from provided the set and insurance. The method of paying for it was provided by a box that was built into the set. They used to put two one shilling coins into it when they wanted to watch. Golly can't remember how much the rental figure was but he thinks that it was probably about 12 shillings a week, or something close to that.

Every three months a bloke would come and empty the coins and place them in £1 stacks, for Carol and Golly to check. They were always a £1 or two short and they shouldn't have been. So they would give him the difference, then he would give them a receipt. They always thought it was strange because they were sure that the amount they were putting in was correct. So one day when the bloke came to empty the TV he did his usual thing. He emptied the coins from the TV and put his little stacks of coins in line and then said, "You are short again."

This time Golly was having none of it, he stepped forward and picked up and counted one of his stacks. Instead of there being £1 in each stack there was 22 shillings, (Only 20 shillings in a £1 remember). When Golly pointed this out to him the bloke said, "Oh I must have miscounted the first stack and just made them all the same height." A neat trick but Golly had caught the cheating sod. He never tried to pull it on Golly again, but Golly said, "I bet he used it on plenty of the other poor suckers."

Anyway back to happier things. Not long after they got back from their Honeymoon they went round to Golly's Mam and Dad's house, where there was good news Golly had quoted 'The Grand Hotel' for cleaning the windows and their reply had come. They had got the job. Getting this contract was one hell of an achievement. 'The

The Grand Hotel

Grand' a promenade property, was now being used as an Ex Miners Rest Home. Golly had priced the job at £35. This was a ridiculous amount back then but they got the job. They used to take two and a half days to do the job and they were doing it on a monthly basis. As Golly said, "A pension in itself."

Golly had also tendered for schools and he had pulled a few round the Preston area. The business was flying high but Golly was wanting better things. Some of the things he would do was to buy window rounds from various people who weren't too successful and then advertise and re-sell them to people who fancied having a go at the job. Buying and Selling has always been in his blood. Deep down he had always fancied having a shop. He was starting to think now was the time.

Austin A35 - Golly's first van

Golly's business partner Alan had just passed his driving test and fancied doing a driving job so Golly bought him out. Golly himself was still taking driving lessons and after nine of them he took his test and passed first time. He immediately bought an A35 van.

So now, Golly made it known that he wanted to sell the window cleaning business and move on to other things. Within days he had it sold to two local blokes who wanted to expand. He can't remember the exact price but it was a few hundred quid.

Golly had seen an empty shop on Alexandra Road, Morecambe, so he went to see the landlady and agreed to take it on for £3.10 shillings a week, not cheap. In the 1960's. Many of you reading this book, will no doubt remember those shops that were selling cheap hardware. These were popping up everywhere, selling plastic buckets washing up liquid, tons of cheap lines.

Golly's shop on Alexandra Road

In the North West, Bury New Road and Cheetham Hill, Manchester, were the best places to go and buy wholesale. Golly had learned about this from an old Jewish shopkeeper in Morecambe who had a wool shop. "Get yourself down to Manchester on a Sunday morning, that's where all the Jewish warehouses are" he said.

So they had the shop, the van and the money. By having these means, it meant that Carol and Golly would make the journey down to Manchester every Sunday morning, to buy stock. They would fill up the van typical lines of stock. Washing up liquid, three bottles for half a crown, Four toilet rolls for 1/11d and big black buckets 4/6d all that kind of stuff. As Golly says, "Business was OK but not brilliant." Further up Alexandra Road was Bob Skelly's second hand shop. Golly got to know Bob quite well and he told Golly, "Alexandra Road was never any good, not busy enough." Bob had another shop down the other end of town on Morecambe Street which did really well. Golly will tell more of the Morecambe Street, years later in the book.

A funny story that Golly told me, was when he first got the shop, there was all sorts of junk in the cellar and he needed to clear it. It had previously been a dress shop. One item for dumping was a lady manikin. A nice Art Deco one, as Golly recalls and he wishes he had it today. Anyway, Dave Winn a very good local musician, but a bit weird, used to call in the shop regularly. He spotted the dummy and when Golly told him it was going to the tip, he said "I'll have it" So Dave carried it home, bored a hole in it and she became his companion.

Several months later, on the front page of the local newspaper 'The Visitor' was a picture of this armless dummy stuck on top of a rubbish pile and titled 'Venus de Ovangle'. To explain, the local rubbish tip was on Ovangle Road. Golly recognised it right away. The next time he saw Dave, he asked him if he still had his girlfriend. "No, She was OK in summer, but a bit too cold for winter, so I gave her to the dustbinmen." He said.

Another of Golly's relics made the front page a few years later.

'Hercules'......You'll get to know about him later in the book.

Golly had now progressed to a 15cwt Ford Thames Van, which stood empty outside the shop all day.

Ford Thames Van - Golly's second van

The shop business that Golly had always fancied was becoming boring, some days he didn't even go to open up. He had better things to do.

Scrap metal was at a premium and Golly used to wander about picking it up in the van. Down the road at the other end of town, Euston Road, they were demolishing all the shops and Golly had a deal going with the demolition men. If he slipped them a few quid he could go in and help himself to whatever he wanted. Well that was a good deal. So most days Golly would load the van and drive to the scrapyard for a 'weigh in.'

One day a bloke came into the shop and was telling Golly about some allotments near his house. "All the tenants have to be off within the next few weeks, to make way for the school extension. For the benefit of the readers who don't know what an allotment is. It's a strip of land let out by the local council or sometimes British Rail, at a peppercorn rent. These strips of land were for agricultural use only (mainly growing vegetables or flowers). The bloke went on to say "There's tons of stuff down there, they've just walked away and left it all. I saw a copper boiler and I know they're worth a bit." He was right, there was tons of it. You might know, Golly didn't hesitate. He went down as fast as a bullet from a gun. These allotments were above average. Not only gardens but piggeries, hen pens etc. Sheds full of old stuff and there for the taking. Golly was there for weeks and had it all to himself. Not only scrap metal but a few antiques to boot. Another bonus was when a bloke asked him if he knew where there were any old 50 gallon oil drums. Well of course he did, there were loads scattered around that had been used for water butts. This bloke had a touring caravan site in the Lake District and wanted a dozen oil drums to spread around the site to be used as litter bins. Golly delivered the bins and collected 30 bob each for them. £18, not bad in the 60s, a nice days pay. But even better than that, on the way back he passed a school and in the yard he could see all this stuff piled up. Golly pulled into the yard and enquired. They were clearing out the kitchens and all the stuff was being scrapped. Golly bought the lot for a tenner. Stainless Steel, Aluminium, Copper etc, all heavy duty, commercial, catering equipment. He weighed in the next morning for £35. Maybe all this stuff sounds trivial today, but remember in those days a working man's wage was around £15 / £16 per week. That allotment was a real boost and added more capital, which Golly needed to further his career as an Antique Dealer. In his words "A Godsend."

Carol used to work the shop on a Saturday and customers would say, "Ah you're open, I came earlier in the week and you were closed." As Golly says, "It didn't matter, he was earning plenty from his trips to the scrapyard. In the mean time Golly put a notice on the shop door, "Light removals." Golly says, "I used to get all sorts of jobs in the evening." One day a bloke came into the shop and wanted a piece of furniture picking up from Lancaster and dropping off at his house in Morecambe. Golly says, "We will get to that later."

Anyway this bloke was called Kevin and it turned out that he was an Antique Dealer who had moved into the area from Leicester. He had also lost his driving licence for some reason. Thinking about it later, Golly thought that Kevin must have done something serious to leave his home town and come up North. It was almost as though he was getting out of the way of something.

So Golly agreed to pick up this piece of furniture for Kevin and he came in the van with Golly to this address in Lancaster. When they got to the house they went round the back to an old Coach House, went in and there was a piece of dirty, wood wormy junk, it was dropping to pieces. Well they got it in the van and delivered to his house in Limes Avenue, Morecambe, then carried this piece of crap into his front room. Golly later found out that the 'Piece Of Crap' was a genuine 'Queen Anne, Walnut, Chest on Chest' worth maybe £50/60 then. Kevin had only paid a fiver for it, but you see, he knew his game.

Kevin started to put adverts in the wanted section of local newspapers and he started to get calls. Golly of course was shifting the stuff for him and picking up knowledge all the time. To be fair Kevin was teaching him about the game. After a few months they were getting pally and they became kind of business partners. Kevin had the knowledge, Golly had the transport and they both had a few quid to work with. We have now reached 1968, this was the start of G.G. Antique Dealing. Golly lived the job, it was exciting, never knowing what he might find.

The first thing they ever bought together was a 'Georgian Mahogany Bureau' for £5. A little Antique shop had opened up in Ingleton, a village about 20 miles outside Lancaster, the bureau was in the shop window, Golly had no idea of its value, but Kevin said "It should bring about £15." The hard bit was trying to sell the bugger, they hawked that bureau around all week and couldn't get a bid. Eventually they dumped it in Golly's Dad's garage for a few days. Golly's Dad looked at it and asked, "How much did

Mahogany Bureau

you pay for that?" "A fiver" Golly replied. "You must be mad." His Dad said. Golly and Kevin eventually sold it for £8, ten years later it would have sold for £400.

The thing was in those days there was plenty of stuff around and it was easy enough to buy. Antique Shops in those days was just a posh way of saying 'Junk Shop', that is what they were known as when Golly was growing up. That said Golly and Kevin were doing pretty well and going out on the road two or three days a week. Golly remembers that one day they were up in Kendal. On the main street in Kendal, there were three or four Antique Shops. They were in one of them mooching around and a girl came in with a Musical Box that she had inherited. She asked the shop owner if he was interested, he wasn't so she left.

Half an hour later Golly and Kevin saw the girl on the street, because no one wanted to buy the musical box from her. They offered her £15 for it she was delighted and took the money. The Music Box was a lovely thing, it had eight tunes with bells, housed in a rosewood case. Golly and Kevin sold it for £35 later the same day. Any one of those dealers in Kendal could have done the same thing, but they just weren't brave enough to have a go. That is just a taste of Golly's first days in the Antique business.

Golly still had the shop but he was hardly ever there and the business was fading away. Luckily Golly managed to sell it as a going concern and the lad that bought it did really well. He had been made redundant and having put his redundancy money into it he worked really hard to bring the business back to a healthy state. So now with the shop out of the way Golly was dealing full time in the Antique Business.

As Golly said earlier anybody can buy the stuff, getting rid of it is the hard bit. Nevertheless it was a great way of scraping a living and scraping a living is what it was. It was a good thing that Carol was working and earning decent money, because that enabled Golly to find his feet. It has been said many times that behind every great man is an even greater woman and in Carol's case this is certainly true, because there is no doubt in the authors mind that Golly is a great man.

There were many good dealers out there who were doing well, using their knowledge and their contacts to do good business. Golly knew that if he could just get a foot on the first rung of the ladder he would be OK. Golly like a lot of other blokes we all know, liked to go and have a pint at lunch time, no breathalyser then. Golly used to go into 'The Dog and Partridge' where he would meet up with Pete Hayes, he was a successful dealer in those times. His son Paul Hayes would go on to have great success on telly with the programmes such as *'Cash In The Attic'*, *'Put Your Money Where Your Mouth Is'*, *'Antiques House'* and many others. He even did *'Crime Watch'* and *'Breakfast News'*, with an audience of millions.

Well, Pete and Golly would talk about what they had seen and what they had bought etc. Pete had a shop on Morecambe street next door to Bob Skelly's second hand shop, he always had money in his pocket ready to buy. He didn't do much furniture though, mostly Bric-a-brac, Jewellery and Pictures etc. He used to get some 'good touches' as they say in the trade. Pete knew that Golly was a learner and hungry for success and he used to say to him, "You'll be OK Golly, you will make it" Golly used to think, "Bloody Hell, I wish success would hurry up."

CHAPTER 11

PROUD HOME OWNERS
WITH HARD TIMES AHEAD

We are now in 1969 and Carol and Golly's caravan was nearly paid for. Golly was now 22 years old and old enough to get a mortgage, so they started to casually look for properties. By early 1970 their caravan, their beautiful home was paid for £650. One Wednesday morning Golly looked in 'The Visitor' their local paper and he spotted an interesting property, priced at £1,100. 18 Main Street Kirkby Lonsdale. 'Graham Nunn' was the Agent. Golly and Carol were anxious to view the property, it consisted of a double fronted shop, with Large Living Room, another Living Room upstairs, Kitchen, four

Kirkby Lonsdale

or five Bedrooms and two Cellars. There were two staircases one each side of the property, it had a large back garden with a private road leading to it. Plus it was only a few yards from the town square and there was the added bonus of free rent for a Market Stall every week.

The property sounds fantastic doesn't it? They agreed to buy it subject to Golly getting a Mortgage. In those days a wife's wages were not taken into consideration. The first thing they had to do was sell their caravan, this they did easily for £350. What a good job they hadn't lived in a flat or they wouldn't have had the capital for a deposit. As Golly says, "Good thinking, Carol and Mam."

Golly with Carlo

So they had about £400 for the deposit which was well over the required sum. Now how does Golly get a Mortgage? He made an appointment and went to see Graham Nunn who asked, "What do you do for a living?" "I'm an Antique dealer" said Golly. "You will never get a mortgage, come up with something else," Graham replied. "OK, How about Window Cleaner?" "How Much are your earnings?" Graham asked. "£40/£50 a week" replied Golly. "My God" said Graham, "I'm in the wrong business, that'll do". He filled out the paperwork and Golly got the mortgage. Carol and Golly were now the owners of a nice large property. As dilapidated as it was, they loved it.

It had been Golly's intention to open the shop and sell all the swag stuff like they had in the shop in Morecambe. But after living there for a few months they both realised that Kirkby Lonsdale was like a ghost town in winter. Carol was still working in the drawing office at the Electricity Board. She had left her job at 'Morecambe Electric' because there was a rumour that the company was struggling and likely to close down. This proved to be a good decision because they did close down, not long after Carol had left. Golly would take Carol into work every morning and then stay around the Morecambe and Lancaster area doing the antiques and a bit scrap metal. Then he would pick Carol up around 5pm, more often than not he was late. But the truth is that without Carol's wage they simply could not have survived.

Carol and Golly had bought the house/shop from a Mr Williams, he was a decent old bloke who did a bit of dabbling in antiques and he would sometimes let Golly and Kevin take some of his stuff to try and sell, sometimes they were successful sometimes they were not. Golly can distinctly remember a set of eight oil paintings in gilt frames being among the items he and Kevin took out to try and sell. They were a set of eight Seascapes, lovely paintings and a great subject. Golly has no idea who the artist was and they hawked these bloody paintings all over the place but they just couldn't sell them. Golly thinks that Mr Williams wanted about £35 for the set, but it was no good, they had to give them back to him. Victorian pictures were at a premium in the 1980's but we're still in the early 1970s remember.

Winter 1970 and 1971 was a rough time for Golly, business was really bad. Golly used to go into the pubs at night selling Christmas Trees, and Holly, just to earn a few extra quid. Another thing Golly used to do was call in on a 'Fruit and Veg' merchant in Lancaster and Golly used to called in regularly and buy maybe 150 boxes of tomatoes for next to nothing, as little as £5 for the lot. The only reason being that these were on the turn. So if Golly didn't buy them there and then, they would be on the tip the next day.

Golly had a mate, Bill Cunliffe, he was a bit of a wide boy from Bradford. Bill would be 20 years older than Golly and he kind of looked up to him. Bill lived in a caravan with his Mother on a bit of land just off Westgate, Morecambe. Everyone thought he was a Gypsy but he wasn't. So Golly and Bill would go and get this bloody van load of tomatoes then start sorting through them. They would throw all the rotten ones to the pigs, who were in a pen near Bill's caravan. Then make up boxes of the decent ones. Say out of 150 boxes they might get 20 or 30 boxes of saleable tomatoes which they used to sell to café's and boarding houses. Although it was a messy job and would take half a day to sort through them, for the investment of a fiver they could make profit of £20 or £30.

So they would sell the boxes of tomatoes, but they would also bag some up and sell them on street corners and round the pubs. That was a good earner. Of course there are always people who find fault and someone who had a Green Grocers shop wrote to the newspapers complaining, they said, "These tomatoes must be stolen because I can't buy them from the wholesalers for the price they are being sold at." Well of course he could have done it, if he'd have had the brains to do what Golly was doing.

Getting back to the Christmas Trees and Holly. Golly knew two Irish brothers, Derek and Gerald Fitzpatrick, they were a right couple of characters and they used to bring him Holly. Golly never asked where they got it from. There was one very strange incident while Carol and Golly were still living in the caravan, which needs to be told at this point. One morning Golly and Carol came out of the caravan, to find a gigantic Holly Tree, not a bush, a proper tree, lying outside the caravan, with a note nailed to it saying, "A present of Holly for Golly". Golly had to start sawing it up there and then, there were van loads of it.

A few days later there was a picture of a tree stump on the front of the local newspaper. The story that accompanied the photo was to the effect that someone had sawn down a Holly Tree in the garden of Morecambe Grammar School. Golly never found out who had done it but it was a bit of a coincidence. Like Golly, you can probably guess who would be the likely suspects.

As Golly said, the winter of 1970/71 was a tough one and Golly and Carol had been living at Kirkby Lonsdale for about six months. Hard times. One evening Graham Nunn the estate agent called round to see them. "When are you opening the shop?" he asked. "We're not, it is too quiet in winter," replied Golly. Graham then asked, "Do you want to put it on the market because I know someone who could be vaguely interested in buying" he said. Golly and Carol agreed to let him have a go.

So Graham advertised it for sale at £2,400. A few days after that a knock came on the door and a bloke offered to pay the asking price. That was a couple of hundred quid profit, a lot of money in those days. He wrote them a £1000 cheque there and then. Well Carol and Golly were chuffed to bits. The next morning Golly went to see Graham Nunn at his office, to tell him the good news. Graham looked at Golly, "Give him the cheque back, I can get you more". "How much more?" asked Golly. "£2,500" he replied, which was a £100 more than the asking price.

That night the bloke came back to see them, when Golly said, "I'm giving you your cheque back, we've had a better offer." The bloke said, "Well I'll give you £2,600." Wow, this was unbelievable and the offers went on like this all week. By the weekend they had been offered £3000. Graham said "I have never known anything like this before, the only way to settle it' is to get both of the potential buyers, into the office on Monday morning and have a bit of an auction." This was done and the buyer ended up paying £3,300. That was £1,100 profit after only nine months. Golly and Carol sold up and moved in with Golly's Mam and Dad for a few months, while they were looking for a suitable property.

Just before Christmas that year the Cylinder Head Gasket went on the Transit Van, No garage would look at it until early January, this would mean Golly being off the road for a couple of weeks. Golly had a good friend Barry Robinson, who is still Golly's friend today, he said buy the gasket and I'll fit it for you. So on Boxing Day Barry came to the house and spent the day fixing the van, it was perfect when he'd finished. As Golly says "On a cold winters day, Barry worked on the drive outside the house and fixed my van, God Bless You Barry." What's more, he wouldn't take a penny for doing it. "A real mate!!"

Getting back to property hunting. Golly had always fancied a small-holding. Graham Nunn knew this and one day he came round to see him at his parent's house saying "I think I've found the spot for you. It's a bungalow with two acres of land." It seems that Graham had been informed by 'The Otley Building Society' that this property had become available, the owner had got behind with his mortgage and they were going to repossess the place. 25 Middleton Road, Middleton, Nr Heysham. Carol and Golly went to see it and it was definitely a big Yes from Golly. It was his dream come true. The price, £5,550 not cheap. They could have bought three semis in a good area for that kind of money. Nevertheless Carol and Golly wanted it, so they put down the deposit, all their savings, even with that they still had a mortgage of £4,000. Different friends of Golly and Carol had mortgages but none of them had a debt of more than £1,200.

25 Middleton Road

They had gone in deep, but they had everything. A detached bungalow, sat in two acres and loads of out buildings. This was perfect for someone like Golly, because he could use the outbuildings for furniture and he had somewhere to keep the scrap etc. Right at the bottom of their field, there was a block of Piggeries, they had been purpose built by the previous owner. These buildings were clean and dry, ideal for storage.

Of course 1971 was another tough year, Carol and Golly had a big mortgage to pay and they were trying to do the place up as the saying goes. Remember Golly mentioning Mr Williams, who they'd bought the house from in Kirkby Lonsdale. Incidentally before we go on it is worth mentioning that the above property recently sold for just under half a million! Anyway back to Mr Williams. Golly had stayed in touch with him because he dabbled a bit in Antiques. Whilst visiting him one day he said, "Golly I've got a deal for you, I've got a piece of property I want to sell." Well dear reader, hold on to your hat, because what you are about to read now will blow your mind!!

Mr Williams went on to say, "It's a detached farmhouse on the moors, the roof has caved in a bit but all the materials are there to put it right. It has water and electricity and it sits on two acres of land with a private road leading to it and it has grazing rights for 200,000 acres of moorland. Oh, and it has got a pub a mile and a half away on one side and another pub a mile and a half away on the other side." "How much do you want for it?" asked Golly. "I'll take a hundred quid for it," he replied. It sounds fantastic doesn't it? But it's the Gods honest truth!!

So Carol and Golly went to look at it, situated just outside Hebden Bridge on the borders of Lancashire and Yorkshire. Well they went up and down this road and they couldn't find it, then Golly spotted a farmer and asked him about the place. "Oh you mean Johnny House" he said. Then he gave them directions. Well sure enough it was there, a big old property in a couple acres. The roof had collapsed and the road had been washed away by flooding. They couldn't drive up to it, they had to walk. Of course it was a bloody shambles, but a hundred quid? Well Golly and Carol did not have a spare £100, so they didn't bother with it.

What Golly did try to do, was sell it and hopefully earn a bit of commission, but he couldn't even do that, no one was interested. Mr Williams ended up taking £75 for it, lock stock and barrel. Well there it is, it's an almost unbelievable story. Over the years Golly has told people about it and he knows that they think he is exaggerating, as the author of this book and Golly's friend, I can tell you he is not. Carol and Golly have talked about it many times over the years and they actually went to look for it a few years ago. They found it easily enough, it is now a beautiful property and it appears to be a Kennels and a Cattery.

Like a posh pets hotel. To think that Carol and Golly could have had it for £75 eh!!

So back to Middleton, as Golly has stated, 1971 was a tough year and a very cold winter, he swore that by the following winter they would have central heating in the property. Central Heating was still a rare luxury back then, but that bloody bungalow was cold.

A little Antique Shop opened in Morecambe it was called 'Collector's Corner'. A lovely couple called Jim and Dorothy owned it, Jim was actually a heating engineer who collected pewter and other items. Well Jim offered to put Gas Central Heating in the bungalow in return for Antiques of his choice. The deal was that Golly would pay up front for materials and Jim would work in lieu of Antiques.

So in the spring of 1972, central heating was installed in the bungalow. It was a Godsend and the perfect deal. Jim just took the Antiques he wanted from the stock Golly had accumulated.

Golly knew a fellow called Frank Lancaster, 'Lanky' was his nickname. Well Lanky had a Caravan Site and Piggeries just out of town and he told Golly about this new scheme that was being introduced by a 'Provine Company', Provine is a day feed for livestock. Anyway Lanky said, "You've got those Piggeries at your place and they are doing nothing, I'll tell the rep to come and see you." So this is how the scheme worked, 'The Provine Company' would provide Golly with 120 piglets, which he would fatten up with their product, then the company and Golly would split the profit after six months. The good thing about it was Golly would not have to lay down any money for livestock.

This arrangement would be subject to a few conditions. The first condition being that he had to have running water installed in all the bays which Golly agreed to. The second condition was that the correct lighting had to be installed, once again Golly agreed.

In fact it was a major plumbing and electrical job. First of all Golly had to get water and electricity down to the bottom of the field. After a few months the work was completed and the rep came to inspect the buildings. He liked what we had done. So a week later a lorry load of Provine arrived, followed by a another lorry, loaded with 120 piglets.

Carol and Golly didn't know what they were letting themselves in for. They had to feed the pigs every morning before Carol went to work. And then muck them out and feed them again at night. They didn't mind the work, they were young and fit, both Carol and Golly shared the work, they were then and they are now, a team.

The hardest part of the job was getting rid of the muck, barrow loads and barrow loads of the stuff on a daily basis. Golly reckons they spent three to four hours a day moving all the muck. Then they had the odd piglet die on them, this, as Golly learned was quite

Pigs!

normal out of a hundred and twenty piglets they lost just ten which was pretty good, so they were told. Every time one died Golly had to go out into the field and dig a hole that he could bury it in. That could take Golly a few hours, when he had to do it. Another great chore for Golly and Carol was weighing the piglets on a weekly basis. Imagine having to weigh one hundred and twenty live animals. Not easy but they did it.

On one occasion Golly had to inject them, can you imagine how hard it was to ram a needle through the thick skin of one hundred and twenty piglets? Then again there were the Provine deliveries to be unloaded once or twice a week, all unloaded stacked and stored by hand.

After about six months the pigs were ready for slaughter. A large wagon arrived and Golly and Carol had to herd the pigs up the field to be loaded. What a bloody fiasco that was, anyone who knows about pigs knows how stubborn they are. They had electric prodders, they had to whack them and all-sorts to get them into the wagon, that was heading to the slaughterhouse. Then when all came to all and it came to settling the finances Golly and Carol's share worked out at £5 a week, for all that work. The only winners were the 'Provine Company'.

So now Carol and Golly had all these fully equipped empty Piggeries. What were they to do with them? They still didn't have a proper road leading to them, just a muddy track. Golly's next task was to have a road installed. He knew some demolition lads and they would dump a load of rubble every now again. Carol and Golly would then handball all this stuff. When they had a few yards put down Golly would order a load of hardcore which they would spread on top of the rubble.

Incidentally this hard work was all done with wheelbarrows and shovels. It took months and Carol and Golly felt as though they were working on a chain gang. Throughout all this Carol, super trooper that she is, was still working at her day job. Golly was trying to build up the Antique Business and playing in the evenings with a group he had put together called 'Blues Workshop'. Just a three piece, Golly on Lead Guitar, Jim Ward on Bass and lead vocals and Richard Hoather on Drums, they were pretty busy playing the usual spots, 'Hunting Hill Lodge', 'The Redwell' and every Sunday, they played 'The Britannia' in Lancaster.

**Hunting Hill
Country Club**
CRAG BANK - CARNFORTH
LANCS.
Tel. Carnforth 2480

◆

Membership Card
NOT TRANSFERABLE

EXPIRY DATE

-1 DEC 1968

• CHAPTER 12 •

BETTER TIMES AND SUCCESS

It is now 1972 and Golly is starting to feel that things are changing for the better. He had got to know a Joiner called John Dixon who had a yard down in Morecambe. John had a desk for sale so Golly went down to his yard to see it. He looked at it and bought it. While he was there he had a look round the yard. John had the usual stuff there, piles of wood, some of it only fit for burning. In one corner of the yard there was a pile of old wood, nothing much there. But then Golly spotted something else between the wood, it was an old wooden horse. Golly went over and pulled it out. He asked John if he could buy it. "There are loads of them," said John, "I can't sell you them because they are in for repair, I've just never got round to doing the job." Well Golly looked deeper into the pile of wood and he could see loads more of these horses. Golly could see that they were Victorian Carousel Horses, very ornately carved, beautiful.

Wooden carousel horse

"Who owns them? Golly asked. So John told him the owners name and address. Golly went round to house and met the owner and offered to buy the horses. The bloke said no, he wouldn't sell them because they had been in his family for generations. It turned out that they were fairground people who had stalls and rides at the 'The Winter Gardens Fair Ground', so that was the end of that, or so Golly thought.

A few months later John Dixon rang Golly to tell him that he had bought 'Fair-

Winter Gardens

field Laundry' and was moving premises. "If there is anything you want down at the yard, just take it, I need to empty the place this week," he said. Golly went down and took a few things and he noticed that the horses were still there, "What about these" Golly asked. "Just take them" John replied, the owners had said they would be too expensive to repair. So Golly loaded them on to his Transit Van, there were about a dozen or so of them, legs off and heads off, really only a nail up job which Golly did easily, 90% of the pieces were there. So Golly had all these wooden horses lined up in the garage at home. But where could he sell them and what were they worth?

He was looking round for the answer when the activities of a tribe of Gypsies came to his attention. They were camping on the old tip in Morecambe and Golly knew a few of them as they were all in the antique job. They were pulling loads of stuff out of Scotland and everyone was curious to know how they were getting rid of it.

Golly also knew a feller called Jack Lum, he had an Antique Shop in Galgate, a village just outside Lancaster. When Golly asked Jack how the Tinkers were getting rid of stuff, he said, "They're peddling it to 'Trade Antiques' in Wigan." Golly had never heard of them but he got their number and phoned them up. Golly told them "I've got a dozen fairground horses that I want to sell, are you interested?" "Not really in our line" the bloke replied. "Anyway, leave it with me and I will call you back later." Well Golly waited all that day but there was no call back.

Well as Golly has said, he had nailed the horses back together and he was just about to start painting them when the phone rang. It was Jim Collins from 'Trade Antiques'. "Have you still got those horses?" he asked. "Yes" said Golly, "I'm just going to paint them." "Don't Touch them" he replied. "How much do you want for them?" asked Jim. Well as Golly says he hadn't got a clue so he took a punt at it, "£25 each" he said. "OK" replied Jim, "Bring them over in the morning." Golly couldn't believe it £300? Was it too good to be true? He couldn't sleep all night, he was too filled with excitement.

The following morning Golly loaded the wooden horses into the van and took them through to Wigan. Jim looked at them and then he paid Golly out with new £20 notes, this was the first time Golly had ever seen a £20 note. Golly later found out that Jim making allowances for the time difference, had phoned a customer in California and sold the horses that evening. "Good for him" says Golly.

Jim was a nice bloke and he was curious about what Golly did. He showed Golly around his warehouse and more importantly told Golly the prices he would pay for items he was looking for. This was the boost Golly needed to get him established. 'Trade Antiques' were one of the first companies to ship antiques by the container load. This was because up until 1970, everything that was exported had to be taken to the port, crated up, then loaded by crane on to the vessel.

Containers hadn't been invented until then. When they were invented, it created a cheap way of getting volumes of stuff to overseas customers. You loaded the container yourself and then had it transported to the Port, then it was shipped out. The Americans came over in their droves buying up all the stuff for peanuts. Which was good because no- one in the UK wanted it anyway.

So things were really looking up for Golly, he now had the knowledge and he had a buyer for certain stuff. What's more he knew exactly what he could sell it for. This knowledge gave Golly tremendous buying power. All this was thanks to Jim showing him around and educating him, Golly says "I owe Jim everything, he was the bloke who put Golly Goulding on his feet."

Golly was on a roll, he used to take a van load through to Wigan two or three times a week. All he had to do was unload and sell the stuff.

He had a pocket full of money, an empty van and back on the road. Golly was finally up and running. 'Trade Antiques' started sending him a list of desired items, with prices given.(Photo). Of course 'Trade Antiques' didn't buy everything, just the stuff they wanted. But Golly had other outlets for the things that 'Trade Antiques' wouldn't buy. These things included 'Old Oak' 16th century Country furniture. Golly had a customer in Yorkshire who would buy that kind of thing.

Golly's old mate and Drummer Will from 'The MBQ' days, had also gone into the antique game. Will had opened a shop/warehouse on North Road, Lancaster and he was specialising in 'Stripped Pine'. He would buy this old painted stuff, put it in a tank of caustic soda and scrub the paint off. Then dry it out and sand, wax and finish it. So that was another outlet for G.G.

They were pulling down streets of terraced houses in Blackburn and Golly used to buy stuff from the demolition men. There was plenty of old pine furniture left behind in the houses and the lads used to keep it for him.

Another thing that happened around that time 1972/73, all licences changed for slot machines. Such as the old penny fruit machines, which previously had been considered amusement machines but were now classed as gaming machines, gambling in other words. This meant that every machine had to be licensed. Even the penny 'All Win', the one in which you won a cigarette or a free go if you got the ball in the right hole. A seasons takings for some of these machines, wouldn't even cover the cost of their license fee and so they became obsolete.

Speaking of stuff becoming obsolete for some reason 'The Winter Gardens Theatre'

Vintage arcade machines

decided to close down. Well
they had a massive fairground
at the back, Golly loved going
there as a boy. There were six
or eight acres of rides, arcades
all the stuff you used to see on
a fairground. Remember the
fairground horses? Here we
had another great opportunity
for GG!!!

Some of Golly's old slot machines

So Golly went down to the
Fairground to have a mooch around. He walked into this arcade and
saw a bloke who was dismantling a kiosk. Can you believe it, he offered
Golly all the machines for a fiver apiece. Now Golly knows that will
now sound like peanuts, but let's not forget a fiver in those days was
still a decent amount of money. You could have a decent night out for
that much money. But these machines were still cheap at that price.

There were all sorts of machines, real Gems! Machines such as 'What
The Butler Saw', this one is self explanatory. 'The Fortune Teller', that
was the one where you put a penny in the machine and a card came out
with a forecast of your future, fortune, or luck.. There was 'The Lucky
Elephant', this machine promised a prize every time, you put a sixpence
in and an elephant brought you a small box with a plastic brooch
in it or something similar. There was loads of stuff remember 'The
Crane'?, that used to grab a prize, but only if you were exceptionally
lucky! Not to mention 'The Ice Hockey, which had two metal figures
that spun around. Then the old football machine, this had twenty two
metal players all in knitted jerseys. There were Two or three of those
machines, which would be worth £3,000 or even £4,000 today, if you
could find one.

Then there were the slot machines, loads of fruit machines, the
mechanical 'One Armed Bandits' as they were commonly known.
'Penny All Wins', 'Test You Your Strength' etc. etc. Many, many, more

that even Golly can't remember the names of. He had them all. Golly did the deal for the whole lot and that entailed quite a few van loads being collected from the Fairground. Over the next few days he was to and fro emptying the arcade. Other people spotted him running about and asked him if he would be interested in their stuff, which he most definitely was.

Golly would bet that he was there for over a month buying and shifting stuff. Funnily enough, no one else seemed interested in the machines. If Morecambe had been a bigger town, there would have been all sorts of dealers trying to out-bid each other. Then again, there wouldn't have been this amount of stuff in most towns, only in Seaside resorts. This was winter 1975 in Morecambe and there were really only three dealers of any significance, the three G's, Golly, George and Gino.

So Golly's routine was this. Nip down to 'The Winter Gardens' every morning and load the van. Then drive through to Wigan in the afternoon and sell it to Jim at 'Trade Antiques' Golly was selling the stuff as fast as he was buying it, as he put it. "Too fast." But that didn't matter, he just put his bit of profit on and got rid. Over the years Golly has sold hundreds of thousands of pieces, mainly run of the mill Antiques. This to Golly, is just an everyday thing, he just buys it and sells it and most of the time he doesn't have any particular fondness for it, that's how it is. But every now and again he remembers certain items that he has handled and thinks to himself, "I wish I still had that." The Winter Gardens stuff falls into that category. Golly just loves Fairground stuff and he went on to buy much more of that stuff from other places. As he says "We will get to that later."

Going back to the slot machines Golly used to buy lots of these from the arcades for a few quid apiece and then flog them on. He had loads of them and they all went to 'Trade Antiques' and then shipped out to the States. Today those machines bring hundreds of pounds each and are very desirable. Of course most of them are gone now, although Golly does still have a couple of dozen or so, which are part of his own private collection.

However there was a time when a collection of slot machines did not do so well for Golly. These machines involved a guy who had a Handbag shop in Heysham Village, Gordon Bell, AKA 'The Flying Fox'. Well Gordon was a bit of a 'Jack the Lad' who always had an eye for a bargain. We should just pause here and remember what a busy

Heysham

place Heysham was in those days, you could hardly move it was so packed with holiday makers. A quaint little village known for its 'Nettled Beer'. People would come up on the bus from Morecambe which is only ten minutes away. There was also the attraction of 'Heysham Head', which was a kind of Edwardian Theme Park. Another attraction was a small circus that was run by the Ross family. There were a few arcades, Rose Gardens, a small zoo and a café, etc. etc. making it a very popular place to visit.

Going back to Gordon Bell (Foxy), Golly called to see him one day, he found Foxy in the back garden with his mate, they were smashing up a load of fruit machines, the real early ones from the 1920's. These machines were fabulous things and these two were breaking them up because the aluminium cases were worth a few bob for scrap. "Don't touch them" Golly shouted when he saw what they were doing, "I'll take them as they are". Of course as he says, he had got there too late the damage was done. But Golly

Slot machines broken up

hadn't realised just how much damage at that point.

Foxy had been given the slot machines by his friends the McNulty Brothers, they were quite well known in the area having made a start in the fifties. Trading under the name of Miami Music, they were first in with Juke Boxes and slot machines etc. So Golly bought this pile of what could now only be described as junk and matched up the bits and pieces as best he could. It was clear though that a good mechanic or engineer could put them right.

The next day Golly took them over to Wigan, 'Trade Antiques'. He unloaded the machines in the yard and married up the pieces as best he could. He then waited for Jim Collins and his partner Max to arrive back from lunch. When they finally turned up Golly thinks they'd had a few, (Drinks that is). The first thing Jim said to Golly was, "I'm not buying that crap." Golly was a bit hurt and offended, because of all the good, rare stuff he had brought Jim over the years. Golly had really thought Jim would like these machines, obviously he didn't, he apparently couldn't see the potential in them. Golly could, but just thought, "Who am I to judge?"

Golly put them back in the van, drove away and never went back to 'Trade Antiques' again. Was that his loss? maybe, but it was certainly Jim's loss. To this day Golly can't for the life of him remember what happened to those old slot machines. All he does know is he sold them to someone. Jim however had never even asked how much the machines were, they could have been two quid apiece for all he knew. Golly wonders if Jim every regretted his actions, sadly he will never know.

One thing Golly will say and he has said it hundreds of times, Jim Collins, 'Trade Antiques' was the man who put him on his feet and he will never ever forget it. It is sad that their business relationship had to end the way it did.

We are slightly ahead of ourselves here, but the machines just seemed to lead us on the route that included fairgrounds etc..

Golly was earning good money and what's more he was taking care of it too. He always remembers Bob Skelly saying to him "Anyone can earn money, it's a clever man that can keep it." Carol and Golly had been married for six years and Golly was now in the position that he had always wanted to be in. It had been his desire to be able to let Carol pack up her job and he would be the bread winner, they had also talked about starting a family and early in 1974 Carol quit her job.

The Godfathers

Then on June the 11th their first son James was born, He was a big lad, all of Ten and a half pounds. Golly sent half a gross of red roses to 'Queen Victoria Hospital' Carol was the talk of the ward. While we are mentioning James, it would be a good time to mention that Gordon and George are his two God fathers, something that James is still very proud of.

Well it seems that it was all work and music for Golly at this point, but there was time for some relaxation. On these occasions Golly would go for a drink in the previously mentioned 'The New Inn', this was a pub in Poulton Square, Morecambe. 'The New Inn' was well known as a 'Dealing Man's' hang out, so having said it was relaxation, I think we all know by now that Golly would not pass up a deal. Any way all the Scrap Men and General Dealers would congregate there to socialise and have a drink. Golly used to sit with George Tyson, and Dick Long. Dick had a scrap yard 'Morecambe Metals'.

So were else would Golly be on the 11th of June 1974 but in 'The New Inn'... 'Wetting the baby's head', as the saying goes. It was getting towards the end of the evening and George's son Andy came in. Andy was about sixteen then, and had just left school at the

The New Inn

time. Anyway the conversation had just turned to Dick's shaven head, Dick always liked a bet and someone had said that they would give him £20 if he would shave his head. Well Dick didn't think twice, he just did it, collected his £20 telling the bloke, "That's the easiest £20 I've ever earned in my life, thank you!"

Well that set Andy off, "that's just what I'd have done," he said. "You're bluffing," Golly replied. Going on to say, "I'll give you £20 if you shave your head." Andy took him on, saying, "I'll do it." They left the pub and all went back to George's house, which was just around the corner. When they got there George cut Andy's hair off and then shaved his head with a razor. Of course George, Dick and Golly were all giggling because Andy looked like a right pillock. Then George smeared Andy's head with aftershave, Andy said it stung like hell. Nevertheless Andy had done it and Golly was happy to pay him the £20.

Another silly story that Golly remembers from 'The New Inn' days. The story concerns a plasterer Olly Oliphant who was one of the regulars. Olly was itching to get into the Antiques Business and he used to do a bit of part time dealing. He had a small shop called 'Steptoe's Cabin' on 'York Bridge', which was only a stones throw from the pub. Golly thinks he must have been worried about his stock as he always left the lights in all night.

Olly was a man who thought that he knew more than he actually did and so he slipped up on a regular basis. An example of this was the morning he bought a little desk, as he described it, off the dustbin men, for £2. Then he sold it to Peter Maudsely, another local Antique Dealer for £5. Peter took it round the corner and sold it to George Tyson for £35. George then sold it for £75 to an out of town dealer, all this happened in the space of a few hours.

That night in the pub Olly in a loud voice was telling the entire pub about his 'steal'' from the dustmen, "I've had a right deal this morning, I bought a little desk for £2 then sold it for £5 straight away. So I made £3 for five minutes work. George Tyson was in and he shouted back across the pub, "Yes and I made £40 for five minutes work and Maudsley got £30 for five minutes work." Poor Olly was 'Flabbergasted' , What he didn't know was that the little desk was a 'Walnut ,Victorian Davenport'.

Anyway back to Golly's part in Olly's story. So there was poor Olly shot down in flames, trying to save face. He proceeded to tell Golly about this 'Pedestal Table' he'd bought asking "Do you want to buy it?" "Is it the one in your shop window?" Golly asked, he had seen it earlier in Olly's shop owing to the lights being on. "Yes." said Olly. "No" Golly replied, "I can't sell them with square tops, they need to be round." "It is round!" Olly said in an angry voice. "What the one in the window?" asked Golly. "Yes"!! Said Olly, in an even angrier voice. "It's square!" said Golly.

Olly stood up, he was a pretty big bloke and announced to the whole pub, "I'll bet my house against yours, it's a round top!" He was clearly trying to make a real man of himself. "OK" Golly said, "Definitely the one in the window"? "You heard!!" Olly replied. Golly shook his hand and the bet was on. Golly would like to make the point before going further that he is not a gambler.

Golly arranged to meet him at the shop at 9am the next morning to resolve the bet. Everyone in the pub was so excited and wanted to be at the pub the next morning to see the result of this almighty bet. It never got that far, after half an hour or so Olly said again in front of everyone, "I don't want to take your house kid, let's make it a grand." He was cooling off Golly would have taken his house. "OK , a grand," said Golly, ten minutes later and so on until it finished up at a fiver. By this time it was about 10pm, this bloody big idiot had tried to belittle Golly.

So Golly said "I've just about had enough of this, get in the F***ing Van and take me to your shop. Olly reluctantly agreed, because after all his shouting and bawling, he couldn't say no. They went to the shop and sure enough the table had a square top, just as Golly had said. Golly picked up the table and said, "Right take me back to the pub,"

Olly did. Golly marched into the pub carrying the table, showed it to everyone and asked, "Round or Square?" Golly's point was proven, Olly had changed from being a roaring lion to a little lamb! He paid Golly the fiver. As Golly says, "Talk about a let down, from a house to a fiver!" Anyway back to the matters in hand, by this time Golly had dozens of business contacts, and friends. One of them being Gordon Dyson, and the other, George Tyson. Both of these men were a generation older than Golly and they were both 'Antique Dealers'. Golly starts with his description of Gordon. Gordon came to Morecambe from Bradford in 1971 and opened an Antique Shop on Westminster Road. He was like a lot of Yorkshiremen, a bit wide. Meaning, he was alert and crafty, no flies on him. Gordon knew every trick in the book, Golly thinks he wrote it. Golly learned a lot from him, having said that he learned a lot from Golly also. Golly was no dummy, he would go to Gordon's shop and camp out for hours. Camping was hanging around, killing time and yapping about all sorts.

Eventually they started working together and once a week they would drive over to Yorkshire to sell or try to sell a bit of gear as they called it. Gordon had plenty of contacts over that end, and Golly had plenty over his end.... Lancashire.

They would load up the day before and set off about 6.30 am. First stop was Settle to see a dealer called Mr Clough who used to always start early in the morning, so they always caught him about 7.30- 8am. This bloke dealt in 'Period Oak' and if Gordon and Golly had any they would show it to him. He rarely bought from them but usually had a bit for them. You see in those days 'Victorian Furniture' was frowned on by some of the old school dealers. The way they worked they would get a certain amount of stuff from house clearances and if they thought it wasn't good enough for their shop, they would keep it out of sight then when blokes like Golly and Gordon came along, who didn't care what it was just as long as they could make a profit, they would show it to them, in the hope of them buying it. It would normally be in-expensive. After all they didn't like the idea of lesser grade antiques being on their premises. "What an embarrassment" having Victorian Furniture in a Posh Antique Shop........Funny Eh?

Now this Mr Clough smoked a pipe and one of the things Gordon taught Golly and he has never forgotten it was, "You can never sell anything to a man who smokes a pipe." Throughout Golly's career this has been proven time and time again. The thing is, a bloke with a pipe in his mouth is a ponderer, very laid back, thinks about stuff too much and can't make up his mind. Just to name one instance. Golly had a bloke lined up to buy some paintings for £12,000, he had bought them from a serious collector. They were nice paintings and the bloke loved them, as did Golly.

Anyhow the bloke said he was going to bring his mate along for a second opinion. As soon as he got out of the car the blokes mate put a pipe in his mouth and lit it. Golly said to Carol, "We can forget this deal, look at him." Carol knew what Golly meant. Sure enough he told his mate to think more seriously about buying the paintings and that was the end of that. So as Golly said, "Cloughy, as they called him was a nice bloke but very hard to sell to."

Their second stop was breakfast in Skipton followed by Mick Kelly's Shop at Eastburn. Mick was a game lad and about Golly's age. He would have a go at buying from Golly and Gordon or selling to them. Either way as long as he could earn. They had another couple of calls in Bingley and then over to Frank's at Denholme. This shop was famous, it had been featured in a T.V. Documentary. Frank and Jack Weatherall, a right couple of characters but as honest as the day is long.

For starters on the shop door was a notice, it read, "THIS SHOP IS FITTED OUT WITH LOADED SHOTGUNS, OPERATED BY TRIP WIRES. ANYONE WHO DARES TO ENTER THIS SHOP AFTER HOURS IS LIKELY TO BE SHOT."

Inside the shop there were all sorts of oddball items such as, 'The Two Headed Calf'. All stuff bought from Old Victorian Sideshows at Fairgrounds and Circus's. Another quirky thing they had was 'Jesus's

Hands', a pair of hands in a case with nails through them. Other stuff came from freak shows, 'The Headless Mummy' loads of weird stuff, but it was interesting. In amongst these weird items there were antiques, which were for sale.

Frank who Golly knew best, usually ran the shop whilst his brother Jack went out busking with a Barrel Organ and a Monkey tied to a chain. Everywhere Jack went the monkey went with him. Frank always wanted to make Golly and Gordon a brew, but for some reason, they never really fancied one. More often than not they could have a deal with Frank.

Other calls included Jack Bartle in Queensbury, a bloke called Wally down in Bradford and Eddie Carroll who was an Art Dealer, it was very rare that Golly and Gordon could do any business with Eddie, but they both thought very highly of him. While we're in Yorkshire and talking about 'Yorkshiremen' , many of them were wrestling fans, including Gordon. Golly actually believes that Gordon had done a bit of wresting in his younger days. Hence the fact that he knew 'Les Kellet' who at that time was a famous TV wrestler. Les had a little transport / type Cafe in Bradford. Gordon used to go in there now and again when he lived there. He told Golly that it was OK for a cup of tea, but he really wouldn't recommend eating there.

Anyway Gordon and Golly used to go to the 'Central Pier' in Morecambe on a Thursday night to watch the wrestling. 'Shirley Crabtree', who at that time was known as 'The Guardsman' was one of the regulars. He would go on to great TV fame, after changing his name to 'Big Daddy'. All the big names of that era would come to 'The Pier'. Names such as, Kendo Nagasaki, Jackie Pallo, Mick Macmanus and of course Les Kellet, etc.

Golly and Gordon used to stand at the bar and watch the audience as they worked themselves into a frenzy. They were much more entertaining than the blokes in the ring.

After watching the wrestling, Golly and Gordon would sometimes go to 'The New Inn' for the last hour. Of course George was always there. Golly would say to him "We've been to the wrestling George, we've had a right good night. You should come with us sometime" George would reply "No I don't like wrestling, it's a put up job, it's all fixed. Boxing, yes, but wrestling, no."

Well of course it was fixed, Golly and Gordon knew that. And that was the whole point. Just good entertainment, although the audience took it all very seriously. It's all about good guys and bad guys. Old ladies whacking the bad guys legs with umbrellas and walking sticks. The bad guys could be just the same. One night they saw Kendo Nagasaki snatch a stick from an old bloke and snap it in half over his knee, then throw it back at him. The audience really believed in the whole thing, they didn't have any idea. After the match, the guys who appeared to be tearing bits out of each other, would be in the dressing room having a beer together. Golly says "It was so, so, funny."

Back to being on the road, Antique Dealing around Yorkshire. Happy times and fond memories. But they were very long days and Golly couldn't wait to get back home to Carol and Baby Jay.

Talking of Baby Jay. Golly kept a Grandfather Clock in the bedroom, which was close to the baby's cot. Baby Jay would always wake up very early and stand up in his cot, shouting at the top of his voice. He wanted to be out and he had a real temper on him. One morning Golly and Carol heard this almighty crash from the next room. They both leapt out of bed into Jay's room. There, they saw this seven foot clock, lying flat out, all in pieces. It was smashed to bits. In temper, Jay had pulled it away from the wall. "What a Bloody Mess" Golly said. Even at 18 months, Jay knew that he'd been naughty, so for his punishment, Carol took his dummy away. She'd been trying to figure out a way of doing it and now she had the perfect excuse.

Baby Jay

Back in Morecambe Gordon managed to acquire a much bigger and better shop from a fellow called Jack. Jack was from over Blackburn way and he had previously worked for the Gas Board. When he retired he came to Morecambe and bought an old established Antique and Jewellery Business. Well poor Jack had little knowledge of the business. He got fed up and moved back to Blackburn. So Gordon ended up with the shop after only parting with little money. The shop was on Albert Road, just off the Promenade and was in a prominent location and was pretty big, so Golly went in as a partner. Well not long after opening, Gordon and Golly went over to Chorley, checking out the Antique shops and they came by this little insignificant shop with a bit of junk in it. They went in for a look round but they couldn't see much. Then the owner spoke to them asking, "Do you buy clocks?" "Yes" they answered. "Well I've got a few round the corner", he said.

He took them round to this stable kind of place, with a loft. They climbed up a ladder into the loft and there they saw a room full of Grandfather Clocks. "They have got to 20 Quid apiece", the owner said. Gordon and Golly could do deals and make decisions without looking at each other. They both knew they were on a winner. "We'll have them", said Golly. He went and brought the van round and Gordon passed the clocks down from a door with a hoist above it. Of course they couldn't use the hoist for the clocks, the clocks had to be separated, Hood, Case, Movement, Weights and Pendulums.

Why the clocks were there? Golly has no idea, they should have been snapped up years before. Even back then they were worth £260/270 apiece. They brought them back to the shop and stood them around the walls. A lad called Joe had opened a Boutique further down Albert Road. He called it 'Joseph's', it is still going. Well Joe used to come into the shop now and then, he would buy a chair, a book shelf or something to decorate his Boutique. He'd seen this kind of stuff in London, decorating and setting things out... like a fancy shirt draped over an old chair, I'm sure you get the picture.

Anyway Joe came in one day and said, "I need something nice and I fancy having a Grandfather Clock, can you give me a couple of prices?" So Golly pointed a couple out saying, "That's two and a half, that's three", and so on. Joe decided on the one at three and pulled out a fiver. Golly looked at him and said, "No Joe £300". As Golly says now, "He doesn't know who was the most embarrassed, Joe or himself."

Gordon and Golly also used to do house clearances, there was always plenty of stuff in Morecambe as it was a bit of a retirement retreat for people from Yorkshire etc. They would get calls from Estate Agents and solicitors to go and clear houses. Some of the stuff wasn't much good so they used to pass it on to the second hand lads. That would usually be Tom and George from Lancaster. They had a good little business going especially with the University. They could never get enough beds.

Anyway one day Gordon and Golly went to look at this particular house, it didn't have much in it but there were a few bits that they didn't want to miss. The thing was if they had bought the stuff they wanted, they would then be committed to empty the house and they knew that Tom and George wouldn't be to bothered about the stuff either. So they needed something to tempt them. In one of the bedrooms there was a box of costume jewellery, loads of it but it wasn't worth anything. Well knowing how Tom and George worked, Golly had a sure fire plan. The first thing they always did was to go upstairs and check out the beds, they wouldn't take any with stained mattresses.

With "a map of Ireland on" as they used to describe them. Then they would spin the mattresses over to check the other side. So Golly planted all this costume jewellery under the mattress. It looked like a hoard of hidden treasure. Tom went straight upstairs. Golly knew what he would do. Tom looked under the mattress, saw the jewellery and quickly dropped the mattress back into place. Tom came down stairs, "Yes it will be all right Golly, we'll take it." So they paid up and that was that. They thought that Golly had missed a load of gold and diamonds. Fancy thinking that about poor Golly!

On another occasion Carol and Golly were driving to Lancaster, when Golly noticed that someone had dumped a mattress at the edge of the lane. Golly pulled up, got out of the van and checked out the mattress for the "Map of Ireland", it was stain free. So he put it in the van and took it to Tom and George. They looked at the mattress and bought it, for a fiver. Pretty good deal, because a fiver then would buy you ten gallons of petrol!

Like Golly said he and Gordon did lots of house clearances together. The trouble was there was so much good stuff that was considered worthless and Golly really means worthless. An example of this would be a magnificent Inlaid Mahogany Bedroom Suite. Golly can remember knocking it to pieces with a hammer then, throwing it out of the top window of a house. Simply because there was so much work involved in picking it up and carrying it down the stairs. It was only going to the tip anyway. Bedroom furniture was a "No, No" as were mirror back sideboards, lovely carved Walnut Edwardian sideboards, smashed up. They weren't worth tuppence. Ornate leaded glass windows, Golly used to jump on them to smash the glass so that he could weigh in the lead.

George Tyson used to break up Brass Beds and weigh them in. George was an ex scrap dealer but even before that he had Horses and

Edwardian Sideboard - back then worthless!

Carriages, known as 'Landaus' on Morecambe Promenade. George made his full time start in 'The Antiques Business' at roughly the same time as Golly. He lived near the market in Poulton Square, Morecambe and he had a shop. He would sell anything he could lay his hands on.

When Golly got to know George and his wife Shirley the shop was full of shoes. George said to Golly "I've got to get rid of this lot." Golly replied, "Let me see what I can do." So he loaded the van and off he went, he had no idea where he could place them. Golly asked around for a couple of days and then he saw a mate of his, Mick Tew and he said, "Hey Golly I was taking to a bloke in the pub last night name of Leo, he said he may be interested in that job lot of shoes."

So Golly tracked Leo down and sold him the load of shoes, made a few quid on the deal. Then Leo sold them to a stall holder on Morecambe Market, just a few yards down from Georges shop. Shirley, Georges wife saw them the next day and said to George, "That bloody little Golly Goulding, how does he do it?" George and Golly have had thousands of deals over the last forty odd years, which must run into millions. Golly went to see him every day and always sold him something or other.

Golly remembers that one day he bought a pair of "Staffordshire Dogs", you know the spaniels that you would usually see on the mantelpiece in old houses. Anyway the thing about these dogs was that the glass eyes were missing, so Golly got felt tip pen and drew a pair of eyes on both dogs. Then he went to see George to try and sell the dogs to him. George looked at the dogs and then he put his thumb on the eyes and they smudged. George just looked at Golly, laughed and bought the dogs anyway.

Another time Golly bought a Roll Top Desk with a drawer missing. So he found an old piece of wood of similar colour, cut it to size and nailed to the desk. It didn't look too bad really because he had a spare handle which he fitted to it. So remember this is just a drawer front that didn't open. Golly took it George, he started pulling the drawers to check it, when he got to the dummy drawer he tugged and pulled at it. . Then he said "Oh it's only stuck, it must be swollen."

George bought the desk from Golly and sold it on quickly. A few days later he saw Golly and said, "Hey that bloody drawer that I couldn't open was false and the bloke I sold it on to is having a new one made." George knew what Golly had done but it didn't matter that's how it was in those days. 'Buyer Beware'

CHAPTER 13

NEW GROUP AND SURPRISING DEALS

Getting back to the music Golly was now in a new Band, 'Carol Jacksons Hi-Way'. Carol Jackson was and still is a great singer who had come over to Morecambe from Bradford with her boyfriend Ray Bainbridge. Ray was a guitarist and for some reason, after they came to Morecambe, he and Carol split up. So this left Carol without a group. Golly had met up with Sib again, remember Sib? He had been with 'The Milestones' and Road Manager for 'Mel Deane and The Leaders'

Carol Jackson's Hi-Way

when they were down in London. Anyway Golly and Sib had met up again in their local pub, 'The Globe'. Sib said he fancied doing a bit of playing again.

So Golly started looking around to see if he could find the right musicians to form a group. Golly got hold of Ray Illingworth, he was a drummer that he'd known for a few years. He was happy to team up. They still needed a bass player, Sib told Golly that he had been talking to Garry Pugh in 'The Globe' and that Garry was interested. Garry had been playing 'Pro' up and down the country with a very good group called 'Ohio Springs'. But after all the years of travelling they had got fed up, so they came back to Morecambe, split up and went their separate ways.

So Golly had his line up, Ray, Sib, Garry, with Carol on vocals. They did quite a lot of rehearsing up at Golly's place and after a few months they were ready to hit the road and work. It was a good little outfit and they were doing some of the better bookings around the Lake District also a few decent clubs. With a great girl singer up front the group were gaining popularity. Anyway after this good spell had lasted for a while, Carol started developing throat problems and she eventually had to pack it in.

Once again they needed a vocalist, they had plenty of work in the pipeline which they didn't want to lose. Anyway Golly thought and thought about who they could get as a replacement. Then Golly remembered Woodie from his 'Mark 4' days. Woodie hadn't been doing much for a few years, but Golly thought it was worth going to have a word with him. When Golly saw him Woodie agreed to come along for a rehearsal. Well, Woodie fitted in right away just like Golly knew he would. None of the other members of the group knew him or had even

Woodie, Golly, Ray

seen him working. So once again the group had the complete line up, they were good to go.

Like Golly said the group had a good reputation as 'Carol Jacksons Hi-Way', so they decided to keep the name, 'Hi-Way'. One thing led to another and they became extremely busy on the Cabaret Scene. They were a novelty act due to Woodie's great wit. He used to have the audience in stitches. Sometimes on the first set the group might only get through three or four numbers due to all the laughter that Woodie was generating. Obviously the comedy stuff was a real attraction but Hi-Way was a serious band at the same time and people realised that. Golly did quite a few years with Hi-Way on the Cabaret Scene.

As Golly said to the author, "You know Dave in the seventies everything was cabaret, clubs just weren't interested in Rock n Roll Groups" I know that he is right. He went on to say, "Everything had to be middle of the road type stuff, fancy suits etc". Looking back it was a great scene and Golly learned a lot about stage presentation etc. But after doing it for a while Golly started to think, "This isn't really for me." Once again he was becoming bored with everything including the band members. It has to be remembered Golly is doing all this exciting stuff during the day as an Antique Dealer and the evenings were at bit of a let down. They were just too routine and having to answer to Concert Secretaries and the likes. After all his many achievements imagine Golly Goulding having to answer to these people.

One thing that was a plus when the group was going round all the different clubs and venues, was the opportunity it gave Golly to root around the rooms looking for a bit of gear. There were many occasions when he found furniture such as Desks, Windsor Chairs, Pianos etc. all this old stuff that they didn't want or care about. Golly would buy it for peanuts, having got the stuff he would sell it on, he was earning ten times the fee they were paying him, as they say, 'It pays to be in the know'! Of course the other lads in the group hadn't a clue what Golly was doing, they just saw him as a 'Steptoe' which he was and still is.

CHAPTER 14

STEVE SEARLE AND
A NEW WORLD OF MUSIC

Now the 'Hi-Ways' drummer, Ray was doing a bit of work midweek, playing with a keyboard player, called Steve Searle. Steve was a fully trained piano player and a first class reader of music. They also had a bass player called Phil in their line up. Steve and Phil were both employed as Male Nurses by 'The Royal Albert Hospital'. This was a very large Victorian Building, housing patients who had learning difficulties.

On Monday evenings the hospital always held 'The Patients Dance', with entertainment provided by 'The Steve Searle Trio'. Now for some unknown reason, certainly forgotten now, Phil was unavailable and they were stuck for a Bass Player. Knowing that Golly could play bass Ray asked him to play. "Sure no problem said Golly" and he went along and did the job.

Now Golly open heartedly confesses that when he saw some the poor souls, trying to dance he got scared, nervous or something he really can't describe. How can you work with these people he thought. He also thought, Let me get out of here. These in Golly's own words were cowardly, awful thoughts, that he feels ashamed to recount. It is a reflection of the good man he is, that he shares this memory with us.

After the gig Steve asked Golly, "Was it OK?" "Yes" he replied. "Can you do it next Monday?" asked Steve. "Not Sure, I'll let you know" replied Golly. As he says, to be truthful, he didn't want to do it. That weekend Golly was playing with "Hi-Way" and Ray asked Golly "OK for Monday?" "Yes" replied Golly. Everyone knows that it is a rare thing for musicians to work on a Monday night so Golly had no real excuse to get out of the gig. Golly went along for the second time, of course this time he knew what to expect.

At the end of the night when it was time to get paid, Golly noticed that Steve did not receive any money. He asked him why. Steve told him that he wouldn't accept any payment because he loved doing it. The patients looked forward to the 'Monday Dance' and he took as much pleasure from it as they did.

All the patients highly respected Steve and always called him Mr Searle. That night when Golly got home he is not ashamed to say that he became very emotional. He thought deeply about these poor unfortunate patients and the way their faces lit up when the band started to play. As Golly says his attitude towards the patients changed dramatically and almost instantly.

You can see the way this story is going. Golly became the Bass Player in 'The Steve Searle Trio' he played at The Royal Albert Hospital's 'Monday Dance' every week.

Golly is rightly proud to be able to tell us that he really came to love all the patients and the dedicated nurses who looked after them. Now he was like Steve and always looked forward to those Monday nights. He really loved the job. Golly doesn't think he is clever enough with words to describe how he changed his attitude from a man who was 'Shying Off' the job to getting an inner satisfaction from doing it. Well I can assure him that he is, when I was hearing his description of the circumstances I am not ashamed to say that I was in tears. No one should be in any doubt what I fine human being Golly Goulding is.

As Golly says whenever he sees handicapped people he gets upset and wants to help them. These feelings all stem back to his days with the 'Steve Searle Trio' at The Royal Albert Hospital. Golly asks the question, "How can a bloke change his thoughts over night??" He answers his own question, "Without getting too religious, I know who is behind it all." "Jesus." God Blessed Golly with his understanding of the people and the situation. In my opinion God also blesses us by bringing people like Golly into our lives.

Golly went on to do much more with the trio because Steve used to get a lot of private bookings. Steve used to do all the singing and Golly learned so much from him about music. Steve also knew that Golly was really a Guitarist, not a Bass Player, so he asked him to drop the bass and come in on Guitar..

Golly went along with that and the trio did all sorts of stuff together, ranging from old time dancing to stuff from the charts. Imagine playing the old time dance music on an Electric Guitar? Well Golly played it even though he hadn't heard most of it before. Steve used to write all the parts out for Golly and Golly being a quick learner would play them.

Sometimes, indeed most times the trio would get a booking and Steve would present Golly with a load of manuscript and say, "This is what we are playing tonight." If Golly struggled because the music was an obscure tune, Steve always covered for him. As Golly said, "I owe Steve so much for introducing me to a whole new world of music. His experience with Steve enabled him to arrange all the parts for the other band members and work out all the chords, etc. That is one of the great things about Golly, he is always willing to learn both in life and in music.

Golly bought a house in Lancaster, just a terraced house but it was a decent little thing. Anyway Steve rented it from him and he would invite Golly round now and again, with a few other friends and they would have drink and discuss music. Golly says, "Steve was an upright, first class decent bloke." So it was no surprise when he later joined The Salvation Army. He would be spotted round the pubs from time to time selling, 'The War Cry' magazine.

Steve also became the resident organist at a working men's club in Carnforth. Because of that, the trio broke up and Golly lost touch with him for a while. Then one day Golly read in the newspaper that Steve had died. The funeral was held at 'The Salvation Army Headquarters' in Morecambe. Good old Steve was "Promoted to Glory". Golly thinks of him frequently and he misses him so much, as he says, "Steve was one of life's 'Pure Gentlemen'.

Anyway Golly had been playing with "Hi-Way" and the trio, then he was dealing during the day, he was very busy. As he said he was getting bored with Hi-Way, so was Woodie and they both left the group, Ray followed their lead. Incidentally 'Hi-Way' went on performing for another twenty years, that's been the story of Golly's life , he forms a Band, then gets bored, leaves and the Band carries on.

Golly had the idea of putting the idea of putting together a little outfit, playing Jazzy type stuff. Not real Jazz but an intricate type of music a bit more cultured and serious than some of the stuff he had been playing. The desire to change the style of music was down to Golly having played with Steve in the trio.

So Golly, Woodie and Ray reformed with a Bass Player called Tony and Golly named them 'Free At Last'. Golly feels this was an apt name because they really were free at last from all that Cabaret stuff that they had been doing with 'Hi-Way'. As Golly tells us 'Free At Last' was a serious band, they chose their bookings wisely. They did this by only going to the right places and playing to the right people.

CHAPTER 15

DEALS, ROLLS AND SNOBS

We will get back to Foxy at this point, as far as Golly can gather Foxy's friends the McNulty brothers, had done exceptionally well and made a lot of money from siting Jukeboxes and Fruit Machines in Pubs, Clubs and Cafes around the Country. In a way they were like local celebrities. It seems that they had bought the old bowling alley in Morecambe and turned it into a Night Club, known as 'The Morecambe Bowl', Golly will have more to say about that as we progress. They also acquired part of Heysham Head, Golly is not sure whether they bought or rented it from the council. Whichever it was, they opened a night club there as well calling it 'The Beach Club'.

Remember Golly saying that Heysham Head was like an Edwardian theme park. So when it closed down there was a lot of stuff to be cleared and Golly would obviously be interested and Foxy was supposed to get first shout. He rang Golly up one Sunday asking him to come over and buy some stuff from him. Golly doesn't remember what, but he thinks it was probably some furniture. While Golly was there Foxy told him that he was getting a very large stuffed bear, apparently it growled when you pressed its belly. He said he was getting it that afternoon, well you can imagine Golly's inner excitement, he was on pins all day, he really wanted that bear.

Foxy had told Golly he would ring him about it later, he never did. He told Golly much later that he couldn't get it, Golly didn't believe him, so he never heard any more about it. However it did turn up many years later, but that is a story to be told later in the book.

Musically in the late seventies Golly was still playing with Woody and Ray in 'Free at Last'. This continued until they folded around 1979.

Golly did not play much after that until he met Derek Jackson. So we will carry on with the other aspects of Golly's life for the time being.

Golly as you will remember mentioned The Circus at Heysham being run by the Ross family. Well Golly knew the sons pretty well Tony Ross was a tight rope walker and he was also a guitarist and country and western singer His younger brother Terry was a bass player, Golly worked with Tony a few times and he was in a couple of groups with Terry. They had a younger brother referred to by them as 'our Michael'. All three brothers had previously worked in the family circus, they were a nice family.

One day Terry came round to the house with about half a dozen stuffed rabbits. They were all stood up and dressed in little suits Terry told him they had come from Heysham Head, they all had instruments and were called 'The Bunny Band'. Of course Golly bought them, held on to them for a while and then sold them.

Golly has always had a liking for the unusual and Taxidermy in general. It is frowned on today by some people, but in Victorian times it was very fashionable. You only have only to look back at Big Game hunting and the taking of Trophies etc.

Taxidermy is an art and has always been an expensive process. Golly once bought a stuffed dog, it was only a mongrel, it still had its original collar and name tag. It had been an old ladies faithful companion. When it died she had it stuffed and it sat in her fireplace for many years. It wasn't uncommon in the old days to have your pets stuffed. Golly's had dogs, cats, sheep etc, you name it, he's had it. At one time he even bought a stuffed alligator. It was a huge monster of a thing. Golly later sold that to a pub landlord and he had it hanging over the bar.

One day Golly and Carol took some rubbish to the local tip, when they pulled up Golly saw this gigantic stuffed lion standing outside the workmen's cabin. Naturally Golly asked them if he could buy it. "Buy it" one of the blokes said, "I'll give it to you. Just take it away." Golly had recognised the lion straight away. It was the one that had been exhibited at Heysham Head for over eighty years or more. It was a real struggle to get it into his van, he only managed it with help from the workmen.

Jay with the alligator

Carol-Anne with the alligator

"I must pay you." Said Golly, "No we don't want anything" they replied. Golly really wanted to give something for it but they just wouldn't take anything. Then one of them said, "Put something in that tin, it's the brew money." Golly had about £2.50 in change in his pocket so he gave them that. These blokes were delighted by what they recognised as Golly generosity, but strictly speaking it was forbidden to sell anything.

Golly and Carol took it back to base and somehow got it out of the van. This thing was 9 foot long it was the biggest lion that you have ever seen in your life and it weighed a ton, (if not a ton it was bloody heavy.) The lion wasn't in the best of nick, all the heavy stitching was coming apart under its belly. It was lined with iron rods you could see them coming out through the feet, it was filled with sawdust, stank and was full of maggots.

Because the lion was too heavy to manoeuvre, Golly made a frame for it to stand on with four big piano casters so that they could wheel it around. He cleaned the lion out the best he could but he just couldn't get rid of the smell. As luck would have it Golly had cleared out an old chemist shop in Lancaster a few months before and he had a box of carbolic soap, so he pulled a load of sawdust out of the lions belly and replaced it with blocks of carbolic soap. If anyone remembers carbolic soap they will know how strong it smells. Having done that, he was able to stitch its belly up with wire. It did the trick. It killed the pong!

The other problem with this lion was that it was moulting, losing its hair in places. Carol always quick thinking and quick witted said. "We should spray it with hair lacquer" So Golly bought half a dozen tins of the stuff and drenched the lion in it that solved that problem. There was still one more problem it had lost its eyes. Golly solved that problem too. He had recently bought six old rocking horses from George Tyson so he nicked a pair of eyes from the biggest horse. When Golly and Carol had finished doing all this refurbishment the old lion looked pretty smart.

Now Golly had a section of warehouse where he used to hide a bit of stuff that needed attention before being sold on, repairs etc. So he put this curtain up and had the lion stood directly behind it. Now remember this was a real lion, a ferocious looking thing. Golly put up a notice saying 'Keep Out'! He knew that if he wasn't around someone would always be nosy and take a peep behind the curtain. So he would let the customers into the warehouse, saying, "I'll follow you in a minute." The first thing they saw when they moved the curtain was this bloody big lion looking at them, there was always the same response, they would yell and then say, "F***ing hell I nearly Sh*t myself." He eventually sold the Lion for £450, a decent price but still cheap. Today Golly's estimate would be £5,000 to £10,000.

So Golly had got the lion from Heysham Head and the stuffed 'Bunny Band', but what had happened to the bear? We are still a bit away from finding out about that, but we will. There is another funny story that involves Heysham Head in a roundabout way.

There was a group that Golly remembers as being very popular from his school days they were called 'Pythagoras and the Squares' (mentioned earlier) and there were still a couple of these characters around, Graham Harrison and Gordon Buchannan. These two were very funny guys and they were now part of a group called 'The Hairy Fairies'. Sometimes they used to come on stage in their underclothes with a pair of wings stuck to their back. They played the early Rock and Roll stuff and drank pints in 'The Kings Arms' pub which was on the Promenade Morecambe it was next door to 'The Tivoli Bar' where the often played.

When they'd had a few pints they would make themselves a sandwich apiece. This involved a beermat which they would empty an ashtray on to, then put another beermat on top and eat the whole thing. Then they would drink another pint, and for dessert and eat the glass, All of it. They were bloody mad! They used to do it regular.

One night after they had been playing at 'The Tiv' one of them Graham or Gordon, Golly doesn't remember which one, came up with an idea that would get them a couple of quid. They went up to Heysham Head, climbed over the wall and took off their pants, shoes and socks and jumped into the 'Wishing Well'. It was maybe three or four foot deep, they scrambled about in the dark for as long as it took, til they had found all the coins. Golly says. "It can't have been that much money, pennies and halfpennies mostly. Be that as it may the money gathered managed to finance the next afternoons drinking session. Golly remembers that one Friday afternoon Graham Harrison tapped him up for a fiver, he has never seen him since.

In among all the many things going on in the mid to late seventies was something that should really have a chapter to itself, Golly and Carol already had their wonderful son Jay who was nearly three years old when on the 20th of February 1977 their son Rob was born. As Golly says, "He was the most beautiful baby you have ever seen." The family was growing and their happiness with it.

The Goulding family

Rob's brother Jay was as we say nearly three years old by this time and he was a very precocious child. Everywhere Golly went the whole family went with him and even at that early age Jay wanted to help his Dad. He could carry small chairs and bits of furniture and of course Golly let him and encouraged him. By the time he was about eight years old people were asking his advice, because he had an amazing knowledge of antiques. One lad, Derren used to bring Golly various bits of stuff and he would say to Jay, "How much should I ask your Dad for this?" Jay's school teachers were also fascinated by him and his abilities.

Carol-Anne, Jay, Rob

But as we tend to do with this book we are getting ahead of ourselves and Golly still has quite a bit to tell us about 1977/78. The antique business was booming, every day they would go out in the empty van looking for stuff, Carol, Jay and

Rob were always with Golly. They always had plan of where they were heading for. As soon as they had the van full, and as Golly says, "That meant tightly packed", plus a full roof rack they would go off and do some family things together, this is how it always was.

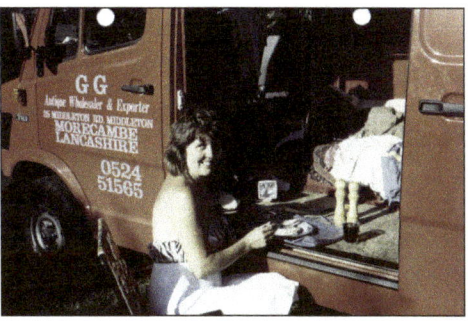

Carol preparing a picnic

Sometimes they would take a canoe and find a river to sail on or swim in. If they were in the Dales or such, they would go for a picnic up a mountain side. Every possible kind of outdoor family fun.

Wherever Golly went the family went with him, there were no seat belts or rules about passengers in those days, so the kids could be in the back of the van, perhaps Jay would be sprawled on top of a wardrobe and Rob would be in a little slot under a chair or something. They hardly ever had a seat for the journey home.

So as Golly was telling us, business was really good. So good that Golly decided to buy a Rolls Royce. One or two of the older dealers around Skerton were buying Rolls Royce's, really a lot of that was just them trying to outshine each other. Someone would buy a Roller and every one would admire it stood outside their semi-detached house. Then someone else would buy one with the Silver Lady and other fittings Gold Plated and so on.

The cars were worth three or four times the value of their houses, can you imagine a £30,000 car parked outside a £5,000 house, but that is just the way it was. People in the travelling community have always been prone to trying to get one up on their associates. This attitude is even more prevalent today, on an even larger scale. These days people compete to see who can build the biggest flashiest house. For example someone will build a Two Million pound house in a £200,000 neighbourhood. Mind you, as Golly says, most of these houses are beautiful but some are well over the top and just look vulgar.

Golly guesses his desire for a Rolls Royce may have stemmed from the one- up- man- ship that he was seeing being displayed by the people around him. He is not so sure about that, because he had always fancied one. But he thought it was just a dream, he never saw himself being in that class.

So when Golly got the opportunity to buy one he did. It was a dark metallic blue "Silver Shadow" (Photo), he felt like a 'Million Dollars' driving around in it. The big thing was, Golly had actually paid for it, not on payments like a lot of the others, who were just poseurs. Especially the people Golly knew in the Blackpool area. Was Golly a poseur? Possibly? But he would like to think not, although he supposes there could have been a bit of that in it. Here he was, Golly Goulding only in his early thirties, driving around in a Roller, it just didn't seem right.

Rolls Royce, Frog-eyed Sprite to side

There is a story that Golly remembers about the influence that driving a "Roller" can have on people. At the time Golly was still with the group 'Free at Last' and they were booked to perform at a local venue, It was at a nice restaurant, probably a Dinner Dance or something similar for 'The Round Table'. The owner of the restaurant was a real arse hole who treated them like sh*t. Ray said "You should have come in the Roller Golly!. All the lads in the group had a good laugh.

Well it came round and 'Free at Last' had another booking there. So they took the gear down in the afternoon using the van as normal. When they went back at night to do the gig they went in The Rolls Royce, the owner didn't see them arrive because being winter time it was dark early on. Golly got parked up on the car park and went in without being seen. The owner hadn't got a clue who the car belonged to. Golly heard him say to his wife, "We've have got a Rolls Royce on the car park tonight, I wonder who's it is?" He naturally thought it belonged to one of the guests. It was clear he was getting a real kick out of the car being outside his venue, it was showing that he was attracting the right type of clientèle.

This guy was clearly a bit of a 'Basil Fawlty' type of bloke. As the night came to an end the car park gradually emptied, all the cars were gone except for the Rolls Royce. While the guys were dismantling the gear and stacking it up near the door Golly heard the owner say, "I haven't found out whose car it is, whoever it belongs to must have had too much to drink, he's left the car behind. Then he turned to Golly saying, "How long are you lot going to be?" "I need to lock up." "Only a couple of minutes" Replied Ray. They finished stacking the gear by the door ready to pick up in the morning. Then they went out on to the brightly lit car park.

The owner was standing by the door and saw them walking towards the Rolls, "What are you doing?" He shouted. "Going home" replied Golly as he opened the car, "Is that really yours?" The owner asked. "Yes and it's paid for" answered Golly. Well if you've ever witnessed a bloody snob changing his attitude, this was a classic case. He came over and started yapping to them, he wanted to be Golly's best mate. He just wouldn't let them leave, in the end Golly said "We really must go, it's been a long night."

The next morning when Golly and the lads turned up in the van to pick up the gear, sure enough the owner was there and made coffee and biscuits for them. This was the same bloke who wouldn't give them the time of day 24 hours earlier. It was a real education for the lads in the group. Of course Golly had seen this kind of behaviour countless times, people that just don't want to know, until they find out that someone has a bit of something about them, then they change immediately.

The Rolls Royce type of incident happened again at another local venue. There was a famous comedian who used to come to one the pubs where the group played, after his show ended. He always had a couple of old birds with him. Well Golly and the lads, being musicians used to stay behind for a drink, he doesn't think this comedian bloke had much time for Golly, Ray and Woodie. He thought he was the star, they were just working lads.

The Landlord, although he was a decent bloke always made a fuss of this comedian Golly supposes that a celebrity coming for an after hours drink was a big deal, nothing wrong with that. And Golly is not knocking it. This comedian, Golly doesn't wish to name him, had just got himself a new TV show and of course he made no bones about advertising the fact around the pub.

Due to his success he had bought himself a second hand Mercedes and everybody had to go outside and admire it. Fair play to him, and well done, but he did have an ego and an attitude. He really believed that he had the best car in the world. So one night Golly took the Rolls to the gig. Well when he saw it the Comedian said, "Who's is the Roller on the car park?" "Golly's." The Landlord replied. Golly and the lads were sitting at a table away from the bar, this bloke just looked at Golly and never said a word, you could see he was gutted. He just couldn't accept that anybody in the pub could have a better car than his. He had one drink then left. To Golly by saying nothing, he was saying everything, jealousy was written all over his face!

After about a year the novelty of having a Rolls Royce was wearing off for Golly. Carol had never really felt comfortable in it, but she did feel some satisfaction in the fact they had been able achieve having a Rolls Royce. Anyway the beginning of the end for the Roller was when it developed a minor electrical problem. Golly can't remember exactly what the problem was but he took it to an auto electrician, he should really have taken it back to Rolls Royce but he wasn't going to pay them a £1,000 just to look at it. Make no mistake that is the sort of figure that they would have wanted.

Anyway this auto electrician was chuffed to bits when Golly brought the Rolls to him to be sorted out. He kept it in his garage for two weeks just for status. Golly wasn't too bothered by this as he didn't use the car very much anyway. Well the auto electrician told his dad about the Rolls Royce he had in his garage to do a job on. So his Dad wanted to know who owned it. So he said "Oh it's Golly the Antique Dealer". That rang a bell with his Dad, because he had worked in the drawing office with Golly's wife Carol. Now Carol always described this bloke as "A horrible man and pompous snob." Now let me tell you anyone who knows Golly's wife will tell you that she would never say a thing like that against anybody, unless she had a very good reason.

Golly had never met him but, he had heard plenty about him. This was because when he knew that Carol was getting married to this rag and bone/window cleaning/ musician and going to live in the caravan it was a big office joke for him. There were other incidents too, Golly knows that Carol detested this pathetic excuse for a bloke.

So this pillock now knows who owns the car and why it is in his son's garage. The reason being because Golly doesn't want to pay out a load of uneccessary money for a minor job. Anyway this false excuse for a man is now telling his son, "Oh yes I know Carol well she worked in the office, nice girl, I know her husband too, I always knew that they would do well." All that sort of flattering insincere claptrap! All this just because of that bloody Rolls Royce!!

So Golly decided that he had enough of the Rolls and started thinking about selling it. The big problem was who was going to buy it? Plenty of people would like to have it, but paying for it, that's a different thing, a completely different story. Well one day an old Gypsy mate by the name of Mick Darling, called to see Golly. He brought a very well to do Antique Dealer with him. Mick was taking this bloke around the general trade introducing him to new contacts. Golly says Mick needs his own chapter in order to say everything about him.

As the two of them walked into the yard and the first words from the antiques bloke were "Is that a Rolls Royce? He had spotted it parked with a few other cars that Golly had around at that time, Three Vintage Motors, a couple of Sports Cars and one or two vans. " Wow, I've always wanted one of those, do you want to sell it?"he asked. "Sure I'll sell it" said Golly.

They struck a deal there and then. So much in money, the rest in antiques and jewellery. It was very quick deal and they were both happy. That was the end of Golly's Rolls Royce! He never missed it and he has never wanted another. He forgot to mention that he picked Jay up from school in it now and again, what he never knew for years was that Jay hated it.

CHAPTER 16

MICK DARLING

Mick and his family were the real hardy, rough living Gypsy family, although Golly did hear that Mick came from a fairly well off background, but had turned his back on it all to go on the road. Mick used to deal in scrap metal and antiques, when Golly first met him he was living on the old tip. Golly mentioned the old tip earlier in the book. The old tip was a big camp site especially for the Irish Tinkers.

Mick had six kids and only one small caravan, three of the kids slept in their own detached bedroom outside the caravan. This room was just four old doors nailed together in a square with a canvas wagon sheet over the top for a roof. That was their home winter and summer. In the winter the kids used to stick to the doors, because of the frost. They must have been tough little buggers! Mick always had a camp fire going with a tripod from which he hung a big black iron kettle. He always made Golly welcome and they did a hell of a lot of trading over the years. Mick always had one or two horses and Golly bought a few off him over the years for the kids when they were younger. He had a few chickens and ducks he kept those for eggs and eventually meat.

Mick would stay around Morecambe for a few months and then move on to somewhere else, but he would always keep in touch. Golly would get a phone call saying, "I'm camped near Skipton", or such- like then he would describe where he was. It would usually be down a lane or a bit of a lay by or similar. Golly would go and meet him and buy his items, which usually filled the van. Mick had a few favourite stopping off spots, illegal of course but the locals didn't mind, because he always left the place clean and tidy. They had got used to him over the years, he was an attraction and a bit of a novelty. He also used to go around the pubs at night busking, he played a Mandolin and a Ukulele, they were his favourite instruments. He even appeared on TV a couple of times. As the years went by he started getting on his feet a bit and he progressed to a 'Living Wagon', this is what the rest of us know as a four wheeled, canvas topped, horse drawn Gypsy Caravan. Mick painted it, using traditional decoration and colours. It was spectacular.

When Mick bought his first one it was a bit of a wreck and he spent the whole summer renovating it. Mick was a talented bloke he would carve the wood and then paint it up in the right method and traditional way. He built the cabinets for the 'Crown Derby' and 'The Royal Worcester' to be displayed in. China ware is a tradition amongst Traveller folk. It gives them the opportunity to show off their wealth and status.

Mick has had several different 'Living Wagons' over the years, he would buy a rough one, do it up and then sell it on. As his kids got a bit older he used to sort them out with a pony and a flat cart to pick up scrap metal and antiques with. This allowed Mick more time to work on the 'Living Wagons'. In the wintertime he would make cane walking sticks and shepherds crooks.. Baskets from twigs and all that type of stuff, he would stockpile all of these things to sell in the summer at Village Fêtes, Markets and Fairs etc.

All in all Mick was doing pretty well and of course Travellers don't know the meaning of Income Tax, Rates, Utility Bills etc. They have a head start on other businessmen. But of course their lifestyle is not for everyone, you've got to be pretty tough to spend the winter in a 'Living Wagon' using oil lamps and cooking on a fire.

Like Golly said he has done hundreds of deals with Mick over the years, not to mention some great laughs. Yes he is a mate but if he could bull Golly, (stitch him up) by selling him something that was not quite right and get away with it, he would. Golly's view is that if he buys something that is not right, he should have looked harder. He put himself into that situation.

Do you remember Golly talking about Frank at Denholme the bloke with the trip wires in his shop? Well Mick once bought an Enema kit, a nice Victorian one in a Mahogany box. He sold it on to Frank as a Victorian Piping Set for putting icing on cakes. Frank put in his shop window on display, he soon found out what it really was, when a lady walked in and told him it was disgusting.

When Mick and his family used to come and visit Golly and his family, they would stay for hours. Mick's kids would play in the field with Carol and Golly's. Mick's kids always wanted to use the toilet, because they had never had a toilet, just a hole in the ground behind the bushes.

Another funny thing that Golly bought from Mick was a Victorian Nursing Chair. This bloody chair was just one mass of lumps and bumps. Carol was attending night school for upholstery lessons and she used to do all sorts of things, repairs and refurbishments for Golly. So she said she would take the stuffing out and re-upholster it. She started to pull out the stuffing. It looked like the contents of a jumble sale. It was just one mass of old clothes. Everyone in the class had a good laugh at that one. But of course as Golly says the watchword for anyone in the business, should always be 'Buyer Beware'!

• CHAPTER 17 •

DEREK JACKSON
The Blues

Well we are now around 1980 and Golly and Carol's third child had been born in November 1979. They christened her Carol-Anne, after her Mum Carol and Golly's Mam Anne.

Anyway Golly had heard about this fantastic Blues/Harmonica player called Derek Jackson, who had just moved to Lancaster. Derek was a mature student who was studying at Lancaster University, he was also working as a part time barman at 'The Greaves Hotel', Lancaster. 'The Greaves' used to put music on three or four nights a week. The Manager John Cockerton, had been Manager of Morecambe Bowl and he was well connected with a lot of the famous Cabaret Acts who were touring

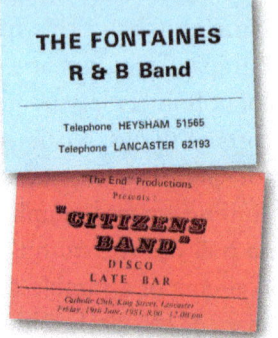

Golly and Derek - Fontaines / Citizens Band

the UK. Acts such as Heinz, Vince Eager, Karl Denver and Golly would think Tommy Bruce. He thinks I might enlighten him, well the answer is probably yes, we did Morecambe about twelve years ago, as Tommy said, *"I did some gigs in Morecambe in the early eighties, they take a long time to book you back'.* He told me he used to do a pub mid week when he was there, so it was very likely 'The Greaves'.

Anyway Golly had heard about Derek who worked behind the bar, because now and again he would get up and sing. Golly felt that he needed to check him out, so he did. Ray, Garry and Golly arranged to meet Derek at 'The Shrimp' in Morecambe. They discussed forming a group and arranged a run through. When they got going and Derek started singing and playing, Golly was 'Knocked Out' and that is putting it mildly.

The lads of course unanimously agreed to put a band together. Golly had been itching to get to some real music of his choice, as he had been doing middle of the road stuff for many years.

So the guys needed a name, Garry had always admired Golly's old band 'The Fontaines' all those years ago, he had liked the name, the way they played, everything about them. So it was decided that they would use the name again, after all it was Golly's group. They went out on gigs and did really well, so well in fact that that they took the whole area by storm.

They were doing 'The Greaves' a couple of times a week, quite surprising really because John, the venues manager did not like them. The music they were playing did not appeal to him, He loved the middle of the road cabaret stuff. He had to be realistic though, because he knew that 'The Fontaines' mark two would fill the place. It was quite funny really because John moaned and bitched every time he paid them, he was a good manager but he really was a miserable old sod!

They kept that group together for a year or so, but then Golly got an offer to play with another group called 'Buddy And The Heartbeats'. These lads were out five nights a week and they were being paid pretty good money. The line up was Dave Barlow Singer/Guitarist, Terry Ross, from the old circus on Bass, Eric Broadbent on Drums. We can recall from earlier in the book that Eric had been on Drums for 'The Leaders' many years earlier, before leaving to play three nights a week at

'The Jubilee Club'. Golly's style of playing fitted in with them perfectly.

Actually Eric and Dave were playing nine gigs a week because three nights a week, Thursday, Friday and Saturday, they went out as a Duo. On a Thursday night after they had appeared as a Duo at 'The Boars Head' in Lancaster they would meet up with Golly and Terry at 'Marineland' in Morecambe to play as a full band, 11.30 until 2am . They followed the same routine on Saturdays but on that night they were appearing at 'The Beach Club'. Golly remembers that he used to get really tired but he was still in his early thirties and so he could handle it. Besides he just loved playing with this group.

Golly with 'The Heartbeats'

CHAPTER 18

FAMILY GROWING UP, THE TRANSFER MARKET AND HERCULES

Carol and Golly's children were growing up a bit by this time, Jay was around eight years old, Rob was five and Carol-Anne would have been around two or three. Golly hardly saw them in the morning during this time as he didn't get up until 10 or 10.30 am. Of course he always picked them up from school at 3.30pm. Quite often Golly would pick them up from school in the van, usually with the roof rack loaded with Antique furniture.

Golly's son Jay told him years later that he used to get a bit of stick off the older lads. They would call him 'Gypo' or say to him, "Your Dads nothing but an old Steptoe." He told his Dad that he had secretly wished he worked at the 'Power Station' like most of the kids Dads who came from Heysham.

As Golly said, "God what a thought, a job like that with regular hours." Golly told Jay that he should be proud of his family, after all his upbringing was quite a bit more privileged than a lot of the other kids. As Jay grew older he came to understand things better and he realised that he really was much more privileged.

For example if any of Golly and Carol's kids wanted anything, like a new bike, they only had to ask. Golly would reply "Certainly, you can have two if you want, all you have to do is a bit of extra work, that way you can save up and buy one." Golly and Carol had put charts up on the wall and the kids would get points for doing little tasks around the place. The points soon added up and they would get their reward, then they would be accused of being spoiled. They weren't, it was good schooling and it taught them to appreciate the value of things.

Golly has recently seen his children using the same method with their own kids, Golly and Carol's grandchildren. Yes it has to be said that Golly and Carol did a good job raising their children and they have all prospered from their upbringing..

Back to the job. Pine Furniture was becoming more and more popular during the 1980's and Golly used to buy dressers and other stuff from a guy in town called Steve Clarkson. He used to buy Old Lancashire Dressers, then he would strip the paint off in large tanks of caustic soda. He had few joiners working for him and they would make up 'Pot Racks' to stand on the back of the dressers. They made these racks out of old floor boards. What you got from doing that was a product commonly known as 'Welsh Dressers'. Steve and his lads were knocking out these items of furniture on a daily basis and Golly was buying them just as quickly.

Steve had one particularly good joiner called John Chadwick and Golly knew that someone with John's skill would be a useful asset to his business. So, one day he said to Steve, "I could do with John working for me at my place." Jokingly adding, "Can I buy him from you?" Funny how things work out because he really did buy John from Steve.

You see Steve always worked on a shoestring and he struggled to pay his lads when it came to weekend. Golly has known Steve to ring him up late on a Friday afternoon and offer to sell him a couple of dressers cheap. Not the best of quality, but cheap, Steve knew with Golly that he would be paid the money in cash there and then. So going back to John, Golly said to Steve, "If you can persuade John to come up to Middleton and work for me, I will give you a couple of hundred quid." So Steve did just that, saying to John. "You would be better off at Golly's place, your money will be guaranteed every week." So that is how Golly ended up employing John, of course he never knew that Golly had bought him, but he had. It was as good move for both of them. John was much more than just a joiner, he had been a shop fitter in London. Although he knew nothing about Antiques, he was a quick learner and Golly showed him how to renovate the furniture, such as making a leg for a table, or

162

renovating a desk and so on. Golly would buy a piece of furniture and then look for the right material to repair it. John would do the rest. After John had been working for Golly about a year he had become a first class cabinet maker, he worked for Golly for over three years. That became a problem because almost all of Golly's stock had undergone repair work, which was too much. Having a little bit of renovated stock is acceptable to any dealer, but not a whole warehouse full. (Photo of a Penny Farthing). This photo has a relevance that becomes clear as we continue. The problem was Golly had fallen into the trap of spending all his time looking for and buying the cheaper items that needed work doing on them. This was a situation that Golly had slipped into without noticing what was happening, he had to put a stop to this trend. This meant that Golly found himself having to let John go. In some ways it was disappointing, because as Golly says, "Bloody Hell we had turned out some interesting stuff over the years."

Examples of this include the following. Golly bought a carved oak bureau and he fancied having a bookcase made for the top. If this was possible then the piece of furniture would become a 'Bureau Bookcase'. John made a bookcase from scratch and then did the carving, in fact he made two. Golly liked them and had them in his house for many years after John had ceased working for him. On another occasion, Golly bought an old bath chair with iron wheels. The wickerwork in the chair had perished but the two large wheels were in good nick. Golly wondered what he could use them for. Anyway it happened that Golly bought an old Victorian Bassinet, (pram). This had this had small iron

Carol-Anne with the carved bureau bookxase

163

wheels that matched the ones from the Bath Chair., as he looked at them Golly came up with the idea of making a Child's Penny Farthing Bicycle, you know large wheel at the front, small wheel at the back. So Golly got some old iron steam pipe and John shaped it up and made and created a great looking Penny Farthing Bicycle. He even made pedals and carved out an oak saddle. You see John could work with whatever you gave him, not just wood but metal too. The bike was so good that he made another one a few months later. Golly wishes that he still had them now.

Carol-Anne on penny farthing

Another time Golly bought a miniature set of Religious Books, tiny things about one and a half inches, there were probably a couple of dozen of them. These were beautiful examples of their type and in perfect condition. They would have been hard to sell on their own, so John made a beautiful glazed bookcase to house the books in. He made it to scale, very accurately, John was a real craftsman.

Tiffany lamp

Golly still has a Tiffany Lamp in the house from those days which is also testimony to John's craftsmanship. The story behind this lamp goes as follows. About thirty years ago Golly bought a Tiffany shade, just the shade on its own. He already had a lamp base which he'd had for many years. What was needed was a Brass Gallery to hold the shade on to the base. So Golly got a

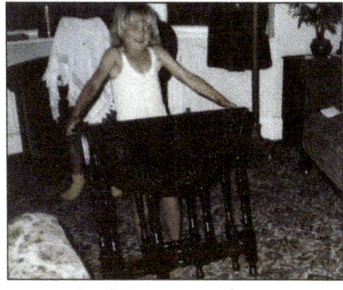

Carol-Anne moving furniture

sheet of brass and John cut it with a fret saw. It took John a full day to make it, but as can be seen from the photo it is perfect. It was a job that required a great deal of skill, because the lamp and shade were not symmetrical, John of course was up to the job. As Golly says he and Carol have had that lamp at home since the early eighties. Golly thinks that it is interesting to know that there will be stuff all over the USA secretly marked 'Renovated by GG Antiques.

We mentioned 'Hercules' earlier. 'Hercules' was the nickname of a very large stone statue, that stood in the garden of 'Bare Hall'. Bare being an 18th century small village in an area of Morecambe. We say Morecambe, but there was no such place back then. This statue was a landmark. It resembled a Roman Centurion, no one has ever come up with its identity, just 'Hercules' to the local people. Golly remembers it as a boy and was always fascinated by it. 'Bare Hall' stood derelict for many years, but the statue never left, although it had lost its head and arms it was still stood up. In the late 1970s early 1980s the Hall was sold, it was to be renovated and become a dwelling once more.

Hercules at Bare Hall

A second-hand dealer in Lancaster named Jack was called in to clear the place. There was hardly anything worth taking but Jack bought the stuff, 'Hercules' included. Jack being Jack, rummaged around the gardens and found the head and part of an arm. He searched and better searched, but couldn't find the missing bits. Well! You can guess who bought it from him. "Got it in one" Mr G. Golly didn't pay much for it, "maybe fifty quid or somewhere around that figure" he told me. That may not seem much money, but in those days Architectural stuff wasn't in vogue, there wasn't much of a market for it. As you know, Golly remembered the statue very well and was delighted to own it. He wanted to keep it for himself, so he had no intentions of selling it. That was until one day, a good few years later, he saw on the front of 'The Visitor' (local newspaper) 'THE HUNT IS ON FOR HERCULES'. Golly smiled to himself. 'Bare Hall' had been re-sold and the new owners were desperate to find the statue. Golly did nothing about it. It wasn't for sale, as far as he was concerned. Articles kept popping up in 'The Visitor'. They knew it had been sold locally and the people of 'Bare Hall' were keener than ever to try and retrieve it. Once again Golly saw an opportunity and he contacted them. "I believe you're looking for 'Hercules." he said "Oh yes, where is it" said the man "I have it and will sell it for the right money" said Golly "OK just name your price" He did. (Authors note, that's all I can tell you).

CHAPTER 19

CARS AND LIVESTOCK

Now one of the things that Golly always used to get was the Exchange and Mart magazine. He doesn't think that the magazine exists in paper form any more, it is possibly an internet magazine these days. But most people of our generation will remember that magazine, you could buy almost anything from it. Anyway Golly was looking through the magazine one day and the number plate, SJG 50 seemed to jump out of the page at him. They of course were his initials, Stephen James Goulding.

The number plate was on an 'Austin Healy Frog Eyed Sprite', at the price of £500. Golly rang up the vendor and bought it there and then on the phone. It turned out that the car was right down on the South Coast of England somewhere, Golly can't remember just where. Anyway Golly's mate and Bass Player Terry Ross hired a car trailer and went down to collect it. Even back then the price was a steal, the number plate alone was worth much more and then there was the car, maybe not classed as vintage at that time but it was certainly a collectors car. Golly used to buy a new Volvo Estate every two years and having sold the Rolls Royce he fancied a Mercedes, so he bought one from a dealer in Blackpool, it was a nice Peach colour. He had the number SJG 50 transferred on to the Mercedes, he remembers that he felt so proud of it.

New Mercedes SJG50

For the benefit of anyone who is unaware of how a registration can be transferred from one vehicle to another the procedure is as follows. If the donor vehicle is more than three years old, as with the Austin Healy Sprite, it must be in possession of a valid MOT certificate. Now the 'Sprite' did not have this document so Golly had to spend a few quid getting it through the required test, which he did. Then he was able to send the registration document and the MOT certificate to the DVLA along with the details of the vehicle you wish to transfer the registration to. Golly was able to do this and sell the 'Sprite' thereby making a few hundred quid profit. Leaving him with a beautiful Mercedes, plus the cherished number plate which stood him at nothing, in his own words "A sweet deal." So here he is GG with a new Merc and a private number plate, as he says "It didn't seem right, it should be some old geezer in his sixties not me." However Golly being Golly, even his new Merc was classed as a working vehicle, so he had a tow bar fitted and bought a twin axle trailer with a roller shutter door for use when collecting stock. As always the family still went out together most days the only difference being, that now all the kids had a comfortable seat to sit in. Golly almost forgot to tell us the Merc also had a sun roof, which when on trips to Blackpool for the illuminations, the kids used stand on the back seat with half their bodies out of the sun roof, giving them the best view. As we have said before no seatbelts at this time. They were delighted with this arrangement because when they had been there in previous years they had seen other kids doing it, always saying, "Dad why don't you get a car with a sun roof?" They got their wish.

Carol and Golly also had plenty of livestock and poultry when the kids were young. Golly remembers many of the animals for example he bought a donkey called Rupert for Carol-Anne. Rupert was a loveable little chap but when he brayed you could hear him all over the village, probably in the next county. Carol-Anne also had a Shetland Pony called Tommy. Rupert and Tommy were great companions spending all their time together.

Other animals included Woolly, Carol-Anne's pet lamb. Woolly was a rare breed and the deal with the farmer was that they took him home when he was a few days old and bottle fed him, when he matured he would go back to the farmer. Anyone who has had a pet lamb or just knows how sweet they are when they are very young will also know that when they have grown a bit bigger, they become very strong and bossy. They always want to come into the house, because they love company. All in all it was a good thing that when Woolly was six months old he went back to the farm.

Rob and Rupert the donkey

It is a long list, they had a giant Boar called Patrick, the biggest male pig you ever saw.. Then there was Toby, he was a Shire Horse. He was really big, massive in fact and hard to control. There were loads of Goats, Pigs and Calves, plus hundreds of Geese, Ducks and Hens, etc. Of course like anyone who has kept poultry they lost hundreds and Golly really means hundreds of birds over the years to foxes. Golly hates foxes and he would indeed. He has shot some dead.

CHAPTER 20

INTO THE 1980'S
AND NEW LESSONS TO BE LEARNED

By the time the mid eighties came around Golly had parted company with John and more significantly had quit playing in the band. At this point he didn't know when he would play again. Having said that the Antique Business continued to thrive.

Then Golly met a lad called Kenny Vaughan, he had been living in Blackpool but was originally from Bournemouth. He was a bit flash, but as Golly got to know him a bit he seemed to be OK. Now Kenny had decided that he was going to live in Ontario, Canada and said that when he got there he would set up in the Antique Business. That being the case he asked Golly if he would send containers full of English Antiques. Naturally Golly jumped at the chance, what a great opportunity he thought. Golly and Kenny both had an excellent guy in mind to pack the containers. His name was Derek Tomlinson, he knew his

Derek on loading bay

job, having packed hundreds of containers for Charlie Allison. Charlie was the head of the Allison family from Blackpool and they had been in the Antique Business for many years. They had earned a fortune when you could still buy stuff for next to nothing. Derek told Golly that he had packed containers with nothing but Grandfather Clocks. Imagine that, a forty foot container filled with maybe 250-300 clocks every time.

Golly has no idea how much the Allison's were selling them for in those days, but what he does know is that his first Grandfather Clock purchased from 'The Trading Post' (Fielding's Antiques) in Blackburn around 1970 cost him £12, which other Dealers saw as expensive. Eight or ten years previous they were buying them for two quid apiece. Golly got to know Fielding's quite well and will speak more of them later. So going back to Kenny Vaughan, he moved to Canada and his first container arrived about a month later. He wired Golly the payment and re-ordered. This arrangement was ongoing for about a year.

Then Golly told him about a vintage car that he had, it was a 1936 Singer. Anyway Kenny asked Golly to include it on the next container load, which he did. Having said that it was no easy task getting a vehicle into a container when it's six feet from the ground sitting on a trailer, but they managed to do it by using a skip wagon.

Incidentally over the years Golly has exported quite a few old cars, especially 'Reliant Robin's. Anyway getting back to the story, it would be a good idea to explain the best way to safely and cost effectively ship a car in a container. First of all remove and drain the petrol tank, disconnect and remove the battery then get the car into the container. When you have done that, fill it up with what is commonly called 'Bric-a-brac', this is a selection of small items of china, glassware, etc. etc. You see the use of space is very important, because even if you shipped an empty container you would still be charged the freight bill. So they get the car wedged in place with a few old mattresses and then nail a block of wood to the floor next to the wheels of the car, to prevent movement. (Interesting to note that all metal containers have a wooden floor.) The next step is to fill up the container with suitable furniture and so on. So Golly shipped out the fully loaded container.

There was a problem though, Kenny's payments were slowing down, Golly was eventually getting paid but not until the stuff had been sold. This meant that Kenny was working on Golly's money, not the desired state of affairs. So the container arrived in Canada and was unpacked by Kenny. Golly didn't hear anything for a few weeks then he got a phone call. "I can't sell that bloody car", said Kenny, "That's not really my concern, you ordered it", replied Golly. The conversation quickly became quite heated, Kenny going on to say, "Also business hasn't been very good lately." Golly knew what was coming next, the writing was on the wall. Kenny had no money and couldn't pay him. The figure he owed was £18,000, quite a sum of money back in the early eighties. Golly had to think fast, "I'll try and get him to send it all back" he thought and to Golly's way of thinking, he would be better off paying an additional £3,000 or £4,000 rather than lose the full £18,000. So knowing he hadn't got a cat in hell's chance of getting paid Golly said, "Send it all back to me and I will pay the return freight." Kenny replied, "I'll think about it and let you know."

Golly never heard from Kenny again, his phone was disconnected and he moved, leaving no forwarding address. So that was that, Golly put the whole sorry business down to experience and he had to write off the debt. About nine months went by and then out of the blue, Golly was contacted by the Port Authority in Felixstowe. Apparently there was a container down there awaiting collection and Golly was named as the importer. The trouble with that was Golly had not been notified of this and as a result there were Demurrage Charges payable of around £12,000. (Just a brief explanation of demurrage, for those who have never imported or exported anything, this charge is imposed if an importer or registered owner of said container fails to load or unload their goods within a set time). Basically the container hadn't been collected within seven days so the charge was imposed on it. Then having still not been collected after another seven days an astronomical charge is incurred on a daily basis. Well of course Golly knew nothing about this, so it meant that the combined Freight charge of £3,800 and the Demurrage charge of £12,000 had to be paid straight away or the container contents would seized and then be sold by the Port Authorities.

This does happen from time to time and the consignee usually pays up because a lot of the time the containers contents have high value items in them. In Golly's case he didn't know what was in the container, all he did know was whatever was in it wasn't going to be worth the charges, It just didn't warrant paying them. You see Golly should have received all relevant paperwork, the Packing List, Manifest and the Bill of Lading etc. etc. all these should have been sent to him in point of fact he got nowt!! Things were not going well so when about about a week after that Golly received a letter from the Inland Revenue demanding payment of £12,000 within fourteen days , it was just the icing on the cake.

The problem was that Golly hadn't been filling in his tax returns because he had always done his own books and never had an accountant. This meant that he had been getting and paying estimated bills for about three years. Golly just figured this was an easier way than doing serious book keeping. So this demand was the result of that assumption. Very little actual tax to pay, it was mostly interest and penalties. So with this £12,000 to pay and the £18,000 that he had lost on the container Golly was about 'Thirty Grand' down, a lot of money and he wasn't very happy.

Still as he looks back he remembers that the business was doing OK so he soon made up the losses. But as he says "What a lesson!!" Anyway moving on from these setbacks, Golly knew a guy, they called 'Big Roland' (six foot eight). He had a tipper wagon and he used it to do bits of jobs all over the place and one day he called to see Golly to tell him that there was a building being pulled down in Lancaster. Golly wondered why he was telling him this so he asked him, "Why would I want to know about a bloody building being demolished?" "Well" said Roland, "There are some good iron roof trusses." "Roof trusses" replied Golly, "What the hell do I need roof trusses for?" "Well if you ever want to build another warehouse this is a full roof, you put it together like a Meccano Kit" said Roland. So Golly bought them, deciding that he did need another warehouse.

Roland dismantled it, numbered the pieces and delivered them. Golly thinks it was 'Big Roland' that decided Golly needed another warehouse, or were the trusses speaking to him? A bit of both, Golly suspects. Right thought Golly the next question is, who is going to build this warehouse? Well he knew a lad called Tony Bell who was an Antique Dealer, he did a bit of dealing around the Lake District and he in turn knew a good builder. This builder had been complaining about the lack of work. So Tony told the builder where there was some work, building a warehouse for Golly. The builder came down to see Golly to discuss the project. The first question he asked was, "Have you got planning permission?" "No" said Golly "we don't need it because, this is a registered small holding of more than two acres in size and it is the required number of feet from the road and therefore we can put up an Agricultural building without planning permission." "OK" The builder said. "Where are the plans"? "I ain't got any plans" replied Golly. "Well how the hell am I supposed to put up a building without plans?" he asked. Golly's answer was typically Golly, "Don't know, try and figure it out."

We know by now that Golly is a practical man who doesn't recognise problems, only solutions. So the builder looked at this pile of old iron and figured out how to put it together. A week later he laid a concrete slab as a base and started to build. Within a few weeks the building was up, the roof had been assembled. Then a crane was hired and the roof was set straight on top of the building. It fitted perfectly, the guy had done a great job, all his calculations were spot on. He added two large doors that could be driven through and a personnel door. That was it. No windows. It really was a perfect job.

Golly got a Bass player called Les he knew, who was a qualified electrician to wire it for him. Golly paid Les by giving him a Fender Telecaster Guitar. This warehouse is still in use today 35 years later.

Now remember a few pages back Golly mentioned 'Fielding's Antiques' in Blackburn. Well he used to call and see them every few weeks and they usually did some kind of a deal. The Antique game is all about buying and selling, you could buy stuff off somebody and at the same time sell them something. People outside the business couldn't then, and still can't now, figure it out. Really it is just one man pitting his wits against the other. Nothing has a price, people would ask, "how can you buy something from one antique shop and sell it to another antique shop and earn money?" Well Golly has been doing it success-fully for more than fifty years and so have a lot more besides him.

CHAPTER 21

ARNOLD FIELDING AND FAMILY

Going back to Fielding's, Arnold, the old man was very tough and he wouldn't suffer fools. There are plenty of people in the business whose word is worthless, but Arnold sensed right from day one that Golly was a straight shooter. Arnold had brought up his son Andrew to be strong and wise and the two of them knew every trick in the book. They were very down to earth decent people and Golly did an awful lot of business with them over the years. The two of them often used to have a run out on a Sunday and when they did they would always call to see Golly.

On these occasions, more often than not, Golly would sell them a few bits. As Golly got to know them better he would call to see them at home, often taking Carol. Mrs Fielding a lovely Irish lady would be there on these occasions and she would always make them most welcome. Their home was packed with Antiques, one room had Grand-father Clocks, (The nicer ones) all around the four walls of the room. There was also a Queen Anne Walnut Bureau Bookcase that would have been worth eight grand thirty years ago.

On one occasion Arnold said to Golly, "Open that drawer". Golly did and he had never seen anything like it in his life in the drawer were two or three hundred gold and silver pocket watches, as Golly says "Unbelievable!" The other thing that Arnold told Golly was that he had bought the house a few years ago then he bought the house next door because he couldn't stand the thought of having neighbours, Golly gets that, no problem.

Sometimes Golly would take the whole family for a ride over to Black-burn, he would drop Carol, Rob and Carol-Anne in the centre of the town and they would do a bit of shopping. Then Golly and Jay would

go to visit Arnold and Andrew at their home. Then meeting up with
Carol and the kids a couple of hours later at 'Tommy Balls'. Tommy was
a working class lad who had made it pretty big in the Shoe Trade. He
even used to advertise his shop on TV, good businessman. Tommy was
also a good mate of Arnold's. They used to sit around talking and one
day Arnold said to Golly, "I've only been a millionaire once and that
was the day I bought a motor bike". You see when Arnold was 14 years
of age he was working in a Cotton Mill about five miles from where
he lived. He had to pedal his push bike up and down the hills around
Blackburn, winter and summer alike. Arnold worked hard, saved his
money and eventually saved enough money to buy a Motor Bike. As
he said, "What a day, to know there would be no more slogging and
trying to pedal up those bloody hills, I really was a millionaire. It was
the best day of my life."

Arnold Fielding

Arnold was a very wealthy man, but he knew what was important, so
because of this Golly and I think the readers of this book know exactly
what he meant when he said that the day he got the Motor Bike was
the best day of his life.

Now Arnold always liked to keep poultry, especially rare breeds. One
day Golly went to visit with Jay and while they were there they bought

half a dozen 'Indian Runners' from Arnold. They are white ducks that walk around with their heads in the air, this purchase was fine. But on another occasion that they visited Arnold, he showed them some prize racing pigeons. Jay really liked them and asked his Dad to buy them, Golly did. They took them home and Golly put them in an empty chicken coop that was suitable to keep them in. "Leave them locked up for a few days before you let them out, they should be fine", Arnold said to Jay. So that's what they did and when they opened the coop all the pigeons flew away and they never saw the buggers again! Golly phoned Arnold and told him what had happened. His response was, "Well, I can't understand that". The next time they visited they saw what looked like their pigeons in Arnold's shed. So Golly asked him, "Are they ours"? "Aye" He replied, "The came back a few days ago." He gave Golly his money back. The question Golly has always puzzled over is. Did Arnold expect them to come back? He will never know the answer.

As the years passed Arnold became very bad on his legs, with arthritis, this meant that he needed a couple of sticks to walk with. He wouldn't go to a doctor or do anything about it he just got on with it. A lot of older people took the view that you were only ill if you saw the doctor, so if you didn't see the doctor you were fine. Well at some point somebody, suggested to Arnold that he and his wife went on holiday to somewhere warm. Well Arnold had never been out of the Country in his life but, the idea appealed to him as it was mid-winter at the time. So he went to a travel agency. When he got there he asked the question, "Where can I go that is warm" Going on to say. "I want to go tomorrow." "We've got Tenerife, it's always warm there." Replied the Travel Agent. Well Arnold as he later said didn't know where the Hell it was, but he said, "That'll do, I'll take two weeks for the three of us." He paid for the holiday there and then and they flew out the very next day. Just and so having the time to get their twelve month passports from the Post Office. Arnold absolutely loved the place and came back home completely pain free.

Unfortunately the pain returned after a few days, he was in agony. However the theme was set and Arnold and family continued to fly out to Tenerife for many years. This happy state of affairs carried on until Mrs Fielding sadly died, this was catastrophic for Arnold he couldn't cope. He was lost without her. The thing was, she had done absolutely everything for him and he lost the will to live. It wasn't long before Arnold passed away himself. Golly felt very sad as he says, "God Bless Em, they were lovely people." Having said that Golly was aware that not everyone felt the same way about Arnold as he did, some people thought that he was a grumpy old sod. Well that was because he wouldn't put up with any crap or bull sh*t, those people never really knew him. Golly feels that he sees a lot of Arnold in himself.

CHAPTER 22

PROPERTY AND SWEET DEALS

A brief word from the author: Golly Goulding is quite simply a brilliant businessman. He sees opportunities that ordinary people like us go through life without noticing. It can be a piece of Antique furniture, a house or a piece of land if there is a potential profit, Golly sees it, he is like no other man I have ever known simply because of the diverse nature of his abilities and talent. So we come to a period of time, the late eighties when Golly was making quite a few interesting property deals. He will tell us about some of the most unusual and interesting deals he made, during this chapter.

There was an Auction Room in Morecambe, 'Yeadon's' they had been around for years. They had an office and from there they used to collect a few rents from people, if ever anything interesting came on the market they would tell Golly about it. They knew that Golly would have ago at something that no one else would touch.

On one occasion they told Golly about a tenanted property in Cavendish Street, Lancaster. This was not a bad little house in a fairly decent area. Now as Golly said this place was tenanted and the rent was 50p a week, fixed for life. Golly went to view it. The elderly couple, nice people, Golly thinks that they must have been in their mid sixties, who were the tenants were quick to tell him what good payers they were when it came to the rent, saying, "We have never missed a payment". Well of course Golly thought about buying them out, but he was told that had already been tried and they didn't want to move. "No bloody wonder" says Golly at a rent of ten bob a week. As you might guess as we are getting to know Golly he bought it anyway. Then he spread the word around that he was looking to sell it, this led to him being approached by a bloke who was a bit younger than him. Apparently he had been left a few quid and wanted something to invest in. Well Golly sold the house to him and in the process doubled his money. The funny thing was Golly had never collected a penny in rent, he simply couldn't afford to go and collect it!

There was another deal that Golly remembers, this time involving a bloke he knew who had a second hand shop in the area. This bloke in turn knew an old bloke who owned a terraced house in a street close to him who was skint, really hard up. So the guy with the shop suggested to Golly that he went round to see if the old bloke wanted to sell the house. So Golly went round and the old guy asked him to come in and have a look around but Golly didn't cross the doorstep. As Golly said, "There was no way I was going in. The bloody place reeked, the guy had rabbits, pigeons, dogs, cats, you name it they were all in the house, it was foul." Anyway the old man said give me £5,000 and let me live here forever. "No problem" said Golly.

He then sold the house for £20,000 two months later. The two houses just mentioned are worth £300,000 today, Golly says maybe he should have kept them, but he was buying and selling houses like selling furniture. Just turning over money and reinvesting. On one occasion Golly bought a forest, it was situated just outside Kendal, he advertised it as 'The Gateway to the Lake District'. The forest was on a main road, it stretched for about a mile and a half and had two streams running through it. Golly sold it to some people who had an Antique Shop in Kendal. Unbeknown to Golly they owned the land adjacent to it. Conversely they didn't know that Golly owned the forest. What a happy coincidence that was, leading to another very sweet deal for Golly.

Then again how about this one? Golly knew a 'Knocker' called Gus. Now for those of us who don't know, a 'Knocker' is someone who mooches around calling at farms, old houses and such like looking to buy Antiques. It seems that Gus had gone to live in London a few years before and he had made a good living pulling stuff out of skips that other people had thrown away, he did this all around the West End and in the City. Now Golly knows that this was true because if ever he was down there himself he would often see loads of stuff being dumped as he was walking past the houses and business premises. That had made him wish he'd had a van available. There was not just scrap metal, there were antiques as well.

Anyway while having a successful time down there, Gus had found himself a girlfriend and decided to move back to Morecambe. When he got back he rented himself a shop on Morecambe Street. Funnily enough it was the same shop that Pete 'I Buy Anything' Hayes, had rented back in the 1960's. You will remember from earlier in the book that Pete was Paul Hayes, of 'Cash In The Attic' fames Father. Anyway the landlord offered to sell Gus the shop for £8,000, but, Gus didn't have £8,000, but Golly did. So they struck up a deal Golly would buy the shop and give Gus £2,000 cash as commission plus letting him stay in the shop, rent free for a further twelve months.

Gus trying to sell Golly some crap

This was no hardship to Golly. So when the year was up Gus moved out and Golly found him a place on Middleton Industrial Estate, (more of that later). Golly knew a Dutchman who lived in Carnforth, just a few miles away from where Golly lived. Now this man was doing OK as an Antique Dealer and he told Golly he had some money that he needed to spend, fancy telling Golly that! He went on to say that he wanted to invest, this was music to Golly's ears. "You have come to the right place, I want £30,000 for the shop on Morecambe Street" said Golly. They shook hands. The completion date was set for about six weeks later and Golly and family were due to go on holiday, which they did. Golly said to Carol, "We'll never pull this one off, it's too good to be true." But sure enough on their return from holiday the cheque was waiting in the letter box. How about that for a deal?

Well it gets better, not only one cheque but two were in the letter box. The reason for this was even as the Morecambe Street deal was going through, there was an even better one taking place at Granville Road Morecambe. Billy and Lily Pugh parents of Golly's long time Bass Player and mate Garry Pugh, lived in a house on Granville Road and wanting to move, Billy had put the place up for sale. The snag being that it was a commercial property, a corner shop with a house at the side and accommodation over the top. The problems with it were the cellar was permanently flooded and the whole place needed modernising. Because of these things no one could get a mortgage on the property. However Golly had an idea what he could do with it, if he could get the right deal, At this time Golly had purchased and was driving a 'Niva' four wheel drive vehicle of Russian manufacture. This not a bad vehicle at all in fact these days it is described as a 'Classic'. However having bought it from the showroom in Barrow and had it for twelve months Golly was ready to sell it but he couldn't get a buyer. His problem was that this vehicle wasn't listed in the car dealers bible, 'Glasses Guide'. Without that little book, car dealers are useless because they only know what they read and then they cut it in half. So having an idea what he might do with Granville Road, Golly went to see Billy in the 'Niva' Billy liked the look of it and commented about it. So Golly said "Look I'll buy your shop outright and give you the car as a deposit." Billy instantly agreed, Deal Done. Golly filled the shop with second hand furniture and got a retired bloke who lived nearby to run it for him. The house section of the shop was let out as a holiday cottage. While all that was going on Golly applied for planning permission to convert the shop and the rooms above into a private house and luckily it was approved. The cellar was filled with hardcore and concrete, that ended the flooding problem. The plumbing and electrics all got sorted out and "Bingo" two houses on the market and they sold very quickly.

Incidentally the end house which had previously been the shop was sold to a Mr John Brown. John was a character from Manchester, he had a shady past and had come to Morecambe to open an Antique Shop. Golly got to know John quite well and took the view that he was not a man to be trusted, he told Golly that he had done a lot of time in prison for what he termed 'White Collar Fraud'. Naturally, John had always wanted to own a house, but of course no one would touch him, so it looked like a mortgage was out of the question. Anyway Golly showed him round the house and John fell in love with it. Somehow he scraped together a deposit. By a sheer fluke he managed to obtain a mortgage from some building society or other, solicitors were given instructions and the sale went ahead. Golly said much the same words to Carol as he had said about Morecambe Street, "This will never happen, something will go wrong." But it went right. The two properties sold whilst they were on holiday, "Bloody Hell."

As it happened Granville Road was repossessed three months later, John Brown had never made a single mortgage payment and was evicted. It didn't bother him, he had fulfilled his ambition of buying a house and he was used to living that kind of life. He would take on a shop for a couple of months, pay no rent and hang on until he was kicked out. John Brown would never pay attention, never mind money, as Golly said, you couldn't trust him. Having said that, he did send him to Texas on one occasion to hunt out a few clients for him, which he did. The thing was with John you would meet him and think what a nice bloke, but if he could get the better of you he would. He really tried to catch Golly out on loads of occasions, but Golly was always on his guard, because he knew what John was capable of, so he never got an opportunity to put one over on our Golly.

John is still around and still doing what he has done all his life, trying to put one over on people. His regular saying was "Would these eyes lie to you?" Well of course they never did. But his mouth did.

While we are still on the subject of property, Golly remembers that there was another very good deal, this time a corner plot of land close to where they lived. This land at Heysham was put up for sale by a building company who had built a load of bungalows nearby. It had decided by the local authority, that they couldn't use this three quarter of an acre corner plot, because there was an underground sewer pipe which went right across the site. Anyway Golly being Golly bought it for a few hundred quid. Then he appointed someone to check out the potential with the Planning Department at Lancaster, with the view to build. The response from the Planning Department was that "They had no axe to grind with regard to the site and its use as a building plot." So Golly applied for planning permission to build a bungalow on the site, and permission was granted. Funny really, because the big building company that Golly bought the plot from said that there was no chance of building on it. Well Golly did build on it. He built a very large detached dormer bungalow, set in the three quarters of an acre. It is still standing there for all to see. Golly didn't do too badly on that deal either.

There was another very similar deal taking place for Golly around the same time. Once again another builder had built a row of houses in Heysham during the 1960's. He ended up with a small plot of land that he didn't consider large enough to build a house on so he put a fence and gates on it and used it as his Builders Yard for the next twenty to thirty years. When he retired, Golly bought the yard. Once again seeking planning permission to build a house from the Planning Department. The response from the planning department was a positive one, they said, "As it is a residential area with houses on either side of it, we are willing to consider your application, providing you come up with a decent, acceptable drawing for a dwelling, we are happy to look at it.". Well of course Golly did just that and once again he received their approval and he built another house. So there you go, two nice pieces of property bought from building companies who both thought they had useless pieces of land. Golly Goulding, 'Antique Dealer', quite simply 'Beat Them At Their Own Game'.

Golly tells me that there were plenty more oddball property deals, some commercial and some residential, but he says we need to move on as he doesn't want to bore his readers. I have a strong feeling that one thing the people who are reading this book are not going to be, is bored.

CHAPTER 23

EXPANSION AND OVERSEAS DEALINGS

During the mid to late Eighties, Golly and Carol's Antique Business was really growing. They were still located at 25 Middleton Road, just to remind you this address is a bungalow in two acres of land, Golly had had the new warehouse built and he had also bought a block of five garages. You know the type, they are made of concrete slabs all bolted together. Golly had bought them already dismantled with delivery thrown in. He got a couple of local brothers to assemble them and block up all the doorways and make one main entrance in the centre. Then they pebble-dashed the front and the sides of the resultant building, the whole thing looked quite smart at the time.

We should also remember that they had the Piggeries at the bottom of the field. At this time no pigs, so they too were used as a furniture warehouse. Golly felt that the way things were going and the potential business opportunities that were opening up, it was time to smarten up

The piggeries

his act. So with these things in mind they laid a new twenty foot wide concrete drive. Next move, they jacked up the roof on the piggeries, knocked down all the pens to create another warehouse. These refurbishments took all summer but by winter 1987 they had a beautiful site.

Golly also had a pair of gates made, 20 foot wide opening, with the letters GG installed. They now had 5,000 square feet of storage, not as much as some but more than most. By having the drive widened, they ensured that they could have forty foot containers driven in and turned round at the bottom of the field. Previously they had to be reversed in which was a tricky manoeuvre.

The business was becoming very well established and they were getting clients from different parts of the world. Places like Australia, New Zealand, Canada, clients from many different states of America, Italy and France. These people were all good customers who wanted to spend good money. But there was a regular situation where a British dealer would call and buy all the best lots. This would mean that when a serious Dealer from say America came, he would discover that everything had been picked through. These people were serious buyers who wanted to put container loads together. It was a problem that Golly thought and thought about. Should he close the doors on the English Trade? These lads came in handy but, they only wanted to cherry pick. Then there was another problem if an American Buyer comes and purchases a load of the right stuff from GG, it then becomes a pain to have it transported to another depot where his container is already sitting. He is going to want to have the container at Golly's place, plus he would need to fill it while it was there.

So Golly made one of the hardest decisions of his career, from that moment on GG Antiques was Export Only. Well as Golly says, that was a decision that did not go down well with the English trade. But Golly stuck to his decision and continues to do so right up to the present day.

His decision meant that instead of waiting days for a customer to turn up, they would probably have to wait weeks, before anyone showed up.

This was actually a plus point because it meant that Golly could get out and do more business. It also meant that whenever a client did walk through the warehouse he would find a vast array of goods to choose from.

Consequently people were buying full container loads from GG Antiques. Why would they need to go anywhere else? Golly had it all, he was providing the whole package, overseas buyers didn't have to hire vans or couriers. On top of that some of them even stayed as guests with Golly and Carol. Golly would pick them up from the airport and run them back. So there you have it no car hire, no hotel bills, they could use the money they saved to buy more stuff from Golly, a good plan Eh? It was a bit of a gamble at first, but it soon started to pay off. GG Antiques were attracting customers from all over the world. Israel, Greece and Spain as well as all the other places mentioned before.

Well in 1989 it became clear that GG Antiques needed to expand even further, because they had American customers wanting containers as fast as Golly could fill them. The family was growing up, Jay was now sixteen, Rob was thirteen Carol and Golly were in their early forties and they had Derek packing full time, but they just couldn't cope with the demand. Even though Jay was having a lot of time off school to help out, they still couldn't keep up with the demand. The school and the teachers did not seem to mind Jay's absences too much in fact one of Jay's teachers, Mrs Murphy, who Golly and Carol had got to know well and reached the point that they were calling her by her first name, Rita, agreed that Jay was better off out of school, he'd done his time in education and now he was needed to help out in the family business.

Rita's husband Jim was a lecturer at Lancaster University and they had two daughters in private education, one of them Emma went on to be a TV journalist and presenter for ITN. We all see her all the time, bringing us news reports from all over the world. Rita also became a customer of GG Antiques. Anyway Rita persuaded some of the other teachers to turn a blind eye to Jay's absences, after all he was leaving in the next twelve months and he had a career to step into. Consequently

Jay, Rob and Golly loading a container

Jay was able to be with Golly most of the time making a strong work based contribution to the firm. Jay also spent a lot of time with his best mate Tony, he lived next door but one and he also helped out in the business, he was a good lad who worked hard, which helped everybody out a lot. Of course he really appreciated having the money Golly paid him to spend on the things young lads spend their money on.

CHAPTER 24

PONTINS, JAY'S DRIVING AND
THE END OF THE HEYSHAM HEAD BEAR.

About a mile from Golly and his family's home was 'Pontin's Holiday Camp' this was a place where many of the people from Middleton Village used to work. Golly, Carol and the family would often go in an evening to watch the Cabaret Shows.

Pontins

There was a great atmosphere in that place, always plenty going on. Jay and Tony were able to go to the bar and buy themselves a pint of beer, they had been doing that since they were about thirteen, it is we believe a responsible way to introduce youngsters to alcohol, in the presence of their parents. They grow up with a sensible way of enjoying social occasions and never cause trouble. There was a problem with getting into 'Pontins', they had strict security on the gate, in order to get in you had to have a pass.

As Golly said a lot of the local community worked there and various neighbours were kind enough to take Golly and the family in. But if they decided to go up on their own they always struggled to get in. One local lady told Golly that she knew someone who had shares in 'Pontins' and could get in any time. Well Golly didn't hesitate, he bought some

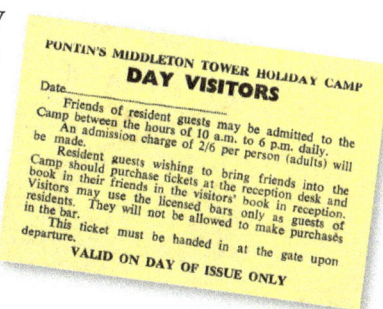

191

shares in the company and thereby gained free admission at any time, Job Done! After that every summer, they would go to up to the camp around 7.30pm and watch all the shows, some fairly big names appeared there. When Golly and his family went in they would be mixing with the holiday-makers, people who had saved up all year to be there. Golly Carol and family would go in free, the holiday makers used to say

Jay and Tony having a pint at Pontins

"Aren't you lucky?" As Golly puts it, they couldn't agree more, the family felt very lucky to have the facility on their door step.

They were wonderful and happy times, great memories. One afternoon a bloke who was staying at 'Pontins' for a week called to see Golly. His name was Phil Brown and he and his family used to come to 'Pontins' Morecambe for their annual holidays, they had been coming for years, they loved everything about the place. Their home was in Bury and coming to the seaside was a real treat. Phil had heard that Golly was an Antique Dealer. He apparently used to dig up bottles from old Victorian Rubbish Tips and some of those things are very rare and valuable. Now Phil had recently taken over a shop in Darwen, Lancashire, coincidently Golly had known the previous owners.

Golly, Phil Brown, Kath & Carol at Pontins

Anyhow, Phil was trying to get into the Antique Business on a full time basis and he was looking on Golly as a good contact. Golly and Carol got to know Phil and his family very well, so much so that they used to go and visit them, attending family events such as Birthdays and Anniversaries. Over the years Phil and Golly went on to do a lot of deals together.

Now Jay had been driving since he was about eight or nine years old, because around that time, Golly had bought an old Sherpa van for about £20 or £30 no MOT or anything but she was a good old starter. Jay would drive it around the field, it was a good way for him to learn and it was great fun when all his mates were in the back.

Jay taught a lot of the kids to drive and one girl in particular Sarah who was about five or six years older than Jay. Sarah now has a large haulage company based in Heysham.

Remember the Bear that Golly was telling us about earlier in the book, the one he was supposed to get from 'Heysham Head' all those years ago? Well one Winters day, late afternoon when the kid's had all come home from school they were watching TV and they looked out of the window. A tractor and trailer went past full of old wood and stuff on it. They were taking up to the village green where the local kids were making a bonfire for the 5th of November. Either Jay or Rob, Golly can't remember, shouted, "Dad, I have just seen Hancock's trailer going past with a big Bear on it. Hancock's had Wagons and Skips nearby and they used take a lot of stuff to the local tip where they would have to pay to dump it. So if they could get rid of any stuff at local bonfires etc, it was a good deal, as they were saving on tipping charges. Anyway, Golly wanted that bear so he said to the kids. "Run after the trailer and get the bear, you can buy the kids up at the bonfire a box of fireworks." So they ran up to the village green but by the time they got there the local kids had ripped the bear to pieces. They had pulled it apart and they were kicking the head around like a football, it was completely wrecked! In Golly's opinion there was no doubt about it, this was the very same stuffed bear that he had been promised all those years ago. He was really sick about what happened, because he had always wondered what had happened to it. Someone must have had it stored somewhere for years. Golly never did find out where it had been stored, but he knows exactly where it ended up. What a disappointment, to be so close to finally getting it, only to have it destroyed as a bit of fun.

Around this time Golly used to have some Manchester Dealers calling on him, 'Britannia Antiques', they were on Stockport Road. Now as Golly has said 'GG Antiques' were now strictly export, but so were 'Britannia Antiques'.

One of their sons had opened a warehouse in the United States, so in their case Golly bent his own rules a little and let them buy stuff from him. They used to send their driver Billy to collect their goods and he used to come in a Ford Cargo Van. It was real smart wagon with a tail lift on the back. They even had his name "BILLY" painted on the front. Jay loved this vehicle. Golly always said to him, "As soon as you leave school I'll buy you one".

So as soon as Jay officially left school in 1990 that's what Golly did. He bought it, and even had it sign written, Jay couldn't legally drive it, so Golly drove it until Jay passed his test at the age of seventeen.

Jay and Carol with the new Ford Cargo van

CHAPTER 25

BIGGER AND BETTER

So here we have GG Antiques heading into the 1990's on the up and up with three well stocked buildings, a seven and a half ton lorry and loads of potential business waiting to be had. Golly starts thinking, "What do we do, Stay as we are, Or take the plunge and get bigger?" Well for Golly there was no contest, because he has never been one to hold back. If ever he saw an opportunity he grabbed it with both hands.

Unloading wagon

Now there was an industrial site across the road from Golly and Carol's, Heysham Business Park. Golly decided he would go across and do a bit of checking around, at that time it was owned by a Local family, the Aspinalls. They had bought the site from ICI and set up their family business there, 'Aspinall Engineering'. Golly went and met the boss and head of the family Paul Aspinall and told him that he was looking to buy a commercial site, preferably with building or buildings on it. Paul showed Golly an acre of land with a Nissan hut on it. These buildings had usually been erected by the Government in time of war, originally as a temporary structure. Anyway the Nissan hut wasn't in bad condition so it would have been a start. Then Paul pointed to some framework of a modern building that he said he had never got around to erecting. So the deal was that if Golly bought the land and the building, Aspinalls would erect it then line and clad it. This being done it would become a brand new warehouse. They then struck the deal and Golly paid him upfront for the dismantled building.

The old warehouse at Aspinalls

Unbeknown to Golly, Aspinalls did not have the title deeds to the land that Paul was offering to sell him. Golly thinks that Aspinalls had gone bankrupt or something a few years previously and they were in the process of trying to buy back the land. "Don't worry" said Paul, "We will get the deeds back soon and then we can complete the deal." Golly thought to himself, "I've got myself into a bloody odd situation here." Paul went on to say. "In the meantime you can use the Nissan hut rent free and you can have that large brick building over there, rent free as well." He pointed to an old I.C.I. building that looked semi-derelict. It had been empty for while and it was due to be demolished in the distant future. So Golly shook his hand. He had nothing to lose. The only thing that bothered him was the dismantled building that he'd bought, still being on Aspinall's site. He quickly made arrangements to have it moved on to his own site. He made the excuse that he was going to have it repainted and then cover it up until it was time to erect it. After all he had bought and paid for it. It was Golly's property and he didn't like the idea of it being on land he didn't own.

Although the deal was supposed to be going through in months rather than years, (Bloody hell, months, that's a hot one)! Anyway, Golly now had the keys to both the Nissan hut and the large brick building, altogether about 12,000 square feet and rent free, don't forget. Golly soon filled them up and made loading facilities for all the containers that GG Antiques were shipping out, right, left and centre. All that space, free storage and electricity. Of course Golly was still yearning for his own site with a modern building and facilities, but that wasn't happening, not for a few years yet. After about three years this situation was still going on but Golly doesn't want to jump ahead as he has more to tell us.

Loading containers at 25 Middleton Road

We are well into 1990, Golly has 5,000 square feet of warehousing on his own site, he also had another 12,000 square feet across the road which was costing him nothing. His son Jay had left school and Jay's brother Rob was going on fourteen. Golly also had another couple of local brothers, the Kitson's working for GG Antiques, plus Carol, Golly and Derek and another packer, this was a formidable workforce and they were working none stop. Golly used to go across the road and speak to Paul every week about buying the acre of land, Paul would just fob him off with excuses. At one point he actually had the cheek to try and put pressure on Golly to bring back the dismantled building from his site so that Paul's men could erect it on the acre that Golly was looking to buy. This would have enabled Paul to generate some cash flow but Golly said no! His actual words were, "I am not having a building put up on land that I don't own!" Going on to say, "Get the deeds, let me buy the land and let me pay you for erecting and finishing the building", which would have amounted to a tidy sum of money. As Golly said,

"Pretty bloody simple, isn't it?" But no, they couldn't produce the title deeds for the land. Golly could see no end to the situation, it went on for another couple of years until Golly was completely fed up of hanging around and being put into 'The Promised Land'.

The way Golly saw it, was that on the one hand he had storage space that was costing him nothing, but on the other hand he was frustrated by the fact that he wasn't making any progress. The level of trading that GG Antiques was aiming for required, Showrooms, Loading Bays, Offices and all the usual facilities that go with a proper business. Now there was a fantastic site right next door to Golly's bungalow, that had been sold by I.C.I. a couple of years previously, to a company called 'Warrington's'. This was a large site with dozens of buildings, yards, and acres of land. All this, at the side and rear of Golly's property. There was a well known local businessman in charge of the refurbishment project, Fred Edmondson, and Warrington's must have spent Millions on renovation work. All the old buildings had been renovated and let out.

The office block had been renamed Newfield House and let out to various companies who required office space. From Golly's point of view the whole thing appeared to be a 'Goldmine'. It finished up as a modern complex and they named it 'Heysham Industrial Site'. There was and still is a security office where anyone entering the site has to report and sign in. So Golly went and signed in so that he could see Fred Edmondson. He wanted to ask Fred about the possibility of buying something on the site from 'Warrington's'. You have to remember that these buildings were for lettings only. Anyway Fred showed Golly a very tall, dilapidated building which they hadn't done any work on because as company 'Warrington's' thought that it would be difficult

Newfield House

to let. Fred said to Golly, "You may be able to buy this one one," for the reasons disclosed. So they established a price and Golly set about moving his stock from 'Aspinalls' to 'Warrington's', putting it simply, he was just so fed up from getting nowhere with Aspinalls. As he says, "It was never going to happen."

So now we have Golly operating from this old building that needed bringing up to scratch. He still hadn't bought it because 'Warrington's' were still undecided about selling it to him. But in the meantime he was using it free of charge. Golly's idea for the place was to buy the building and make it into a four storey warehouse and install a lift. If he could have bought it, he would have spent serious money on the place. Once again this was something that was not to be and Golly could understand why. Warrington's simply couldn't afford to have GG Antiques and all the comings and goings with containers etc. was not a viable prospect for them. They were perfectly right to take this view because GG Antiques presence and all the activity that this successful business brought with it, would preclude any possible further sales or indeed rentals that Warrington's might hope to make.

Just as an aside, that large building that Golly had rent free and had hoped to buy is still there and nothing has ever been spent on it and it is more of an eyesore than it has ever been. So what a situation to be in, Golly Goulding his pockets full of money and he can't spend it, nobody wants it!! After a few more months had passed without Golly having to pay any rent on the old building, Fred came to see Golly and said, " Sorry Golly you will have to move out of this place, I'm sorry it didn't work out. At first they were keen to sell to you, but then they stopped and thought about the complications that might incur, with having you stuck in the middle of their site." Golly said, "It's OK I will just have to find somewhere else." Fred replied, "You can have that building there". He pointed at one of the modern units. So that's what Golly did he moved everything into the modern unit and started paying rent. But all the while he was thinking this is not me, paying rent, is not my style, I need my own place.

Golly doesn't want us to get him wrong this was a beautiful warehouse, he was proud of but it wasn't his. Golly thinks that we have progressed to 1992 now and he had purchased twelve acres of land in Middleton, it was roadside frontage and was right next door to 'Greendales Caravan Park'. Golly had a couple of ideas for this site, he would either put a dwelling on it or just sit on it in case Greendale's ever decided that they wanted to expand at some time in the future. In the end he got an architect to draw up plans for a stable block. Golly was working on the theory that he could, if he wished, at some time in the future, easily convert it to a bungalow. Golly successfully applied for planning permission and then went ahead and built the stable block. He installed an access road, which ran up to the building from the main road and when you looked at the building on approach, it had the look of a private house. Golly financed the building and the access road with the sale of a redundant corner of land that he owned. He sold that to a lad who wanted grazing land for his horse, Golly was able to get top dollar for it.

So, getting back to GG Antiques and Golly's plans for the future. He was in a position that most businessmen would give their right arm for. He was cash rich, he's never had a bank loan or an overdraft in his life. GG Antiques were trading from 5,000 square feet on their own site and renting 12,000 square feet of warehouse space from 'Warrington's'. This situation went on for the next year or so and then there was a very surprising development. 'Warrington's' seemed to be struggling financially, these struggles eventually leading the company to fold and go into liquidation or bankruptcy. Golly never really found out.

A very surprising thing happened though, Fred Edmondson acquired the main Office Block, "Newfield House" and the six acres of land that went with it, from Warrington's. He was also still taking care of the whole redundant industrial site. Fred being Fred, a shrewd but tricky businessman, used to run a Car Boot Sale every Sunday. Carol and Carol-Anne would go down regularly to check it out for Antiques.

Sometimes they hit lucky. One particular Sunday, Fred said to Carol "Tell Golly I want to see him, I may have a deal for him."

Golly went to see him the day after and he offered Golly the 'Office Block' and the six acres of industrial land that it was situated on. Golly couldn't believe it. He went home and told Carol, "Guess what, Freddie Edmondson has offered to sell me Newfield House." Carol replied, "Buy it"! So Golly went straight back and told Fred that he would have it. Then Freddie put the icing on the cake, he asked Golly, "Do you own that land next to 'Greendale's'? "Yes" replied Golly. "Do you want to part with it?" Freddie asked. Golly said, "Yes it's for sale." They had a deal there and then.

Golly bought Newfield House and used the land as part payment. It was a cash sale and all done on a handshake. Freddie gave Golly the keys without receiving a penny. Golly instructed solicitors to complete immediately. No search, no survey the whole deal was completed in four days, everything bought and paid for. Now GG Antiques were flying!!

Carol on the day we bought Newfield house

The expansion plan was starting to take shape, GG Antiques had now added a beautiful 12,000 square foot office block and six acres of commercial land too. As we know Golly had purchased a dismantled warehouse from Aspinalls, well because he did then and still does now plan ahead, he'd already bought another similar one. That purchase came about, when he heard about a company in Heysham who where dismantling a five year old warehouse building. Their intention was either to take the dismantled building back to their main depot in the

Putting the sign up on Newfield house

North East and re-use it or sell it to someone in the local area. So Golly bought it and took photo's for reference before it was dismantled. The company numbered every part to make it easy for re-assembling , plus they also delivered it for him.

Golly had remained on good terms with Aspinall's in spite of their failure to be able to sell the land to him. They agreed to get their own architect to draw up plans for a new warehouse and then build it for him. The building that Golly had bought from them and the one he bought from the company in Heysham, fitted together perfectly. When they were assembled and stood as one, it looked massive. Golly had spent thousands of pounds to have the concrete floor laid. He hired a specialist company to line and clad the building with new materials and

Bingo!! GG Antiques had a brand new 12,000 square foot warehouse. Within a few months it was full of stock, great, except it just wasn't big enough so Golly put in a second floor, which increased the warehouse capacity to 20,000 maybe 22,000 square feet. Add to this, Newfield House, 12,000 square feet of showrooms, the 5,000 square feet of ware-

The loading bay

housing next door, behind their bungalow, plus a large loading bay. This meant that including the loading bay, they had about 40,000 square feet of floor-space storage and show room property. Now by any business's standard, that is pretty big and very impressive.

For those of us who are unaware of construction details, it is worth mentioning some interesting facts about the construction of a loading bay. It was an eye opener for Golly when Aspinall's architect responded to his request to include a loading bay in the plans. He said, "Golly this is a tricky one, I am not qualified to draw it, you are going to need a structural engineer." He went on to say, "A loading bay is a completely separate and different kind of construction to that of a warehouse. An open fronted loading bay has to be Held Down, to allow for wind pressure etc. A warehouse by the same rule has to be Held Up".

The result of this information was that Golly had to produce no less than sixty sets of drawings all done by structural engineers for the Planning Department in order to obtain the correct planning permission. Imagine it. Golly thought it would be a simple, straight forward job. All he would have to do was to get some steel uprights and a roof. But no, because if he had done that, the first time a high wind blew, he would have lost the lot.

CHAPTER 26

TAKING THE U.S.A. BY STORM

Moving on, GG Antique Wholesalers were now a force to be reckoned with. They had become one of the largest 'Antique's Outfits' in the United Kingdom. G.G. had a young American customer in San Diego, California. His name was Dan Pond who used to buy furniture for regular shipments. He would eventually become one of their best customers. There was another customer, Rob Steeves from Portland, Oregon and between the two of them, they became G.G.'s Antiques best customers. They had Golly and his crew filling forty foot containers with English Antiques as quickly as they could pack and ship them. These two were racing neck and neck in a competition to become the leaders in a buying race. Golly will tell us more of that later.

Golly and Dan Pond

Now a couple of years previous to this, Golly had met a Canadian guy whose name escapes him now. This guy used to advertise his services throughout the U.S.A . Through these adverts he would get clients and bring them over to England on buying trips. Most of these clients were 'One Hit Wonders' (people that thought they could retire off one load). Needless to say, this bloke was pretty good. What he was getting was an all expenses paid trip, plus commission from the clients as well as the suppliers. Also he was buying for himself as he went around. Any way as Golly tells it, "This bloke eventually caught a big fish by the name of Scott Swaboda". Scott was from Washington State and he hired the Canadian bloke to bring him over to England and take him round the general Antique Trade. Well, Scott wasn't too impressed with the places that he was being taken to. Markets, Fairs and the run-of-the-mill, Antique Shops. Scott's sights were set much higher than this bloke could ever comprehend. Anyway after a day or two of disappointment, they arrived

Scott Swoboda, Golly and Dave Morris

in Morecambe and Golly couldn't see them until mid-afternoon. He can't remember why, but he must have been busy doing something or other. So Scott and the Canadian bloke were killing a bit of time, by wandering around a few local Antique Shops and buying nothing.

Scott would tell Golly later he was so bored and fed up, he was just about to call it a day and catch the next plane home. Eventually they turned up at GG Antiques and as Scott put it, "He struck gold." His words to the Canadian bloke were, "Why the hell didn't you bring me here in the first place?" Well of course the bloke knew what he was doing. He always took his clients round the smaller places. In the meantime, he was picking up his own bits and pieces as they went around. He viewed the time as a free holiday.

The fact was that Scott hadn't bought a bloody thing all week, so there was no commission. Delighted to be where he was now, Scott said to the bloke, "This will do me now, I don't need to go anywhere else, I've found everything I need here." He handed the bloke a bunch of cash and said "I don't need you any more." The bloke left. He didn't care, he'd got his finders fee. That was that.

Scott actually stayed at Golly's house for the rest of the weekend, whilst he was there he was almost non-stop buying. This led to many return visits from Scott and over the following year or so, he bought 45

Container loads. Golly said to me, "That's roughly 10,000 pieces". "How's that for a deal??" There was so much activity at G.G's it's almost unbelievable.

Golly and Scott became very good friends, they visited each others homes on a regular basis. Carol and Golly have spent many years touring the USA. On one occasion Scott invited them over, so that they could attend the 'Washington State Fair', he'd also laid on a Hot Air Balloon Trip for them, which they declined. One thing they did enjoy very, very much was a fishing trip out on Puget Sound, this is a lovely bay around Seattle. One of Scott's employees had a fishing boat, in which he used for catching King Crab. He invited Carol and Golly to go out and fish with him. The morning started with putting out these wooden cages, very similar to Lobster Pots. These were dropped around various parts of the ocean. They had markers that floated on the surface of the water. By the time the last one was dropped it was time to go back and pull up the first one and sure enough it was full of crab.

Now the local rule for crabbing is pull out a Dollar bill and if the crab's back measures less than the length of the Dollar bill you must throw it back into the water. A few were short but most were oversized .You then had to remove them from the basket, some of them would nip you and if

Golly at Scott's warehouse

Catching king crab in Seattle

they got a grip, you couldn't shake them off. The only thing you could do was break the leg off. These were powerful buggers! Golly was doing pretty well, handling the crabs but one big one did grab him. It gripped tightly on to his fingernail and he whacked it and whacked it but it still wouldn't budge. Eventually, he broke its leg but it was still gripping his fingernail, so he had to get a screw driver and prize it off. Golly's nail went black and he lost it a few weeks later.

In spite of this they enjoyed a great day out and they caught bucketfuls of crabs. In the evening they were invited to an outdoor party. What a feast King Crab! 'Tons of it' delicious. Incidentally Carol and Golly were filmed by the local news channel while they were out on the water and they appeared on the evening news.

At the beginning of this chapter I mentioned Dan Pond. Dan was only in his twenties when he first came to the UK. Somewhere on the grapevine Dan had heard about GG Antiques and he was anxious to check them out. He arrived at GG's one very cold Winters afternoon and he was frozen. He'd heard about the English climate but wasn't fully prepared for the wintry conditions. After all he had just flown in from San Diego, California. Carol and Golly welcomed Dan into the house and sat him down by the fire. After an hour or so they took him over to the warehouse to check out the antiques.

Dan knew exactly what he was looking for and he quickly found it in G G's warehouse. The next day he picked out a full container load, to be shipped immediately and then a second one to be shipped two weeks later. That's how the business continued. Every two or three weeks, Dan had a container arriving at his base, India Street Antiques. Golly was always well ahead of him. He had to be. The demand was strong. He always had a container on the loading bay being packed and one on the water heading for their destination. And that was just Dan, there were others like him. This continuous flow of goods continued for years. Meaning that Dan had thousands of pieces shipped to him in hundreds of containers.

As with other customers Golly and Carol have become very close friends with him. In Dan's word's, "Carol and Golly are my English family." So much so that when Dan visits he stays with them. 'No Hotels for Dan'.

Golly and Carol have had some great times with Dan and always looked forward to spending time in his company on their many trips to 'The United States'. Dan would always lay on something special when they were there, such as taking them to exclusive 'New York Steak Houses' and other top class restaurants. Now, with San Diego being on the border line to Mexico, Dan would often take them across into Mexico through Tijuana and down the coast to Rosarito. Once there they would spend a few days in a Luxury Hotel.

You see, you get a lot for your Dollar, once you cross the border, especially in the restaurants. For example, all you can eat lobster for about five or six dollars. Down in Rosarito there are several very good eating places, after a great night of wining and dining and it's time to settle the bill. It's always a pleasant surprise, because it is so inexpensive. Consequently the staff always receive a substantial tip.

Another good feature down there is the music. There are dozens of Mariachi Bands, wandering around the place. Just busking really but they all seem to do pretty good. They come into the restaurants and play a few numbers, then pass the sombrero round, collecting a few dollars.

Imagine it, they probably hit twenty or thirty bars and restaurants a night collecting dollars from American tourists, not bad eh?

You're just sitting there eating, then a three or four piece Mariachi Band will walk in and start playing. A half an hour later, another bunch will walk in, that's how it is all evening. The bands take requests from the punters, they get extra money if they play the song. One particular night, Carol, Golly, Dan and a few others were sitting at the table and sure enough, 'The Boys' walk in and start playing. Now, because Golly is a musician, he can pick out the good players from the average, he noticed a young lad playing the violin, his skill was outstanding. As usual they played a few numbers and made the collection then they have a second bite of the cherry asking for requests. Golly tried his hand and requested "CZARDAS", this is a 'Hungarian Gypsy Violin' tune that you would recognise if you heard it, but would not necessarily know the name of it. Golly had to write it down, as none of the band members spoke English. The young violin player had a quick word with the other players, they all nodded and the lad on the violin started to play "CZARDAS", the others quickly followed suit. Well, as Golly says, "Bloody Hell, they

Mariachi Band

brought the house down". They made such a good job of playing it, that everyone in the place stood up and applauded. Even the staff came out of the kitchen to listen and applaud their performance.

You see, these musicians are used to the same old requests, for songs like 'La Bamba' and all that crap. So it came as a great surprise to everyone, hearing them play something so intricate.

Going over the border into Mexico is a great experience, but coming back is an even greater one. Hundreds and hundreds of cars lined up waiting to cross into the United States. Dozens of hawkers trying to peddle their wares, which can be anything from flowers to exotic birds and animals. They just come up to

Border crossing

your car window and offer you kittens, puppies and birds. For example you can buy a large 'Macaw Parrot' for 50 Dollars, these would cost $1000 or more in a pet shop.

All well and good, you can buy them, but as soon as you reach the border crossing, the Mexican guards will take them off you. Golly believes that the guards have an arrangement with the vendors. He says, "I bet they sell these bloody parrots a dozen times a day." A good little earner, eh?

Incidentally, sometime in the mid nineties, whilst they were driving down the coast just over the Mexican border, they could see this massive ship, which appeared to be anchored off the beach. The thing was huge. In fact it was mock up of 'The Titanic', constructed for the Movie. Golly

says, "It was awesome just like the real thing." He supposes, it was the nearest thing you would ever see to 'The Titanic'. Golly learnt, that this was the location where they filmed the sinking of the vessel. It has to be said, Carol and Golly enjoyed great and happy times in Mexico with Dan.

Customers lined up at Rob Steeves' warehouse

At this point we come onto Rob Steeves and his wife Darlene. They first tracked Golly down in the early 90's. They had opened an 'Antique Barn' just outside Portland Oregon. The business was doing OK but, they wanted to explore the possibility of importing Antiques from England and they planned a trip. They'd heard about 'G.G. Antiques' from an auctioneer in Wisconsin, name of Bruce Bieri. (more of Bruce later).

The climate in Oregon is similar to that of the UK, but when they arrived at G.G. Antiques they were freezing just like Dan was. What is it about our weather? It's not that bad, although it seems the Americans just can't take it. Well maybe one of them can, Duane from Alaska, we will hear about him too..... later on.

This would probably be a good time to mention the apartment at Newfield House. Golly had one of the offices converted into a kind of 'Bed Sit' as we would call it. Nothing too fancy, just a couple of single beds, with a bathroom and kitchen, all you need really. This was for the benefit of customers who wanted to stay over for a few nights. Some stayed for weeks, we will also get to those people later.

Anyway back to Rob and Darlene Steeves. Rob and Golly hit it off straight away and have remained close friends ever since. So Rob and Darlene wasted no time in picking out goods for their first container. This was quickly packed and shipped. Another one was brought in to repeat the order and this was how things worked. Golly used to operate what was described as 'The Shuttle System'. Every time a full container left the loading bay it was replaced by and empty one. Doing it that way saves 50% of the haulage charge. Times that by six and it's a massive saving and that was, and still is, the method used. It just makes so much sense. The loading dock has six bays and stock was coming and going almost daily. G.G. were selling close to 1,000 pieces a week. Where was all of this stuff coming from?? Later.

Back again to Rob and Darlene. Their method of selling was through a mailing list. They would send out information on the container they were about to receive, (they were averaging two per month). When it arrived they would unload, clean the stuff up, then set it out in the barn ready for sale. They used to have an opening day sale. Scores of people would line up outside the barn, some waited for many hours. Then Darlene would open up for an hour to allow people to preview the items. To assist the potential customers, all the items had lot numbers.

In the afternoon the doors would be opened and the stampede would begin. Because of the preview, customers would note down the lot numbers. They all knew what they wanted and they quickly snapped up the whole contents of the barn. It usually took the rest of the week for the items to be collected, then Rob and Darlene would have an empty barn again. A few days later another container would arrive from G.G. Antiques and the whole process would be repeated. This carried on for a year or so until 'R&D Steeves Imports' out grew the building. More space was needed, which applies to dealers on both sides of the Atlantic.

Rob heard about an old grain warehouse that had been up for sale for quite a while. It was a little shabby and really needed a face lift, which would mean money being spent to bring it up to modern day standards. But hey, in the antique business who cares? This is just the kind of setting that attracts customers.

Rob Steeves on Golly's vintage Gibson guitar

Rob and Darlene went ahead and bought it, moved in, set up shop and away they went. All their previous clientèle got to know about the move and followed on. Using the same formula but on a much bigger scale, business was better than ever. This of course meant buying more stock from Golly and we know Golly by now, he was delighted. Of course being the businessman he is, he welcomed the extra pressure.

So we come back to the old question, where the hell is all this stuff coming from?? The Americans were continually concerned about how long the supply could last. The question they were asking was, "Surely with a country as small as England the supply of Antiques must be drying up?" Well Golly replies, "You would think so but it never has done yet." Golly and many others like him have shipped out millions of Antiques over the last fifty odd years and are still doing so. Although, at nothing like the rate they used to. As Golly says, "There are still plenty of Antiques around if you know where to look and you're willing to pay market price for them." Golly does know and he is willing to pay, because he also knows who to sell them to.

But back in the day, when the job was manic, G.G. had many pickers out on the road scouring the country for Antiques. Most of these blokes were working off their own money, although Golly did pay one or two of them 'Money Up Front' and they usually played it straight with him. Having said that, now and again he would get bitten. There was one particular bloke from Lancaster who said to Golly, "If I had £1,000 to work with I could get out around the old farms and bring you loads of stuff." Now Golly knew that this person was not 100% but he thought it was worth a shot, so he gave the bloke the money. Of course he never saw him again. This happened twenty odd years ago, Golly says, "Bloody silly really, because the bloke could have used the money to get on his feet and build a strong relationship with G.G. Antiques. We'd have looked after him." Golly's message to him is, "Shot yourself in the Arse Mr L. I hope you read this book sometime and I bet you're still skint."

Golly isn't bitter about it, He just thinks what a bloody fool he was, because he had a great opportunity to get in with the right people, people who would have looked after him but, he blew it.

You see Golly has been responsible for making a lot of people wealthy and successful, by buying from them on a large scale. They had a ready-made market and instant payment. How could they go wrong, and most of them didn't. Equally as Golly says, "I did well from them, without these people I would not have been able to operate at such a high volume."

At this time Wagon loads were coming in to Golly's place every day and he was buying it all. Naturally there were things he didn't want, but he bought them anyway. No one ever went away from Golly's place with stuff on their vehicle, they were always empty. Their pockets were full of money and this enabled them to get out on the road again and buy more stuff. They were doing exactly what Golly had been doing twenty years previously, when he was dealing with 'Trade Antiques' in Wigan. Golly will never forget how they looked after him and put him on his feet.

Golly has built up very strong bonds with his suppliers, and he still deals with most of them. Although there have been a few who p***ed on their chips and once they have done the dirty, Golly won't have them back.

The Japanese market was growing stronger and good quality 1920's Oak furniture was at a premium. The majority of people running stuff into Golly's were bringing average shipping stuff, as they call it. Nothing really tasty. The main reason for this was, that's what he wanted, nothing too expensive, as the Americans like a lot for their money.

So Golly asked his suppliers to up their game a bit, Saying, "If you come across any nice quality Oak for the Japanese Market, pay a bit more for it if you have to, don't hold back. I'll buy it from you, don't be scared to have a go and if you slip up I'll bail you out". Well most of them played ball and they found the odd nicer piece, also they knew

Good quality English furniture for the Japanese market

that they would be safe with the price. Sometimes they really overpaid (so they said) but on the scale of things it didn't really matter. If Golly lost a few quid on an item, he could easily make it up on the next one.

There was one particular bloke from Lincolnshire who used to bring in two or three loads a week and was on good money. Like the others, Golly had asked him to look out for the better stuff, he said to Golly "If ever I do see any of that better quality, clean Oak, I will certainly bring it to you." Well, he never did, he was picking up £3,000 to £4,000 a week from 'GG Antiques' and he never, ever, came up with a stick of decent furniture in years. To be fair, what he was bringing was fine and there was always decent profit to be made, otherwise he wouldn't have lasted that long. Golly used to say to him, "Surely, you must see some of it around." "Never see any of it Golly." He would reply. Golly thought about it and now and again he would ask the same question, "Seen any nice Oak Dave?"

"Never see any of it Golly." He would reply as usual.

He must come across it sometime's, Golly thought. "Something's not right, is he Bullshitting me?" Well of course he was. Golly found out from his friend Luigi, that Dave had a lock up store and in that store, guess what? He was keeping all his best Oak. How did Luigi know? Well, he knew a dealer in Gainsborough called Rod, who used to call on Dave every evening and buy all his best Oak furniture. As Golly says,

"Dave can sell what he wants to who he wants, I can't control that and wouldn't want to, but the fact is, he's been lying to me all these years." "I never see any of it Golly". "Bull Shit".

Well, you can guess what happened. Golly told Dave that his services were no longer required. This is a term that Golly has used several times during his career, never falling out with anyone unless they asked him why. When they did that Golly told them good and proper, in no uncertain terms. Then of course they wished they had never asked in the first place. Interestingly just bring an end to the Dave saga, Golly and his son Rob went to see this Rod bloke down in Gainsborough and bought a wagon full of good Oak furniture at reasonable money. Rod knew about the situation with Dave, he knew that Dave had been bringing in several loads a week to 'GG Antiques' and never anything good. He'd asked Dave, "Doesn't Golly ever question you, on why you never bring him any decent Oak stuff?" "Sure, but I just tell him that I never see any" Dave replied. "How do you get away with it?" Rod asked. Dave replied, "Don't know, I just do." Well, as Golly says, "He bloody doesn't now."

As stated Golly bought a wagon load of stuff from Rod, Dave could have had more money from Golly, than he had got from Rod. As Golly says, "It's his loss." Golly is still visiting Rod and buying regularly from him.

Golly's Rockola jukebox -
identical to Scott's
(see page 207)

CHAPTER 27

GOING FORWARD WITH THE INTERNET

Back in the nineties the use of computers in business was becoming popular and Golly's son Jay made the decision that 'GG Antiques' should have a website, which they did. wwwggantiques.com they still have that website, although now it looks a bit dated. Even so it still gets daily hits and Golly likes the way it looks and doesn't want to upgrade it. As he says, "That website has been good to us, it tells everything the way it is". Golly's motto has always been, "We walk it as we talk it", and they do. Golly has never gone back on his word. His Dad taught him from an early age, "Don't open your trap unless you know what you are talking about and don't say anything you don't mean." Golly's pet hate is people who say something and then they don't do it. He hears it on a daily basis, "Loose Talk" "Pub Talk."

Getting back to the website, granted, it still has that old nineties look, but as he has said it still works. But there has been one small section removed. The one that said, "Overnight accommodation" as was written earlier. Golly and Carol have this room which is fairly large converted into a small apartment for anyone who wishes to use it. Back in the early days there was no shortage of takers. So much so, that if you wanted to stay, you would have to make a reservation. Golly had provided this modest place as he describes it, for the benefit of overseas customers. Any guests were given the keys to all doors and to the outside gates, so that they could come and go at their leisure. This place was and still is very popular with the American customers.

They would fly in to Manchester, drive up to Golly's and maybe go straight to bed. Then they would get up in the middle of the night and start picking out items for their containers. "Midnight Shopping" as they used to call it.

They would usually be suffering from a bit of jet lag, and very often would not catch up with Golly for a couple of days, which was fine by all. Some of them would stay over for three or four days and some even longer. One couple from Kansas, Judy and Ernie, sometimes stayed for a month, it was their annual holiday.

On the other hand there were a few who took the mean advantage. These people had seen the website and saw the apartment as free accommodation in the UK. Golly says, "I suppose it was, but only for serious buyers." Well one or two weren't that serious, there have been a few bluffers, pretending to be dealers. They were never seen again. Can you imagine anyone having the nerve to do that? Golly says, "Believe me those people are out there".

In the cellars of Newfield House was where all the 'Bric-a-Brac' was kept. Hundreds, thousands of pieces of China, Glassware, metalware, etc. etc. everything priced up. Also there was a constant supply of boxes and paper. Golly would say to his clients go down into the basement, pick out what you want, make a list of the items and pack them into boxes yourselves. Golly trusted everyone, he would say to them. "Help yourselves, I don't need to mess around with that stuff." It was a real novelty for the 'Yanks', they loved it 'Midnight Shopping' again and again.

Then of course there have been one or two 'Bad Apples' for example there were a couple of English guys and an American lady who started to visit on a regular basis. They would pick out furniture and then spend all night in the cellar picking out stuff. Incidentally one of the men and the lady were a couple, the other bloke was their friend, they stayed together in the apartment. Now remember there were only two single beds, side by side in the apartment as Golly says, "Bloody strange."

The next morning they would give Golly the list, maybe £200-£300 pounds worth of stuff, but they would have packed thirty or forty boxes. Now it is hard to keep track of all the small stuff and Golly never thought it necessary to check on people but, he had his suspicions about these three. So he went down the cellar and he could see that the place had been blitzed. No way did the list match up to the amount of stuff that was missing. So Golly didn't mess about, he told them to p*ss off and leave right away, which they did Golly knew that on their previous visits they had been robbing him blind. How rotten can some people be, to abuse his hospitality like that. No wonder Golly has taken the free accommodation offer down from the website.

CHAPTER 28

FOOD, EDUCATING THE CUSTOMER AND 'SNATCHEMS'

There was another customer that Golly got to know when he came over from the U.S.A. by the name of Bob Tonks. He became one of Golly's regulars, he was in fact a Canadian who had quite a few connections in the States. Some of these contacts were better than others but Golly will get to that.

Now Bob, was partial to a pint of English beer and after a days buying, Golly would join him in having a drink in the house. This drink was usually followed by going out for dinner in one of the local restaurants.

Their favourite was 'Modleys' this place was owned by Debbie and Tony. Debbie was the granddaughter of the well known Yorkshire comedian, Albert Modley. Some of our readers may not know that he spent

Bob Tonks at Golly's house

most of his life in Morecambe. Debbie ran front of house and her husband Tony looked after the bar. Golly and Bob spent memorable nights there.

Modleys was a great restaurant with excellent hosts, because of this Golly took many of his American customers in there over the years. Such a good place and serving delicious food, Golly felt it deserved to be mentioned.

It has to be said that anyone who knows Golly will be aware of his love of Indian food. In pursuit of this food one of the places that Carol and Golly used to frequent was 'Morecambe Tandoori'. It happened that one night they took Bob along to this place in order to introduce him to Indian Cuisine. Like many Americans apparently, Bob said, "Oh yes, Indian food is just like Mexican food, I'm used to this sort of thing." Well of course Indian food is nothing like Mexican as Bob soon found out.

The first thing he ordered was Onion Bhajii, this came with a small salad. Then he asked for 'Thousand Isle Dressing' which would normally accompany seafood. The waiter somewhat confused said, "We don't have it, I don't know what it is". Moving on to the main course, which Golly recalls was a mild Chicken Korma or something similar. Bob then asked the waiter for 'Tomato Ketchup', which they happened to have. Bob then poured this bloody ketchup all over his curry. This embarrassed Golly as he knew the owners of the restaurant very well. Bob ate the whole thing, Golly says "It must have tasted bloody awful."

Continuing with the food and drink theme. Another of the places Golly would take people to, was a pub called 'The Golden Ball'. It is situated on the back road into Middleton as you follow the River Lune. It is known to the locals as 'Snatchem's'. This pub got it's nickname two or three hundred years ago as it was a place where ships Captains would gather a crew. At this time Lancaster was quite an important port and the sailing ships of those days used to sail up the River Lune and dock on the quayside.

'The Golden Ball' was the tavern on the other side of the river and it was frequented by seamen, ex seamen, or indeed anyone who felt the need to get drunk. It was the job of the leading seamen to go ashore and gather a crew for their next voyage out to the Americas. They would come to the tavern and offer drinks to anyone foolish enough to accept them. Their trick was to drop a coin into the tankard and by accepting the drink and drinking from the tankard the recipient accepted the 'Kings Shilling'. This meant that you had volunteered to be signed on for duty. This is why you often see glass bottoms in old pewter tankards, giving the recipient the opportunity to hold up the tankard and check that there wasn't a silver shilling lurking at the bottom.

If any of the customers in the tavern were wise enough to refuse a drink from any strangers, they still might not be safe from recruitment. If they had drank a little too much ale anyway, there was every chance that you would get a good knock on the head as you left the tavern. They would then be snatched, while they were unconscious. Next thing, they would be put into a small boat and taken on to the main vessel, which was due to sail out to sea on the next tide. Hence the name 'Snatchems'.

Anyway 'Snatchems' is a great little pub and Golly's American customers were fascinated by it. Bob Tonks was as intrigued as the rest were. Now there is a very interesting thing about the area around the river banks. At high tide the whole area gets flooded and looks like a massive lake and the Golden Ball gets cut off. That used to handy in the old days when pubs closed early, you could stay in the Golden Ball for hours until the tide went out.

Anyway going back to story, Golly explained to Bob how hundreds of acres of land turned into a giant lake, twice a day. Naturally Bob was very keen to see it. One bright sunny day, which happened to be 1st August, Golly took Bob to the end of the lane to see the tide at its highest.

When they got there Bob looked and said, "Wow this is awesom!!" Then Golly heard a sound in the distance, he thought at first that it sounded like a seagull. Well it was no seagull. Looking in the direction where the sound came from, Golly could just about see someone's head in the water, about a quarter of a mile away. It was someone shouting for help in a Squawky type voice. Golly and Bob ran along the banking. As they got closer to the person, they could see it was a lady who was up to her neck in water. They then spotted another lady on the banking. They realised it was her they could hear. She was crying "Help, Help." She had a squeaky Scottish accent. This is what Golly had thought was the seagull calling.

Arriving at the scene Golly and Bob could see the top of a car, there was a dog sitting on the back window ledge. It was clear that one lady had been able to wade to the banking, but the other one would not leave the dog. Golly knew the area well and he shouted to her "Grab the dog before it's too late and wade over to this wall as fast as you can! The tide's getting higher, not lower." She did as he said but at the last minute, just as she reached the wall, the little dog, his name was "Rory" jumped out of her arms and started to swim back towards the car. Luckily Rory had a long tail and Bob managed to catch Rory's tail. He pulled him back while Golly pulled the lady out of the water. Within minutes the car had disappeared from view. The lady who wouldn't leave the dog was very lucky that Golly came along, because she wouldn't have left the dog and they would both have drowned very quickly. The other lady was frantic she had only taken delivery of the brand new car that morning.

High tide at Snatchems

Back then not many people had mobile phones, but Golly was one of the few who did., he had called the Police, the Fire Brigade and the Ambulance Service, they arrived pretty quickly, but of course they were unable to drive up to the place where Golly, Bob, the two ladies and their dog "Rory" were standing. The ambulance crew ran along the banking with their stretchers and when they saw the two distressed ladies they wanted to take them to hospital. They both refused point blank to go. The reason being they were too concerned about the car, it was brand new and the cry was, "Where's my new car gone?" "You will see it again in a couple of hours" replied Golly.

The ladies were wet and cold, so Golly offered to take them back to his place, to comfort them and dry them out. The two ladies readily agreed, it was their only choice really. They had refused help from the Paramedics. The Police and the Fire Service couldn't really do anything, so everyone left the scene. Golly took the ladies, Bob and the dog back to his place. Carol provided the ladies with dressing gowns, sandwiches and hot tea. While they got warm and had their refreshment she put their clothes in the tumble drier. Apart from their distress at their new car disappearing underwater the ladies seemed to be OK.

Golly asked them what the hell they were doing there in the first place. Their excuse was that they had picked up their brand new car in Scotland and they were driving down to Blackpool for their annual holiday. They had been using an old map and following the coast line. Well yes, Golly says, you could do that, but in a boat, not a bloody car!

It seems that they had driven past 'Snatchem's' through a bit of shallow water and then hit a bit of deeper water further up the road. This was deep enough to cut the engine out. Apparently they just sat in the car waiting for the water level to drop. The hadn't realised that the tide was coming in, not going out. They soon realised this, but nevertheless, they still sat there in the car, thinking it wouldn't get much higher. When it did, the first lady got out and started shouting for help.

You would have to say that it was a sheer stroke of luck and good fortune that Bob wanted to see the high water on that particular day, because Golly and Bob were the only people in the vicinity on that day and especially at that time. The fate of the other lady and Rory, in absence of the two guys cannot be known, but the likelihood is that they would have drowned. What Golly can say is that he has seen many cars that have had to be written off on that marsh road. It's sad but true. Any car driven into the incoming tide will be written off.

Golly tried his best to assure the ladies that their insurance company would replace the vehicle with another brand new car. He was not sure that they believed him, but they seemed to go along with the idea. After a few hours a breakdown vehicle arrived to tow their car off the marsh and load it on to the back of their truck. The two ladies got in the cab and they, the dog and their car were driven back to Scotland. Before they left Golly asked them to get in touch and let him know the result of their insurance claim.

About a month later he received a letter of thanks from the ladies. In the letter they told him that they had arrived back in Scotland that evening and on the following morning, Sunday, they received a hire car, which they drove to Blackpool and started their holiday. Within a month they had received another brand new replacement car, plus new clothes and replacement luggage. This was exactly what Golly had told them would happen that afternoon at his house. Yes, a happy ending to what could have been a tragic event.

Sadly, poor Bob died a few years later, only a short time after he'd got married. Bob's widow, who Golly had never met, wrote him a letter, asking him to tell her about Bob's trips to England. Golly wrote back with as much information as he could. He also took the opportunity to acknowledge that Bob was a hero. Because he was, if he had not grabbed Rory's tail the dog would have swum back to the car and the lady would have followed. Because of this Golly would like to think that Bob did save the lady's life. So he says, "God Bless you for that Bob."

A great character was also brought into Golly's life when Bob introduced him to Bruce Bieri. Bruce was an auctioneer from 'Wild Rose' Wisconsin. He used to come over to England on a regular basis to buy Antiques from 'G.G'. A real character. Bruce had a handlebar moustache and very often wore a big white Stetson. Golly recalls that he was a 'Tough old sod' but straight with it. He always stayed at Golly's place and by 5 o'clock in the afternoon he was ready for drinking and he always brought his own liquor with him, 'Windsor Bourbon Whiskey'. He would expect Carol to get Pepsi-Cola for him, he definitely wouldn't drink Coca-Cola. For some reason he didn't like it. Most people can't taste the difference, but Bruce certainly could.

He always bought good quality, ornate furniture, 'Fancy, Faggot Furniture', is how he described it. Bruce had all sorts of expressions for things, for example he would say, "Can't cut a fat Hog on that, but, I'll do OK". By this he meant, "I won't get an enormous profit, but I will get a decent one."

Sometimes he would bring his wife Donna over with him, they both took a shine to Golly and Carol's eldest son Jay. So much so that he would go back over to the States with them for a week or so and help them to unload the container. Now Wisconsin is an extremely cold State in Winter time, temperatures get down to around minus 40 degrees. As Golly says, "That is bloody cold!" Jay used to go over there in Winter and Summer alike and Bruce told him, "If you see anyone you know walking down the street, don't stop and talk to them, because they certainly won't stop to talk to you." It's just not the done thing in Winter. If you stood still, you would freeze to death.

Donna, Bruce, Carol, Golly, Bob - Dinner at Gollys

Jay of course got to know quite a few people in Wild Rose, the town had a population of less than 700 people. Plus Bruce had a share in the Restaurant/Bar on the other side of the street. He knew everybody and everybody knew him. Bruce had another string to his bow, he held a lot of real estate sales. When he did this he would mix in 'English Antiques' along with the American stuff. He would always seem to get high dollar returns on his investments.

Golly and Carol went over to 'Wild Rose' a couple of times to see Bruce. The first time they ever went over there, Bruce picked them up from Chicago Airport. This is a six hour drive from 'Wild Rose'. He came in a big old Cadillac that had a bench seat across the front. On this front seat Bruce had put a bucket of ice and two bottles of Winsdor. Down on the floor was a cooler box stuffed with cans of Pepsi. As soon as they hit the highway Bruce said, "OK Golly, the bar is now open, start pouring". Golly poured Bruce a large drink in a tumbler. As he told me, "I kid you not, Bruce did over a full bottle of Winsdor that night, on the drive up to Wild Rose." Golly drank a few beers to keep him company, Carol went to sleep in the back of the car.

Golly and Carol in Wild Rose Wisconsin

Golly, Bob & Buddy playing the Blues

When they arrived in town Bruce pointed to the hotel and up in lights was a sign which said, 'Golly and Carol welcome to Wild Rose Wisconsin'. They checked in to the hotel and then went straight out to the restaurant. They were treated like a couple of celebrities. It was quite an event an English couple staying in this backwood's town.

Bruce's house backed on to a lake and Golly used to take a boat out and row around the lake in the early mornings. This comes as no surprise when you remember that Golly has always been fascinated by rafts and canoes etc. when he was out in the rowing boat, it was as if he was a boy again back on the river Lune. There will be a good canoeing story coming up but as we know Golly likes to keep us in suspense. Bruce Bieri has remained a good friend and customer of 'G.G. Antiques' over the years. Although he has now retired he still keeps in touch.

CHAPTER 29

ENGLISH DEALERS

Golly has more to tell us about the American Dealers that have played a major part in the G.G. story, but as he as he says, "This would be a good time to look at some of Golly's English Dealer friends. Because apart from Tyson's, who Golly has dealt with constantly over the last 45 years. There are several others, although they haven't been dealing with Golly for that long, they have been around doing business for quite a while.

One such person is 'Walter Coleman'. In the 1960's Walter opened up an 'Antique Shop' in a large building in Burnley. The building had previously been a Co-op. Walter and Golly got to know each other in the mid seventies and got on well. One Sunday afternoon Walter came to visit Golly and Carol, he brought his wife Brenda with him. Now it happened to be, that Brenda was expecting a baby, so was Carol, she was pregnant with their son Rob. This meant that the two ladies had something in common and they hit it off straight away. Brenda had her son Michael in early 1976 and Carol gave birth to Rob. After that every Sunday afternoon, Walter, Brenda and son Mickey would call and buy a load of stuff from Golly, they hardly ever missed calling. This routine went on into the 1990's when Walter and family retired to Ireland, where Walter originated from.

Golly wants to give credit to Walter by saying, "He was a gentleman, a good friend and a loyal customer. Over the years they had hundreds of deals together.

Another dealer from the old school was 'Paul Allison'. Paul was one of four brothers who had all been raised in the Antique Business. Together they should all have been millionaires but alas no, they were four brothers who could not get on with each other. Golly didn't really know the other three, but he knew of them and some of what he had heard he didn't like. Paul was no angel either, but if you kept on your guard you would have a good chance of making a deal. Paul had a great personality and was a naturally funny bloke, he could easily have been a very good professional comedian. As Golly says, "Even in general conversation, Paul would have him in stitches." Paul also knew the 'Antique Game' inside out.

On the business side Paul was shipping out loads of containers to the U.S.A. and would visit Golly frequently to buy a load of Antiques. Plus he would recommend 'G.G. Antiques' to American importers. As Golly has stated, a good guy, but he needed watching. The way things went Paul would show up at Golly's place and buy load of stuff, then he would say, "Oh I've forgotten my cheque book." Golly came to expect this. Paul would then say, "I'll send the wagon tomorrow to collect and I will give the driver a cheque for you." The next day his driver, John would turn up with the wagon and Golly would ask, "Did you bring a cheque?" John always replied, "No, Paul never mentioned anything about bringing a cheque." Well, as Golly says, "knowing Paul he wouldn't."

So then it would start with a series of phone calls. Paul always promising to put the cheque in the post. Usually after a few more phone calls a cheque would arrive. It would usually be post- dated for two or three weeks. Finally, Carol would bank it, then a few days later the cheque would bounce. So then it would have to be re-presented. The same thing would happen again, it bounced! The third time it would clear. Paul was very astute, he was actually working with people like Golly's money. By the time Paul paid Golly the stuff was almost in America and Paul would by that time have received the payment for it. Golly always felt that he would eventually get paid, but he always had to go through the same bloody stupid routine beforehand.

Sometimes Golly would have to go looking for Paul, of course he was never able to find him, or could he??? One day Golly and Jay were in Blackpool and Jay saw Paul Allison's car outside Jack Crawford's warehouse. Jack was another of the old Antique Dealers that Golly had dealt with for years. Now as Golly says, "To be fair, I would not have recognised Paul Allison's car but Jay did." They went into the warehouse. Golly saw Jack and said to him, "Where's Allison?" I've not seen him," replied Jack. "Well" said Golly, "His F***ing car is outside!" Jack said "He was here but he's gone." Well Golly wasn't having any of that and started looking round the warehouse, which was pretty big.

There was no sign of Paul until Golly opened a large pine wardrobe and Paul was inside laughing. He said, "I knew you were here Golly, I heard you talking, I only hid in here for a joke, I knew you would find me." "What a load of bollocks, get me paid!" said Golly. Paul went out to his car, got his cheque book and wrote Golly a cheque. Did it bounce? Golly can't remember, after all it was a very long time ago. It was a typical Paul Allison trick. He was an expert at that sort of thing. Poor old Paul died in October 2015 and in spite of all his roguish antics, Golly misses him dearly. Paul Allison was certainly one of life's characters.

CHAPTER 30

THE DITONDO BROTHERS,
LEADING INTO IMPORT AS WELL AS EXPORT

Golly feels that before we get too far into the story of G.G. He needs to mention the "Ditondo Brothers," there are three of them, Johnny, Luigi and Angelo. It was in the 1980's that Golly first met up with Johnny. His parents had come over to Manchester just after the war and settled there. As a youth, Johnny had worked in a Raincoat Factory. While employed there he used to buy raincoats from his employers and sell them to his mates at the weekends. He quickly found out that he could make more money in a couple of days selling raincoats, than he could working in the factory all week. It gave him a taste of buying and selling. This would lead him into his career as an 'Antique Dealer'.

Luigi, Golly and Johnny

Johnny eventually left the factory and started doing a bit of work for Sonny Baron, AKA 'The Baron Antiques', He was kind of his right hand man. Johnny learned a great deal from Sonny and after a while he broke away to start his own 'Antique Business' naming it 'Family Antiques'.

He bought a large shop on Bury New Road, Manchester and he also had a couple of warehouses nearby.

Golly and Carol got to know the family quite well and would visit them every few weeks, always on a Saturday. Golly would buy stuff from Johnny and then they would go out for dinner, usually to an Italian Restaurant. In the meantime Jonny's brother Luigi, who had been doing a bit of part time work for him was itching to get into the business. Luigi was doing OK anyway, he had a couple of Ice Cream Vans and a Burger Bar, all doing good business. But like a lot of people, he had a fascination for the Antique Game. Luigi definitely wanted to be a part of it.

So he sold one of his Ice Cream Vans and the Burger Bar and bought an old school building. There he created 'Partners Antiques'. His wife Kath, carried on running the remaining Ice Cream Van, and continues to do so right up to the present day. Golly would also make a visit to 'Partners Antiques' on the same day that he visited 'Family Antiques'. Then it would be off out for dinner. Jonny and Luigi knew all the best Italian Restaurants around the Manchester area and of course being Italian themselves, they were always, well taken care of. As Golly said, "There are three brothers, the third and youngest of them being Angelo." As a Manchester/ Italian you can guess what Angi did for a living, you guessed it, he had his own Ice Cream Van. He also likes to do a bit of buying and selling of Antiques, but not on the scale of his older brothers.

Golly and Carol are close friends with the whole Ditondo Family and always attend their functions, Weddings, Birthdays etc. They have also been to Italy with them, where they visited the small village where the brothers were born. The Ditondo Family think well of the Goulding Family and the Goulding family reciprocate those feelings. When Jonny finds out about this book, Golly will say to him. "It's no good you having a copy, you can't bloody read." In fact he can, but not very well. This is because of his upbringing. As a boy, coming over to England and his parents speaking only Italian. Attending an English school must have made it very difficult to adapt to. It has to be said he has made a good fist of it.

Golly remembers a story from a few years ago. Golly, Carol, Johnny and his wife Jean were driving to Italy. When they arrived at the border between Switzerland and Italy, Johnny decided to speak to the guard in Italian. The guard couldn't make out what Johnny was talking about, so he asked him, "Do you speak English?" "Yes" replied Johnny. "Speak to me in English then", replied the guard. You see, Johnny had forgotten a lot of his native language and he was obviously better at speaking English than he was at Italian. As Golly said, "We all had a good laugh at that one, including the guard."

Crossing the Switzerland / Italy border

The memory of this European trip gives Golly the opportunity to mention that G.G. Antiques, as well as being major Exporters worldwide, have also done their fair share of importing, bringing in containers from several European Countries. Golly has decided to start with the business he has done in Spain. Golly and a Dealer called Dave Morris from Salford heard about all this Spanish Furniture that was maybe forty or fifty years old and had the look of earlier French stuff.

So Dave and Golly decided they'd go to Barcelona to check it out. Golly had heard of a man called Louis Buenos, more commonly known as the 'Barcelona Bastard'. He had Warehouses around the Antique Market in Barcelona. After a day or so they tracked him down. Golly says "this bloke Buenos was a sharp as a razor and a bit mean looking. Money was his God, he was definitely Spanish Gypsy." But so what?

Golly was well used to dealing with these sort of people and he wasn't fazed by him. As Golly says, "My money is a good as anyone else's."

There was not much of a language problem because Buenos had a couple of young girls with him and they could speak part English. The next day he drove Golly and Dave out into the Country, to a place that was in the middle of no man's land. The drive took over an hour and the bloke was driving like a bloody maniac. He was purposely taking them down back roads, trying to confuse them. He didn't want Golly and Dave to remember the route, because the place they were going to belonged to another dealer and Buenos was obviously being the middleman. That was OK as far as Golly was concerned. As long as the price was right for him he wasn't interested in what Buenos got for himself.

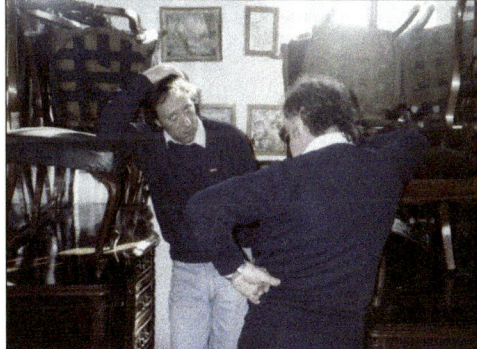

So when they'd reached their destination, Golly and Dave walked into this Warehouse and saw a mountain of furniture, all with the right look and at the right money. It didn't take long to get the buying done and that was it. Cash had to be paid on the spot but Golly was still OK with this, although

Dave Morris and Golly in Spain

the next stage was to get the stuff shifted. Always the good businessman, Golly had set the wheels in motion with his shipping agent back in the UK. They were 90% sure that a container had to be dropped somewhere around the Barcelona area.

So the next day Buenos took them out again, to the place and then wait for the container to arrive. This time he used a different route. More main roads and he was clearly trying, yet again to confuse them. They had been hanging around for a few hours when the container arrived. The driver unhooked and left it there for twelve hours. Golly and Dave worked like hell to load it and they were there until gone midnight. Louis Buenos, thinking that they would have finished loading, had come back to pick them up and he had been there since 8pm and he was just getting madder and madder. But on the other hand he could see how hard Golly and Dave were working to try and finish the job. Even so, he never lifted a finger to help them. It was 1am before they completed the job.

Now Golly knew that they had bought more than a container load, but this quite normal. The idea was to come back a month or so later and buy more furniture to top up the next load and this is what they did. In fact they did it several times, everything was flowing smoothly. Golly and Dave would fly into Barcelona. Buenos would pick them up, then take them out to the place and leave them there to work. When all is said and done he was clearly getting a good slice of commission. After a few trips, things were getting a bit more organised, for one thing the Container would already be in place by the time Golly and Dave arrived. This gave them a full day to buy and pack.

As per usual they overbought. On one particular trip Buenos took them to another warehouse, it was in the middle of a town somewhere in the hills. He had the keys to the place and through one of the previously mentioned girls, he explained that this was where he kept all his best stuff. Whether it really was his stuff Golly never found out, he just went along with it. That said, it really was good stuff, much higher quality than the items that they'd been buying from the other place. Of course the prices were higher too.

Golly waded into the stuff and bought plenty of it, as always, it needed to be shifted. This place was quite a distance from the spot where Golly had been buying from and they already had plenty of left-overs from the last trip. After Buenos had been paid the cash for the furniture he insisted that his items needed to be moved fairly quickly. It was too messy to bring in an additional Container from the UK plus Golly and Dave were flying back the following day. However Golly if nothing else has always been the man with a plan, so rang his pal Brian Curtis in Blackpool. Brian had this large truck and used to do Continental trips on a regular basis. Luckily Brian had a few free slots and said he would be able to go to Spain and collect all the items, or so they thought.

Brian drove to Spain with details of the two addresses, where he had to collect from. He had no problem getting to the first place. That was the old warehouse in the middle of nowhere. Brian arranged to meet Buenos at the second place in the middle of town. Now granted Buenos did turn up and surprisingly actually helped Brian to load his truck, but Brian was expecting his truck to be full. He thought to himself, Golly had said there would be a lot of stuff and it would be a tight squeeze getting it all on. Well Golly was right, the truck should have been full.

When Brian got back to Golly's place and they had unloaded, Golly said, "Where is all the good stuff"? "This is all Buenos gave me". Brian replied. At that point Golly knew that he had been well and truly stitched up. Yes he could have gone back and argued his case but after air fares and Hotels, not to mention the transport costs, it wasn't a viable proposition. On top of that, knowing Buenos as he did, Golly knew he would be getting a load of hassle, it wasn't even worth considering going after the missing furniture. 'The Barcelona Bastard' had scored, by keeping back all the best lots. On the other hand, he'd lost a good customer. "Good Old Louis."

Over all they'd had some good trips and done pretty well out of it, but Golly never, ever went back. As Golly says "Buenos bit the hand that was feeding him and really, it was his loss." He was one of those people that you sometimes meet in life, they just can't play it straight. Buenos just couldn't help himself. 'The Barcelona Bastard' Eh? What an apt title to have.

• CHAPTER 31 •

PORTUGAL AND OTHER CHEATS

So there we have it, Spain, it was the first country that G.G. Antiques ever imported from, but it would not be the last. A few years later they had the opportunity to buy out of Portugal. Golly met a Portuguese dealer, his name was Arnoldo. He used to visit G.G. on his English buying trips. Golly says, "Arnoldo was a tough dealer who wanted everything for little money." On one of his trips he persuaded Golly that it would be a good idea to visit his premises in Portugal. "Come over to my place in Lisbon, I've got a warehouse full of Antique furniture. It will be very good for selling on the American market" he said.

So Golly and Carol thought it was worth a look and made the journey over there. Sure enough 'Arnoldo' did have plenty of items, but his prices were very high. After a couple of days spent negoti-

Arnoldo & Golly in Lisbon

ating, Golly managed to pick out a container load. As usual an empty container was dropped off at Arnoldo's warehouse and his workers would pack it for him. They went through this process several times, now as Golly says, "You can never pick out the exact amount of stuff to fill a container. Sometimes it's over, sometimes it's under".

If and when Golly over-bought, the left over goods would just sit in Arnoldo's warehouse until his next visit and then be topped up with new purchases. When or if it was a case of not buying enough, Arnoldo

240

would top it up himself with Golly's permission. Golly trusted him to do this fairly and at first Arnoldo showed that he could be trusted. But as time went by the top up goods were getting worse and worse. Finally, Golly had to call it a day.

Arnoldo's backyard

Things came to head after Golly had been to Lisbon on one of his many buying trips and he was only able to fill two thirds of the container. As usual Arnoldo offered to fill up the rest. Golly didn't really have much choice but to let him do it and he did. When the container arrived at G.G. Antiques about a week or so later, Golly's lads were horrified to see all the crap that Arnoldo had included, in order to fill the container. As Golly explains. "Talk about scraping the bottom of the barrel. Low end goods, woodworm, plenty of damage, plus a large bill, for the extra stuff, which amounted to several thousand pounds." Golly rang Arnoldo right away saying. "You cheeky bastard, I am not buying this F***ing Crap!!" Arnoldo had no choice but to hold his hands up and go along with it. He had already been paid for the stuff Golly had picked out, but he

Portugese beds bought in Lisbon

would get nothing for the extras. So he said, "I will send Alan to pick up the extras." Alan was a Dealer from Warrington that had introduced Arnoldo to Golly in the first place. Alan did come to collect the stuff and he had to agree that the stuff was worthless.

As Golly says, "Yes the items that he'd picked out in the first place warranted the trip out there but, the freight bill had to be paid and remember it was only two thirds of a load, plus all the work of unloading the crap and storing it until Alan showed up." Yet another case of biting the hand that feeds you! Golly goes on to say, "What the Hell are these people thinking about, they have a bloody good thing going and then the blind bastards blow it!"

Golly says, "But there is more." He got to know a 'French Dealer' called 'Harvey'. He had a warehouse in Brittany and made a recommendation that G.G. Antiques would do well in America with some of the 'French Furniture' from his warehouse. Golly knew the French stuff sold well in the 'United States' and was keen to check it out. He and Carol arranged the trip to Brittany. They decided to drive over and meet up with Harvey. He had a shop in the town and a warehouse in the countryside where he kept most of his stock. As Golly says, "This was very nice stuff a bit pricey but nice." By this time G.G. Antiques had their own articulated lorry and several of their own containers. They had dropping off places in the U.K. and different dealers would fill the containers on trust. (Bloody trust, you will hear more about that as we go on). Anyway, back to Harvey. Golly picked a decent load out of his warehouse and Jay brought out the container, which he dropped at Harvey's yard.

Golly recognised that there was enough stuff around to make it worthwhile carrying out this operation on a regular basis. So a couple of weeks later Jay went out to collect the container, bringing another empty one with him. A month or so after that, Golly and Carol drove over to pick out another load. Jay was scheduled to collect and bring out a third empty container. They had what is known in the trade as a 'Shuttle System' in place.

Everything was fine, the system appeared to be working well and Harvey said to Golly. "You don't necessarily have to make the trip every time, I know roughly what you are looking for and the price you want to pay, I will select and load up the goods for you, so that they are ready for collection." Well he did know these things, so Golly decided to try him out. Harvey did well, he was picking out pretty decent stuff. Golly would wire him the money and Jay would collect the container, always leaving an empty one. A good method of dealing, which should have continued indefinitely.

Of course it was the old story, the standard of the stuff started to decrease. The last lot that was shipped out was so bad, that Golly had to burn much of it. Meaning, G.G. Antiques had lost thousands of pounds by having to sell the remainder at half their cost. If you are following the story correct, (authors note). If you, as the reader are like me, you will be hanging on to every word. You will know that G.G. Antiques still had an empty container, stuck in Brittany. Golly phoned Harvey and told him that G.G. Antiques didn't require anything else from him and stating the reasons why. "You F***ing Robbing Frog I'm done with you." Of course, because he had one of G.G.s containers in his yard, Harvey figured, he had Golly over a barrel. He was sure that Jay would be coming back to collect it and he could then charge him an over-priced storage fee. Golly was ready for him saying, "You can keep the container." "Yes but it will cost me a lot of money to have it moved," replied Harvey, he was out in the sticks. "Pay it then" said Golly. You see for Golly, having to pay for Fuel, Ferry and Jay's wages, it was much more cost-effective to leave the container were it was.

And that is just where he left it, stuck right in the middle of Harvey's yard. For about a year, Harvey kept on ringing up about this bloody container. He just could not grasp the reasons why it was still there. To put the icing on the cake, Golly found out that Harvey, in anticipation of Golly's return, had paid his men to fill up the container. Now he had to pay them again to empty it.

Yes, you would think that Golly had learned his lesson by now, well not yet. As he says, "For every bad deal I ever made, I can show you a hundred good ones". Also it has to be said that at least 90% of the people he has ever met and dealt with, have been pretty decent. But finally in this section, Golly says that he really needs to mention his dealings in Belgium. Now Golly had known this bloke, a Dealer in Blackpool, for quite some time. He used to go and see him every week or so, to check out the stock that he was bringing in from France, on a regular basis. Golly considered him to be "a good call", this is an expression used by Antique Dealers meaning, a good buying source. Although, there was something fishy about him, in the fact that he seemed to move around a lot, for unknown reasons. Eventually, he shifted out of Blackpool and went to live in Belgium. While he was there, he made a few contacts and got himself a bit of a warehouse. With now having a base to operate from, he contacted Golly and suggested that he come over to Belgium for a mooch about and possibly buy from him. Golly, based on previous business dealings did so. Whilst Golly was over there, the bloke, apart from showing round his warehouse, also took him around the general Antique trading places, working on a commission basis. Now some of these places were keen to sell their stuff to Golly, but they just couldn't meet the prices he was comfortable paying. What was the reason for this? Well Golly is pretty sure that the bloke was also getting commission from the sellers. Golly could see them looking at each other in a shifty and guilty way.

It was so frustrating, the Belgian dealers were itching to sell to Golly, but their hands were tied. The money that Golly was offering would not get them the profit that they required, minus the commission that they would have to shell out to the Blackpool guy. So in a lot of cases they just couldn't have a deal. As Golly says, "It was so bloody obvious" this English bloke actually believed that Golly hadn't cottoned on to his scheming and conniving ways. The bloke could have done so much better if he hadn't been so 'Bloody Greedy'.

Everybody was missing out because of this Greedy, Blind Bugger. The biggest loser was the bloke himself, because he didn't have to lay any money out or take any risks. So, moving on from this stupidity. The bloke had stuff in his warehouse and Golly would buy most of it. Golly says, "No fool like an old fool". Once again, Golly started placing containers outside this bloke's warehouse and Jay would collect them and drop them off. The old shuttle system was back in place. And as on previous occasions , things were changing for the worst.

Golly would buy most of the load and the bloke would be trusted to top up the container with the right stuff. Well it soon became clear that he couldn't be trusted. He couldn't resist putting a load of crap on the back end of the containers. To cap it all, Golly had put half a dozen cases of beer on to his container, as bit of a treat for the lads in England. When the container arrived Golly said, "There should be some cases of beer in here somewhere". Well you can guess they had been nicked. When Golly questioned the bloke about the missing beer, he denied all knowledge of it. This bloke has proven himself a liar and a cheat. But do you know something? After all his underhanded ways he is still on his arse and always will be. This knowledge is what gives Golly satisfaction. People like that haven't, prospered and are never likely to.

Why oh why, do they do it? They are so thick, they can't comprehend that other people aren't like them. They are totally blind to the big picture. As Golly says, "If anyone had given him the opportunities that he has given to some of these worthless sods, he would have stuck with them for life." So there you go! Four European Countries where Golly did business and it all went tits up!! 'No more' importing for 'G.G. Antiques'.

CHAPTER 32

THE WORST AND THE BEST OF DEALERS

B ut do you know? Similar things have happened in the UK. We won't be going through them all but Golly wants to mention one instance. It invoked a bloke from Yorkshire who claimed to be a 'Jehovah's Witness'. He asked Golly's sons, Jay and Rob to place one of their containers at his place and as they bought stuff over a period of time he would just fill it. The idea was OK because this bloke, Dave Fox, (Fox by name. Fox by nature) would only pack the items that Golly's lads had already picked out. It is true to say that back in those days Jay, Golly and Rob were buying that much stuff, that they couldn't possibly keep track of it all. They were all pretty sure that some stuff never made it back to base. Say for example, that they had bought sixty or seventy 'China Cabinets' in a week and say, three or four maybe more, went missing, how would they know? It would have to be something unique before it was missed. That's what happened. Rob remembered buying two identical cabinets off Fox because they had special features. When the container was unloaded there was only one. This led to an enquiry and the checking of past lists and as it turned out there was loads of stuff that had not turned up on previous containers.

This bloke remember, was a 'Jehovah's Witness' (good or not so good, depending on one's point of view) but lying through his back teeth, he outright denied it. Golly had no hesitation in telling Fox, "You are a liar!" After a bit more grilling Fox admitted he owed 'GG Antiques a few hundred quid'. He paid bit of it, but they never got the balance. Later on his partner or ex-partner told Jay, that he was right about Fox, saying, "Oh yes he was re-selling some of your stuff to other dealers, he knew or thought, that you would never notice because you are always so busy. OK, at this stage, Golly thinks that we have heard enough of these stories and should concentrate on the nicer people in the business.

Take Larry and Marie for example, they had a great business in Honolulu, Hawaii and were good people. Larry used to come over from Hawaii every few months and buy two or three container loads of Antiques from G.G. Meanwhile, over in the 'United States' his wife Maria looked after the shop. They had two daughters, Mandy and Melissa. Golly, Carol and Carol-Anne would often go over to visit them in Hawaii and Carol-Anne became close friends with Mandy and Melissa. These visits of course were business trips, Honolulu Eh ? Not a bad place to go for business trips. Larry and Maria were excellent hosts and took them to all the best places on the Island.

Antique warehouse, Hawaii

On subsequent trips they also took them to some of the other islands, such as Hawaii, known by the people over there as 'The Big Island' and another beautiful Island is Maui. But Oahu is the most famous one and Honolulu being the capital of Oahu. Everyone has heard of Waikiki Beach etc. Larry's shop was located on 'Nimitz Highway', named after the Aircraft Carrier' USS Nimitz' and was situated pretty close to 'Pearl Harbour'. In fact, a lot of Larry's customers were Military Officers, this meant that whenever Larry came over to England on buying trips, he was always on the lookout for unusual objects and Curios. Co-incidentally Golly also likes what he terms as oddball items, such as Juke Boxes, Slot Machines etc. The majority of Golly's stock is High End, Antique Furniture. Having said that, on the last occasion that I was at Golly's place, he'd just bought a Penny Farthing Bicycle and a Barrel Organ, you could hardly call those furniture.

When he was over in England on buying trips, Larry would always hire a car and wander around looking for different stuff, although he bought most of his stuff from 'GG Antiques'. One day he turned up at Golly's driving a Bubble Car that he had bought from 'Bygone Times' in Lancashire. He had paid about £3,500 for it, a lot of money but as Golly

Larry on buying trip at Gollys

looks back he says it was a great investment. Golly and Larry were chatting away and he told Golly, "No one has ever seen a three wheel car over in the States. They wouldn't be allowed on the roads anyway." "Come to think of it I have never seen one over there" Golly replied. Golly then said "Oh yes there are lots of three wheeled cars over here and you can still buy them brand new." "Really, is that so?" replied Larry. "Yes, Reliant Robins" Golly informed him. "I wouldn't mind trying a couple of those" said Larry. That evening Golly looked through the local paper and found one for sale, about £250 as Golly recalls. He bought it the next morning and showed it to Larry, "There you go" he said, "You could have ten of these for the price of that Bubble Car." Golly had quoted him £350 which was fair enough. Larry couldn't believe his luck, saying, "Oh yes I definitely want it and more of them too, if you think you can find them."

Golly replied, "I will get you a few over the next month or two, they're not common but, there are a few about and usually they are that kind of money, £300 to £400." Larry was delighted. You see to most Americans who have never seen a Three

Reliant Robin

wheeled car, it is not just a car. It is a great novelty. 'GG Antiques' have been, responsible for shipping out a great number of 'Reliant Robins' to many States across America. As Golly says, you hardly ever see them around these days and if you do see one they are usually expensive, especially the vans."

People usually have them painted yellow and then have them sign written with 'Trotters Independent Traders', giving a nod to the TV programme 'Only Fools and Horses'. Needless to say there are one or two around the Blackpool area, outside Car Showrooms. As Golly mentioned to me, "I wouldn't mind having one again, it would look kind of catchy, parked up in 'G.G.'s yard."

After a few successful years, Larry sold the business in Hawaii. He, Maria and family moved to Las Vegas and opened up another Antique Business. Naturally, they still used 'G.G.Antiques' as their main supplier. Golly and Carol had visited Las Vegas many years before, but again

Maria, Larry, Golly & Carol having dinner at Iranian restaurant

had many good return trips out there visiting old friends and clients.

Golly with a Magnum in Hawaii

Business trips, of course. They used to stay at Larry's house sometimes, but more often than not they would stay at one of the Casinos out on 'The Strip'.

One particular afternoon when they were at Larry's place he opened up the newspaper said to Golly, "Have a look on that page and tell me where you want to go tonight" As Golly says, "You can imagine how many big Shows that were on offer in Vegas, you would be spoiled for choice." Of course Carol and Golly had seen some of the shows before on their previous trips. What Golly did spot was that 'The Jordanaires' were appearing at one of the smaller Casinos. Big by U.K .standards, but not on the same level as 'Caesar's Palace' or others similar. 'Guess What'...'No Contest'....'The Jordanaires' Show was a 'Dead Certainty'.

Golly was pretty sure that Larry didn't really know who 'The Jordanaires' were. Golly says, "Of course all you readers know who they are don't you? No? I guess some of you don't'. Well in my opinion and that of the author, You Should. OK, for those of you who don't know, 'The Jordanaires' were Elvis's vocal backing group throughout the 1950's and the early 1960's. They sang on hundreds of records and appeared in dozens of movies.

Elvis first spotted them when they were appearing as a Gospel Group. He was so impressed that he pulled them into the recording studio to back him on one of his early recordings. It was a success and after that they went everywhere with him. Golly has so much respect for them as he says, "Those great, early Elvis recordings would have been nothing without 'The Jordanaires'."

So that night Carol, Golly, Maria and Larry all went to the show and what a great show it was. After the show 'The Jordanaires' came out and sat at Golly's table and they were talking shop. This was right up Golly's street because he has a great knowledge about vintage music. A quote from Golly. "If they'd had that subject at school I would have been top of the class not bottom."

Golly and Carol meet The Jordanaires

You may think Golly is only interested in what he likes, well that in the authors opinion is not entirely true. Golly can hold his own on a great variety of subjects, but if you get on subjects he is really interested in his knowledge is vast and would be difficult for anyone to better. Consequently, they spent a great deal of time conversing with 'The Jordanaires'. They knew that Golly was interested in what they had to say and they were also delighted to find that Golly was interested in them and their career. He was unlike most people they meet, hungry to learn more about Elvis.

Naturally Elvis's name came up, but they could clearly recognise that Golly was not looking to prise information about him from them. One thing they did tell Golly about Elvis was how generous he was and the gifts he used to give to people. For example, on one occasion someone admired Elvis's Cadillac, Elvis just said "There you go, here are the keys, take it, it's yours." Things like that just go to show what a lovely person Elvis was. Extremely generous, he always treated people well and respectfully.

Gordon Stokes, leader of 'The Jordanaires' told Golly."We still go out on tour and can be away for quite some time but when I get home there's always a bunch of Royalty Cheques waiting in the mail box. 'The Jordanaires' were on almost all of Elvis's recordings, between the years 1956 and 1964, 'The Golden Years of Elvis Presley'. How amazing that all those years later they are still earning money from them.

What a great evening it was. Especially after the show. Golly and Carol were even invited out for breakfast the next morning, by 'The Jordanaires'. Golly says, "Thank you Larry for showing me that newspaper, if you hadn't done that, I would never have known that 'The Jordanaires' were even in Town. I would have missed out on a fabulous experience."

Now back in those times 'G.G. Antique Wholesalers' were supplying customers in forty different States. Of course in some of the larger States like California and Texas they would have several Importers on their books. The demand for 'English Antiques' was huge. Golly was actually turning down business because of his loyalty to his existing customers. Authors note, I believe that apart from his incredible business acumen, the reason for Golly's success and longevity in the business is his loyalty to the people who treat him right. He is a credit to his family and himself. Golly would only take on new Dealers if they were operating at least two hundred miles from his existing customers.

In Golly's eyes it would not be fair to have more than one Dealer in the same area. People would say to him, "You are mad to turn business away." But that's the way it is if you do business with Golly Goulding. How come, one Dealer would know where another Dealer was sourcing his supply? Well if they were clever enough and Golly believes some of them were. A Dealer could hang around when a consignment was being delivered and take the container number. Then with a bit of inside information and detective work, it would be possible to trace a container right back to where it was loaded. They would establish that the supplier was 'G.G. Antiques', contact them and try to place an order.

Whenever this happened Golly would do his own bit of detective work by asking them, "How did you find us?" Going on to say, "For an accurate freight quotation, we will need your full delivery address." Sometimes he would discover that they were in the same Town as his regular clients and on the odd occasion he'd find out that they were actually on the same street. "Can you believe it?" Golly would then have to tell them the bad news by saying. "Sorry, I can't supply you, because to do so, would jeopardise my existing clients business."

When Golly told them this, more often than not the enquirer would get angry and Golly would try to explain to them by saying, "Look at it this way, if I was supplying you, what would you think of me, if I started to supply someone else, who was in direct competition with you? Some of them understood, but most of them just slammed the phone down on him. Golly found this a bit hurtful, but he didn't have any choice. As he says "Bloody Hell, I was only trying to do what is right and proper."

CHAPTER 33

NORTH TO ALASKA

One US client who definitely had no competition was Duane Hill of 'Alaska Auction Company'. Duane was up in Anchorage, Alaska. He had a great business going for him. He had an Auction House and large showrooms within the same property. Duane would buy a lot of expensive items from Golly, his containers were really high end goods. Duane would put English stuff into the showrooms and also mix in a few pieces into his regular Auction sales. Out there the things that bring the high dollar return are Native American and Eskimo items such as weapons, tools and traditional clothing etc.

Outside Duane's place, Anchorage, Alaska

But good Antiques do pretty well too. Two or three times in a year Duane would hold a 'Specialist Auction', featuring 'Vintage Whaling Equipment'. This would include harpoons, carved whale bones, and teeth. Anything really, connected to Whaling. Other interesting items that featured in his Auctions were Mastodon Tusks. The American Mastodon roamed the earth millions of years ago. Up in Alaska if you possess the knowledge and you roughly know the area to go to, you stand a decent chance of finding something interesting. It may only be a bone. But now and again you may be fortunate enough to locate an Ivory Tusk. Duane gets several of these Tusks every year and they bring a premium.

Taxidermy is also a big thing in the United States especially in Alaska, the people just love their Trophies, Grizzly Bears, Moose, Wolves etc. Alaska is full of these things. Golly and Carol have been over there to visit Duane and his family. Their reaction is "Wow"! "It is a real eye opener up there, absolutely stunning, it is like no other place on earth."

Now most people who visit Alaska go as tourists, Carol and Golly have never been in that category, they travel as guests to all the places the average tourist never sees. As Duane says, "Imagine setting foot in places where no man has ever been before." Well that is just what Duane and his Son do. They go on regular

Stuffed polar bear - can you believe the size?

Moose hunting trips, taking off for a week or two and bringing back Elk etc for eating.

Golly has been invited countless times to go on Moose Shoots and Hunting Trips. We are aware that from his very early days Golly loved weaponry and guns. Even now he holds a 'Firearms Certificate' not to be confused with a Shotgun License. Golly has 'The Real Thing'. Having them is one thing as Golly says, "You know I would have loved to go hunting a few years back, but now, I just don't think that I could kill a wild animal. I'm pretty sure that I couldn't do it. Vermin? Yes but Moose or Deer? That is something entirely different."

Golly adds, "Bloody Hell, now I know I'm Getting Old!"

On one of their trips over there Carol and Golly stayed in Duane's Winnebago RV. This being one of the giant American Motor Homes. One night they were parked up behind Duane's place when they heard a loud noise coming down the street. It turned out to be a load of kids playing with a remote controlled car. It was turned midnight and still daylight, these kids were out on their bikes running around playing. As Golly says, "I guess that's the normal way of life out there. But then again they do have long winters, very long, with only four or five hours of daylight."

Duane was telling Carol one time that, his wife Christine gets what is commonly known out there as 'Cabin Fever'. Christine, originally hails from California and to keep her sanity, she needs to spend a couple of weeks back there, during mid-winter time. As Duane says, "Not everyone can take the Alaskan Winter." Having said that, they do have gorgeous Summers. Alas! They are very short. 'Break Up' the term used, is when the snow stars to melt. Starting around May, but come mid-September, it's back again. Their Summer lasts for about four months. Although some experts say that Alaska is warming up and are predicting longer Summers. "Maybe So."

Duane is very much an outdoor person, he loves to go fishing and as you might expect he has his own boat. It is a big luxurious thing and he has often offered it to Carol and Golly for their vacation. Golly says, "We have never been able to take him up on his offer because we have such busy lives here in the UK." He goes on to say, "What an amazing situation to be in, we can go anywhere in the 'United States' as guests (and we do fit it in, as and when we can). We'd never have to pay any Hotel Bills, but that's not our style. We wouldn't dream of taking advantage of anyone."

Golly's son Jay adores fishing. In fact he has two boats of his own that he uses out on Morecambe Bay. So it was no surprise that on one particular trip when they were staying in the Winnebago, Duane booked a days fishing out on the ocean. He hired a large fishing boat including the Skipper, to take them out. So about 5 0'clock in the morning, Carol, Golly, Jay, Duane and his son set off to the fishing port, which was a couple of hours drive. The Skipper was waiting with the boat and they set sail for deep water. It took another couple of hours to reach the required depth. The fish, they were aiming to catch were Halibut.

Carol caught the first fish

They were all issued with these short rods and harnessed to the boat. Carol caught the first fish, it probably weighed thirty or forty pounds and was considered a tiddler by Alaskan standards. Every member of the party was pulling out fish, left, right and centre. It so happened, that Golly caught the biggest fish of the day. It was a seventy to eighty pounds Skate. Golly says, "It felt like I was pulling a 'Bloody Piano' up from the depths of the Ocean." It took him well over twenty minutes to reel it in and as he put it. "It was a big as a Wardrobe." Most of the fish they caught were thrown back, as Golly said "The amount of fish we caught between us would have fed the Five Thousand."

So when they got back to port Duane put a few Salmon in the cooler and gave the other fish to the skipper. As they walked round the dock they saw a Halibut being weighed. It weighed in at One Hundred and Eighty Pounds. As Golly commented, "He had thought the Skate that he'd caught was big, but it was nothing compared to the one hung up on the dock."

That evening Duane did Barbecued Salmon. Now if anyone has ever eaten Salmon Barbecued Alaskan style, they will know how good it tastes. For those

Golly caught the biggest fish

who haven't Golly, tells us, "It is so good, it almost defies description. Taste wise it's out there on its own, simply awesome flavour. Yes indeed, It was a very special day and a 'Real Treat', one that will never be forgotten."

Barbecued salmon with Duane and family

On another visit over there Duane took Golly and Carol out to a place where the Wolves lived. There were dozens of acres of land fenced off and the area was full of grey Wolves. Golly loves Wolves so the experience of being in and around them was incredible. Golly said "The wolves were surprisingly friendly." On the same day Carol saw a Brown Bear Cub, a really cute little thing and it just appeared to be wandering around on its own. Duane warned her not to go near it, no matter how cute it was. The reason being, where ever there is a cub, there will be a Mother Bear close by, who would be likely to attack and probably kill you. It should be remembered that a Bear can run at more than twice the speed of a human being, so it is no good running.

Spending time amongst wolves

There were some very memorable times in Alaska. Golly's son Jay and his wife have been over there a few times on their own. There is always plenty to see, plenty going on and they are always made very welcome. Equally, Duane still comes over to England in the winter time and always receives a warm welcome. As he puts it, "I come to try and warm up a bit." As you know, it can be frosty here, then you see Duane walking round with no coat on. He thinks it's warm. Good times with good people, Alaska has been a real highlight of life for Carol and Golly.

CHAPTER 34

CANOES, COWBOYS AND WESTERN ROUTES

So in this chapter we are going to hark back to Golly's love of boats or more specifically Canoes and Golly's childhood dream of owning one. Now Golly has had one or two canoes over the years. As you know he has been attracted to them since he saw the one his boyhood neighbour and hero David Ham used to paddle on the River Lune at high tide. David who we mention quite early in the book has had an unforgettable effect on Golly, in one or two areas.

Now with Golly's love of canoes in mind we find Carol and Golly driving through the 'Ozark Mountains' in Missouri, when Golly spotted a sign 'Log Cabins To Let'. He said to Carol, "Let's go and check these out." 'The Ozarks' run through Missouri, Arkansas and Oklahoma and they are absolutely magnificent. Without doubt, if you go there you will see some of the finest scenery in the world.

Ozark mountains, Missouri

Anyway having seen the sign for the cabins they drove down a track that would be described as a 'Dirt Road' in the 'United States'. As they were driving along, they could see a few quaint Log Cabins, running alongside a beautiful river. On the riverbank, there sat a row of 'Indian

Canoes'. Golly got out of their vehicle and went into the small office to make an enquiry. He was keen and interested in knowing more about these cabins. Golly fancied coming back and renting one for a week, later that year, or possibly the following year. He took a brochure and the following spring, they hired a cabin. The canoe came with the cabin and you could just please yourself where and when you used it.

The cabin by Kings River, Missouri

Now would be a good time to tell you that Carol does not share Golly's affection of canoes, or in fact sailing crafts of any description. So part of the deal when you hired the cabin was that the owners would drive you and the canoe about twelve miles up 'Kings River' to drop you off, then leave you to make your own way back to the cabin at your leisure. "By canoe of course" As Golly says, "What a great idea". Then going on to say. "I was pretty excited." Carol may not have been so excited but she didn't let him know it. So they got themselves a picnic hamper and few cans of cold beer and off they went .

This part of the river, although fast flowing, was pretty calm, but about half a mile along, they hit rapids. There were quite a few sharp bends as well. "Bloody Hell", said Golly. "It was like white water rafting." Well, they managed to keep afloat for a few minutes, but then they tipped over. Golly managed to keep hold of the canoe and because the river was fairly shallow they both managed to wade to the bank. Unfortunately the hamper and both of them were saturated, which was OK, as it was around 90 degrees. They sat on the banking for a while, drying out and they could see other people doing exactly the same thing. Everyone that came round that sharp bend in the river capsized and they were Americans. When Golly and Carol saw this, they didn't feel as bad about things.

The famous canoe trip down Kings river

So, they set off again and hit more rapids. They were trying to manoeuvre through the rocks and they tipped over. This time, losing a paddle. Golly ran along the bank and managed to catch the paddle as it wedged between two rocks. He went back to Carol who was sitting on the bank, she said, "Now you know where that saying comes from". 'Up the creek without a paddle'. Once more they set sail, this time, managing to make it a mile or so further before they tipped again. It seemed that they were capsizing every few minutes, but in fact they only tipped it three times during the whole journey.

The next bit of river got very narrow and there were branches hanging low over the water and they had to crouch down to get through. Then they hit some really deep water with no current at all, obviously there must have been some current below the water, but on the surface it was like a mill pond. Once again Carol came up with one of her proverbs, this time it was, "Still waters run deep". When they'd got about halfway down the river they were clear of rapids and the final 5 or 6 miles was perfect. Eventually they reached the spot where the cabin was.

Carol was so, so happy to reach it, she hadn't said anything but she had been thinking that they would never make it. That evening they went out to a local restaurant for dinner. While they were there Golly got talking to a few people and they told him that they had tipped over seven or eight times, so three, was well below average. That information made Golly feel a lot better. He didn't like the thought of 'The Yanks' taking the rise out of 'The Limeys'.

After spending a week at the cabin Carol and Golly moved up to Branson, Missouri. Branson is a well known resort town in the 'Ozark Mountains', most famous for its street line of Theatres. Golly has been telling me, "Branson is an unbelievable place, there are forty odd Theatres on the main street alone and this is a town in the middle of nowhere. It is a great American vacation spot, there are dozens of Hotels and some good places to eat."

Branson Missouri

People like 'The Osmonds' have their own Theatre in Branson. Golly and Carol have been to Branson a few times, as they have customers in Missouri, Arkansas and Oklahoma, plus all the other surrounding

States. The last time they were there 'The Platters' were appearing there, so obviously, this was a show, not to be missed.

In reality Branson is just one main street that goes on for quite a few miles. There are also side roads and back roads. It was on one of the back roads in Branson that Golly spotted a 'Mountain Lion'. Golly and Carol were in the car driving back to the Hotel and he saw this animal drinking from a stream and as they drove past, it just looked up very calmly and then carried on drinking. It clearly was a Cougar, commonly known as a 'Mountain Lion' in the 'United States'. Unfortunately for Carol she did not see the Cougar, as she was driving. As Golly pointed out, it would have been a good thing to have a camera at that moment. It really was a magnificent creature, right there on the edge of town.

Golly has spoken to many Americans about seeing the 'Mountain Lion', asking them, if they had ever seen one, none of them have. They know they're out there, but these animals seldom show themselves. So Golly counts himself very lucky to have seen one.

Golly and Carol have done and seen some really interesting stuff and be to so many places in the U.S.A. As Golly says, "He could write a book about the place" maybe he should.

People from Golly's era who grew up in the 1950's, will or should have heard and seen about the places and territories that were featured in the Cowboy films and TV shows, places like 'Abilene' and the 'Chisholm Trail'. The readers may be interested to know 'The Chisholm Trail' was the old cattle trail which led from 'Fort Worth Texas' into 'Abilene, Kansas', leading through Oklahoma, (Indian Country). It's roughly a thousand miles. Cowboys would drive the cattle on average, about twenty five miles a day, so the journey would take around two months.

A herd of mostly longhorn cattle would average 3,000 head and ten or twenty Cowboys would be hired to drive them. Each Cowboy would work in shifts and would have three horses each. The cattle had to be watched twenty four hours a day, in order to prevent stampedes and rustling. When the cattle arrived at their destination they'd usually lost quite a bit of weight, this resulted in lower prices. Because of this, there would often be trouble, arguments, gunfights and the like.

There have been dozens of films made about the famous cattle drives and the TV series 'Rawhide' was based on 'The Chisholm Trail'. Have you ever heard of 'Dodge City'? Of course you have, it was named after 'Fort Dodge' and it was one of the wildest cities in the 'Old West'. This place has so much history. It sits on the 'Arkansas River' near the 'Great Plains'.

Now the Americans that Golly knew said, 'Dodge City'? "Oh don't bother going to Dodge there is nothing there." Well there was plenty to go for as far as Golly was concerned, as he says, "What about Wyatt Earp and Doc Holiday? Wyatt Earp as many of you will remember was the Marshall of Dodge City before he moved to Wichita where his brother Virgil had just opened a new brothel for the benefit of the Cowboys, who'd been paid at Trails end."

At this time Wyatt Earp was being paid by the authorities to round up all the criminals, Golly says, "Old Wyatt Earp was not daft when there was money to be made."

'Boot Hill', the famous graveyard, so named because all the Cowboys were killed with their boots on. Well that place just sits on the edge of town and Golly just had to have a wander around it. Another of the famous places in 'Dodge City' is 'The Long Branch Saloon', this was a gambling den and the scene of many gun fights. There is a 'Long Branch Saloon' in 'Dodge City' even today, but Golly says, "It is not the original building, nevertheless Golly and Carol have been there and had a cold beer. The Saloon may just be for tourists these days, but it is still an interesting place and they still have saloon girls, just like we have seen in TV shows such as 'Gunsmoke', 'Bonanza' and 'Laramie'.

Wyatt Earp is famous for the 'Gunfight at The OK Corral', Tombstone, Arizona. Yes Golly has been there too. Wyatt may not have been the TV hero that we have been led to believe, but he had certainly lived a colourful life, Lawman, Buffalo Hunter, Miner and Brothel Keeper, he died peacefully of a heart attack in the late 1920's.

Golly thinks we should briefly return to the business profile of 'G.G. Antiques' in the U.S.A. at this point. Golly had a customer called Jim Kelly who had a vast knowledge of his home State, Montana. This place was the scene of probably the last and most famous of all the Indian Battles, 'The Battle of the Little Bighorn', often referred to as 'Custer's Last Stand'.

Jim and Golly used to talk for hours about the Indian Wars and such-like. Jim had a few relics from 'The Battle of the Little Bighorn'. At one time, anyone could just wander round the battlefield. You would never know what the place was, just by looking at it. Golly informed me that it was just like looking at a scene in the Cumbrian 'Lake District'. Now it has all been fenced off. Golly has two bullets fired from a 'Springfield Rifle' that Jim gave him. 'The Springfield' was the chosen rifle of the '7th Cavalry'. They had been dug up on the famous battlefield. To Golly they are priceless. Photo. Jim has all-sorts of stuff like that in his home and so do lots of other people from that area, as it used to quite

Golly on the banks of the Little Bighorn river

common to find such things. Golly told Jim that he and Carol had been round that area a couple of years prior to this and they had walked along the banks of 'The Little Bighorn' River and eventually found the site of the battlefield. There is also a museum nearby and a monument of 'George Armstrong Custer', with a list of the names of all the people who were killed. This list includes the names of two of 'George Armstrong Custer's brothers who were also killed at the famous battle.

Incidentally the film based on the story of 'George Armstrong Custer', 'They Died With Their Boot's On', starring Errol Flynn in the lead role, is one of Golly's all time favourite films.

Wyoming is without doubt one of Golly's favourite States, it borders Montana. The World famous, 'Yellowstone Park' sits in both States. Cheyenne, Wyoming, is included in Golly's list of the best places he has visited. It's an all time favourite. There is a wealth of historical information about the 'Cheyenne' Tribe and the Indian Wars. Oglala Lakota, Sioux War Chief Crazy Horse,

Wyoming

had relatives on the Cheyenne River Reservation and 'Sitting Bull', 'Annie Oakley' and 'Buffalo Bill Cody' all are known to have spent time in the area.

It is worth mentioning that 'Buffalo Bill Cody' and 'The Rough Riders' put a travelling Wild West show together. This show at one time featured 'Annie Oakley' and 'Sitting Bull'. The show toured Europe and several ships were needed to bring all the horses, wagons and performers across the Atlantic. 'Buffalo Bill' was invited to bring his show to perform at 'Windsor Castle' on the occasion of Queen Victoria's 'Golden Jubilee' in 1887. There was a cast of hundreds, plus

Golly firing musket in Montana and Magnum in shoulder holster

a couple of hundred horses, buffalo and other animals etc. Golly has a fair knowledge of these events, which he gathered from his visit to 'The Buffalo Bill' Museum, in Cheyenne in the County of Laramie.

Golly really does have a pretty good knowledge of the history of the 'United States', certainly more than the average American. In the meantime he is going to quickly skip over a few places such as the city of 'Deadwood' in 'South Dakota' which borders 'Montana' and 'Wyoming'. 'The Black Hills' with memories of Calamity Jane, the movie 'The Deadwood Stage' 'The Black Hills of Dakota' Do they ring a bell? There was the fake Gold Rush which led to the last of The Indian Wars. All these places are packed with history. Golly has tons more to tell but as he says, "This book is not about the history of The United States.

Golly could talk for hours about his experiences and the interesting people he has met in the U.S.A. How about 'Gouldings Trading Post' in 'Monument Valley' Utah? This is the location where all John Ford's Western Movies were made. Maybe, this will all be in the next book as this subject is about Golly Goulding's life, adventures and experiences.

• CHAPTER 35 •

STILL IN THE STATES AND MUSIC

So Golly is still in the States but we will hear a bit more on the subject of Music, rather than Antiques and American history. Although this next snippet, did happen to come about through the Antique Business. Paul Allison had introduced Golly to an Auctioneer customer of his from Houston, Texas, by the name of Jerry. He was half 'Cherokee' Indian and it was clear from his features that he had Native American Heritage. Before they actually met, Jerry thought to himself with a name like Golly, this guy could be Negro. When they did meet up, Jerry said "Thank God, I suspected that you may have been a coloured person." (Golly has put this in a more polite way than the actual words used by Jerry).

Golly and Jay having lunch with Jerry in Texas

Anyway as they began to chat the subject of music came up. Jerry knew through Paul that Golly was a musician. You will remember Paul, the guy who hid in the wardrobe. Jerry mentioned to Golly that he had acquired an old 'Gibson Guitar' some time ago, he said he knew it was OK and would be worth a few bucks. As he only lived a few blocks from his Auction House he nipped over to get it. He came back with this 1967/68 'Gibson Jumbo Guitar'. Like I said, he knew it was worth money, but he didn't know how much. So he said to Golly, "Are you interested?" "Sure" replied Golly and they struck a deal. Golly gave Jerry three English draw leaf dining tables. His cost being £120 to £150. Jerry would easily sell the tables for $800 / $900. Jerry was so pleased with the swap and so was Golly. The Guitar also came with its original case and Golly made the decision to carry it with him as hand luggage.

Gibson guitar that Golly got in a swap

Now Golly can't remember which UK airport he flew into, he thinks it would have either been Gatwick or Manchester. Anyway as he was going through customs one of the customs officers pulled him to one side and asked him, "Where did you get the guitar?" Golly being sharp minded replied, "I had it given to me by a friend." "What's it worth" asked the officer. Golly replied, "I don't know." "Come off it", replied the officer, "This is a vintage Gibson Guitar and you are trying to tell me that you don't know the value, You'll have to put a price on it" "I haven't a clue," replied Golly. "Well you'll have to put some kind of value on it." Golly said. "OK, Two quid." he knew it was a stupid answer. The officer looked at his colleague and sighed, "Let him through." That was that, Golly had managed to bring in the Vintage instrument, duty free.

Authors note: Golly assured me that it had never been his intention to try and dodge import duty. He really had no idea that there would be an issue about paying fees. It was a complete surprise to him. He just needed to think quickly. As he said, "If I had realised about the duty, I could have got Jerry to give me a low priced receipt, which would have been easy enough". But it just didn't occur to him.

Since writing this section, Golly has remembered that it must have been Manchester Airport. The customs officers would have known that he did not have the guitar with him when he flew out of the UK. That will be why they pulled him over on his return.

Today's value of the guitar. Not that much different really, about £800 or £900. Jerry would have sold the tables for somewhere around $350 each, so both parties did OK. Golly still has the guitar. It is at their house in Spain and still plays it daily when over there.

While Golly is on the subject of vintage guitars and music, he needs to mention 'Beale Street' in Memphis, the home of the Blues. 'Beale Street' Memphis, has the same kind of legendary status in the U.S.A. as 'The Liverpool Cavern' does in the U.K. It is just one of those places that all serious musicians long to put on their CV. We are pleased to say that Golly has performed in both of these iconic places. He has only appeared once on Beale Street but he has appeared many times at the most famous club in The World, 'The Cavern' Liverpool.

Beale Street, Memphis

Back to 'Beale Street', Golly and Carol were in Memphis and naturally they wanted to see the famous 'Beale Street'. Co-incidentally they were staying at 'The Heartbreak Hotel' on 'Elvis Presley Boulevard, which is more or less opposite 'Graceland'. They hadn't planned to stay there, it was just a place they had stumbled on. 'The Heartbreak Hotel' a legendary name, but really only a very standard 'Days Inn' Motel. A handy location and not too far from 'Beale Street', so they took a short cab ride and went for a bite to eat in one of the many restaurants there. After their meal they wandered down the street which was lined with Music Bars and Clubs, for example, 'BB King' has a Club there. Also on the street is the famous 'Lansky Brothers' shop. This is the place where Elvis bought all his unusual clothing. It is a fascinating place with an atmosphere that is hard to put into words. 'Blues Music' was coming from everywhere, Golly says, "There is no place on earth like Beale Street, it is magical!"

Golly holding his own with Memphis Blues band, Beale St

The first Club Golly and Carol went in to was called 'The House Of Culture'. There was a Blues Band playing and after he'd had a couple of beers Golly said to the singer, "Is it OK if I get up and play a couple of numbers with The Band?" "Sure" the guy replied. Photo. So Golly got up and did a few Blues numbers with them. The guys in the Band and the people in the audience might have thought that this English

Bloke would know a few chords, well he yes does, but he also knows a few extras as well. Golly brought the house down they just didn't know what had hit them. Golly can't remember who coined the famous quote. 'Everyone will be famous for ten minutes', But he had twenty minutes on Beale Street."

Golly says, "I gave them a good run for their money, I didn't let the side down." Authors note: There was never any chance of Golly letting the side down, he is up there with the greats, Scotty Moore, James Burton, Albert Lee, Hank Marvin, Brian Parker, Ray Fenwick and Bill Parkinson. Golly Goulding's name belongs up there with them and others. Don't take my word for, go and hear him play, you will not be disappointed.

Golly said to Carol, "Bloody Hell, I've played on Beale Street." There are not many Englishmen who can say that. As Golly says, "Memphis is a large city, but it is not a very friendly place. There are only certain places where you can really feel comfortable. 'Beale Street' is one and 'Sun Studios' is another." We shouldn't need to explain much about 'Sun Studios', because he says, most of

Sun Studios

the people who read this book should know as much as he does about the place. But just in case there are any who are not sure. 'Sun Studios' was run by Sam Phillips, it was the place where Elvis cut his early recordings. Other well known artistes who recorded there include, Johnny Cash, Carl Perkins, and 'The Killer himself' 'Jerry Lee Lewis'.

These four mentioned above came to be known as the 'Million Dollar Quartet'. But Sam Phillips had dozens more artistes on his books and they sold millions of records on the Sun Label.

The one time Golly visited the place, he got talking to the lady who was in charge of the record shop. This was interesting conversation from Golly's point of view because, Sun recordings are getting rarer and they are of course very collectable. Well during the conversation, the lady happened to mention, that she was a half cousin to 'Jerry Lee Lewis' and because of that, she had responsibility for letting out the recording studio. Golly found out that right up to the present day anyone can go in to 'Sun Studios' and make a recording. Yes this iconic studio is still open for business.

From memory Golly says that "It's not as expensive as you might think to record there." He actually negotiated a price with the lady, his reason for doing so was at that time, he was playing with the reformed 'Fontaines'. Imagine five Lancashire lads making a record at 'Sun Studios'. Maybe it wouldn't sell. It wouldn't need to. "Who Cares?" But 'Bloody Hell', wouldn't it have been a tremendous achievement.

Just on the subject of 'The Fontaines'. Golly, through Larry in Las Vegas, had the contacts to go out there and play for a couple of weeks. Not in the major Casinos, but in some of the smaller places. These would have been very prestigious venues by our standards. So a couple of weeks playing in Las Vegas and making a record at Sun Studios, it doesn't get any better than that. Golly put the idea to the lads in the group and they got a little bit excited, but the excitement only lasted a short time and they lost interest. As Golly says, "Small minded sods."

Golly & Bill reform the 'Fabulous Fontaines'

The beat goes on

THE Fabulous Fontains are reforming after nearly 36 years to do a special Christmas concert.

The band began performing their brand of rhythm and blues back in 1964 and enjoyed a tremendous two years supporting top acts such as Jethro Tull, Led Zepplin, Deep Purple and Eric Clapton.

Band member, Glen Knowles, said: "We diad a similar concert earlier this year and we expected a lot of people from the Sixties to turn out.

"We were delighted when we got quite a few younger people coming along as well to watch us perform.

"We are hoping to do a Christmas party every year from now on if this concert works and people enjoy it."

The band hope to do more musical work throughout the year to raise much needed funds for St John's Hospice in Lancaster.

The Fontains will perform at Smokey Joe's, Morecambe Street on Saturday December 23.

The doors will open at 8pm and admission to the event is £3.

The Fabulous Fontains during their heyday.

275

Carol holding Elvis' mic

Going back to Memphis, Carol's claim to fame is that she kissed the mic that Elvis sang into. While they were staying in Memphis Golly and Carol went over to Nashville for a few days, as Golly is sure you all know that Nashville is the home of 'Country Music'. Now Golly can take or leave this style of music, but Carol loves it. They did the usual stuff and visited 'The Grand Ole Opry' What really struck them was that there were Dance Halls everywhere that opened in the mornings and stayed open until late at night. There was no admission charge, not back then anyway. So you could walk in to one of these places at 11am and find couples dancing, also groups of people line dancing. The people were all dressed in traditional western clothing.

Whenever they visited the States, which was often, Golly would hunt down boots and he knew exactly where to look. He would always buy at least one pair, very often two or three pairs. He knew exactly what he wanted, 'Black Ropers' size 42 American. These boots were marketed as an everyday working boot but Golly saw them as a dress boot. He had a stockpile of them back in the U.K. Now that stockpile of boots is all used up and Golly and Carol haven't been back to the States since pre 9/11. Golly says, "We probably won't go back there again, because we have visited all the places that we ever wanted to see, many of them more than once. We would go out to the U.S.A. for two or three weeks at a time, Two weeks wasn't long enough and a month would probably have been too long. We always planned where we were going and would hire a car from Chicago, O'Hare Airport. We always flew with 'American Airlines', we qualified as frequent flyers, which had its rewards."

Golly hunting for boots as usual

As Golly says, "Yes great times and very happy memories, we certainly had more friends in America than we did in England." Returning briefly to the issue of 9/11. Carol and Golly had planned a trip, they were due to fly into Las Vegas and spend a week or so with Larry and Maria. Then it was their intention to drive through the desert and stop off in 'Palm Springs' for a few days. After that they would head on down to 'San Diego' to visit Dan. Sadly, tragedy struck on the 11th of September 2001. Now, Carol and Golly had been due to fly out on the 14th of September, but as you will recall all flights to the U.S.A. were cancelled. Nobody knew what was going to happen, so everything came to a standstill After three or four days flights got back to normal, but there were many people, Golly and Carol among them , who were not inclined to take the perceived risk of flying.

There were thousands of people who were trying to cancel or postpone their scheduled flights. Now fortunately or unfortunately, depending on your point of view, Golly and Carol's flight was going ahead, but as he said to Carol, "It is too risky, we are not going". Golly was quite right it was extremely risky. The whole world was in panic mode. They tried to change their flight but they were unable to do so and they volunteered to opt out. They lost all the money that they had paid out. Golly still hates flying but as he says, if you want get anywhere it has to be done. As we write, it is exactly fifteen years since 9/11. It really is unbelievable how quickly time passes by.

Golly would like to let us know that especially in the U.S.A. The Millennium was a big event. In Golly's opinion and I am sure many other peoples,' the Americans have a tendency to get alarmed about things and over-react. There were a couple from Oregon, Don and Judy Lacey, who had been dealing with Golly for about five years. Those two were in quite a panic about January the 1st 2000. Now granted, there had been a lot of talk and speculation about bank accounts ceasing to exist and computers crashing, the question some people were asking was, "Could this be the end of the world?" To hear the Lacey's talk this disaster could well be about to happen. This notion, coming from two highly intelligent people. It makes you think. Just what you're thinking

The Alamo

Alcatraz

is another story though. In fact Don was the 'Principal' of a University in Oregon .

Don and Judy had a second home up in the mountains and they got themselves bedded in late December 1999. They were extremely well prepared having laid in ample supplies. These supplies included six months supply of canned goods, three thousand gallons of water, hundreds of gallons of gasoline, plus guns and ammunition, basically they had the lot.

There were many more like them, can you picture them? All these people, hiding away in mountain retreats looking anxiously at the clock. Then its five past twelve on the 1st of January 2000 and nothing is any different. As Golly says, "What a bloody anti-climax, I bet that they were all disappointed really. Very, Very, Funny."

• CHAPTER 36 •

BACK IN THE UK AND THE FLORAL HALL, MORECAMBE

Golly's keen to get the narrative back to the U.K. Morecambe in particular and the 'Floral Hall'. Photo. This great Dance Hall mentioned earlier in the book was about to close down and be demolished. It had been operating as a Bingo Hall for a few years, but an old mate of Golly's, Joe Waite, brother of the famous John Waite decided to put on a final event.

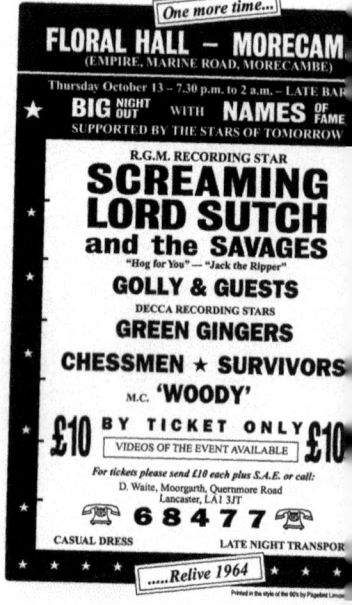

One more time...

FLORAL HALL – MORECAM
(EMPIRE, MARINE ROAD, MORECAMBE)

Thursday October 13 – 7.30 p.m. to 2 a.m. – LATE BAR

★ **BIG** NIGHT OUT WITH **NAMES** OF FAME
SUPPORTED BY THE STARS OF TOMORROW

R.G.M. RECORDING STAR

★ **SCREAMING LORD SUTCH**
and the SAVAGES
"Hog for You" — "Jack the Ripper"

★ **GOLLY & GUESTS**
DECCA RECORDING STARS

★ **GREEN GINGERS**

★ **CHESSMEN ★ SURVIVORS**
M.C. **'WOODY'**

★ **£10** BY TICKET ONLY **£10**
VIDEOS OF THE EVENT AVAILABLE

For tickets please send £10 each plus S.A.E. or call:
D. Waite, Moorgarth, Quernmore Road
Lancaster, LA1 3JT

★ ☎ **6 8 4 7 7** ☎

CASUAL DRESS   LATE NIGHT TRANSPOR

★ ★ ★ .....Relive 1964 ★ ★ ★

Printed in the style of the 90's by Pagefast Lancaster

It would be a 'Rock and Roll' Dance as it was back in the 1960's. His natural choice for top billing was 'Screaming Lord Sutch and The Savages'. Golly wasn't working with any particular Band at the time and Joe wanted him to have second billing. So he put together a bunch of his old playing mates and played under the name of 'Golly and Guests'. There were another three local groups who took part. Well Joe, pulled it off and everybody had a really good night. Golly said, "Good for him." That was the night that Dave Sutch said to Golly "You should have been one of my Savages." "I know" Golly replied. Should he? "You bet he should." If he had, Golly believes it would have been the greatest honour that he could ever have achieved. He confessed to Dave that night "Back in the 60s, if I'd had been offered a playing job, with say 'The Rolling Stones' or even 'The Beatles' and you'd offered me a job with 'The Savages' I'd have bitten your hand off" Authors Note.... "I know this to be the Gospel truth."

On the other hand he probably wouldn't have been the successful businessman he is today. As we know Golly's success has only been achieved because he was a hungry Musician who was desperate to get ahead and make something in his life. Golly is a big fish in a small pool. Is it better to be a small fish in a bigger pool? Really no one will be able to figure out the answer to that question.

Because Golly is a big fish he is fairly well known in his own back yard. Beyond that no one knows who he is. Talking of backyards, Golly was asked to be the judge of a Halloween Scarecrow competition. He was escorted round Middleton Village to look at all the gardens that people had decorated for Halloween. His role was to pick out the winner. So a local lady showed him all the places, then he had to make the choice. Well as Golly says, "It wasn't fair, everybody had tried so hard, in my eyes they were all winners." Now Golly hadn't been asked to donate a prize, but in reading this book we have come to know the character of the man, he has a real generosity of spirit. So, all the contestants received a prize. Golly bought them all gift vouchers from Argos and the kids used them to buy toys and games.

However one particular house stood out from the rest. They had a real human skeleton hanging from a tree near their front gate. Golly informed them that it was valuable and that they should take it down before someone spotted it and nicked it. Where had it come from? Golly seems to think that the young lad at the house mentioned, that his Dad had found it in a derelict building many years previously. So it was no surprise that they came knocking on Golly's door a few weeks later looking to sell the skeleton. Golly was happy to buy it for a few hundred quid. It was a nice thing. "Is there such a thing as a nice skeleton?" This was a Victorian skeleton, which would have been used by medical students. The joints held together with minute brass fittings. It was a very intricate work of art. Can you imagine trying to assemble a fully functional skeleton, with over 200 separate bones? Golly had it hanging by the coffee machine in Newfield House and every time Carol went to do the coffee it frightened the bloody life out of her, she hated it!!

CHAPTER 37

PROPERTY
AND TRAVELLING THE THREE COUNTIES

Another Couple who came into Carol and Golly's life were Naomi and Eli from Israel. Their shop was in Tel Aviv and over the years, they bought many container loads of Antiques from Golly. Eli was an ex pilot who had served in the Israeli Air force. They spoke many times about leaving Israel. They really liked the idea of moving to England, because of all the trouble in the Middle East. They already owned a house in London and fancied one in Heysham in order to be closer to 'G.G. Antiques'.

One day Eli showed Golly a newspaper from Burnley. In the property section there were many cheap houses advertised for sale around the area. Golly said "If you're looking for cheap houses, you need look no further, because there are plenty for sale in Morecambe."

The thing was, Eli had this retirement plan and he had access to a large sum of money. He was looking to invest it and try to secure his future. So he asked Golly to be on the look-out for any cheap properties. Eli tried on many occasions to get Golly to come on board as his partner in the property venture. Golly declined every time Eli asked him. He did however help him to find places and would always check them out.

The very first place that Golly viewed on Eli's behalf was a seventeen bedroom Hotel on the Promenade, West End, Morecambe. The West End used to be a lovely respectable area, sadly, now pretty poor and undesirable. The asking price was £25,000. Golly just happened to know the agent Bob. He told Golly that he had sold the property six years previously for £160,000, he sold again a year or two later for £80,000 and it just kept dropping in price. This was typical of all the properties in the West End, in fact in most Seaside resorts around the Country. Cutting a long story short, Eli bought that property and many more like it.

An example that Golly can remember is, a very large corner property at the corner of Westminster and Alexandra Road. Eli purchased that for £8,000, Crazy, Crazy Money, quite unbelievable. So does Golly regret that he didn't go in with Eli on these deals? You can bet he 'Bloody Well Does Not.' He wasn't interested then and he isn't interested now. Eli probably now, has thirty or forty properties all of which are tenanted by people who are receiving DSS payments. These tenants bring a million headaches. As Golly says, "I wouldn't have these properties as a gift if I had to run them, I would have them if I could sell them on though." Golly goes on to say, "This is a pretty unlikely scenario."

Another good friend and customer is Martin Donohoe from Kilkenny in Southern Ireland. Martin has the largest Horse Auction in Ireland and only deals in high class stock. It is worth noting than 60% of the stock that competed in the last Olympics, passed through his hands at 'Goresbridge Auction Sales'. Martin's Father was an 'Antique Dealer' and Martin and now his son John, still have a passion for the business.

Father and son come to 'G.G. Antiques' about four or times a year to buy stuff. They then sell through their own Auction House. It all gets sold regardless of whether the goods make a profit or not. Some stuff does well and some of it loses money, but that's the way it has to be. They really don't mind, because they enjoy the business. It's not all about money. They, as with Golly and hundreds of others, are in love with the job, once people are bitten by the 'Antique Dealing' bug, you can never shake it off. Golly says "I guess it's like Music, I've had a lifetime of it and I'm stuck with it. "The Best Job in the World."

Golly and his son Rob always pick up Martin and his son John at Manchester Airport and then the four of them begin the two day buying procedure, covering Cheshire, Lancashire and Yorkshire. It should be said that these are two very long days, but they are interesting days. The four of them cover a lot of ground, meeting up with all their regular Dealers. When the buying is done, all the goods have to be collected and taken back to 'G.G. Antiques' in order to be packed and then shipped over to Ireland. This whole process takes about a week.

CHAPTER 38

A HOUSE IN SPAIN

In the summer of 2004 Golly's son in law Nigel asked Golly if he was interested in a share of a large villa in Southern Spain. It seems that the owner of this villa owed Nigel a substantial sum of money for a deal they had done in London. Apparently this man was on the verge of going bankrupt so he had approached Nigel with a proposition which went as follows. He suggested that Nigel buy the villa only paying him the difference between his debt and the value of the property. In this way Nigel would be squared up for the outstanding debt. Of course he would have to fork out money to gain his payment. If you follow, which we hope you do? Golly is sure we do.

Golly has done similar things in the past, but on a much smaller scale. For example putting it in round figures, say a Dealer owed Golly £1,000 and didn't have the money, but what he did have was £2,000 worth of stock. He might say give me £1,500 for this lot, it's a good buy. Golly might turn round and say, "I will give you £1,200." "OK then" the Dealer would say. So Golly's got his money and a bit of cheap stuff. The Dealer got himself out of debt, plus a few extra quid.

Well that is how this property deal was meant to work. Deal was done and hands were shaken. Golly and Carol were chuffed to have the opportunity of being half owners of a large Spanish Villa. With its seven or eight bedrooms and half a dozen or more bathrooms, a swimming pool, large gardens and a couple of garages. "Wow what a magnificent place." The keys were handed over and Golly and Carol made a few visits. Every time they went over they took suitcases full of stuff and left it there. No money had changed hands at this stage, which was OK because it appeared that everybody was good. Then the seller announced that he wanted another 100,000 euro. Naturally Nigel and Golly told him to get stuffed. Golly was even more disappointed than Carol. It's no exaggeration to say that he was bitterly disappointed.

So Golly sent a message to the seller saying, "Get all of my luggage and other stuff sent back to England. To be fair the bloke did bring all Golly's stuff back to him at no charge. So that was that, the dream property had gone up in smoke. Golly had really been looking forward to owning a property in Spain. He couldn't get the idea out of his head. So one day he said to Carol, "Come on, we are going to Spain to look at houses, we will buy our own place." That is exactly what they did. They booked a flight and a Hotel and made arrangements to meet a Real Estate Agent over there. It was September 2004 and they spent two full days looking at various properties, they weren't impressed with any of them.

That was until the Agent took them to see these houses in a brand new development that was still under construction. They viewed the Show House, It was like a dream, it had everything anybody could ever want, Three bedrooms, three bathrooms, gardens front and rear etc and all within a gated community. A very good quality piece of property. In the site office was a scale model of the urbanisation. Eighty five model houses, with little flags on the rooftops. Almost all of the flags were green, which indicated sold, but seven had red flags.

The site manager explained. "The developer has held these back because he wants to keep them for himself, but yesterday he was saying that he may now sell them." It was easily clear to see why he'd hung onto them. These remaining houses were in the best locations. Golly had an 'Off the Record' 'Man to Man' chat with the site manager, who appeared to be a straight-shooter (he was) and he admitted that these seven properties wouldn't take any selling whatsoever. They would sell themselves. Having said all that, the developer did genuinely intend to keep at least one and use it as a holiday home for his family. Carol and Golly could see from the scale model that there was one particular property that stood out above all the others, number 36 and was undoubtedly the best one on the complex. They really fancied this property and Golly told the agent and manager. "We're seriously interested in this one, if it is for sale." The site manager whose name was Phillipe said to the agent "I'll talk to the developer and ask him if he's prepared to release number 36. Come back tomorrow and I will have an answer for you."

Golly and Carol returned on Saturday morning with the estate agent and Phillipe the site agent gave them the good news, "Pay a deposit today and the property is yours." I have to say that number 36 was priced much higher than some of the others but it was well worth the extra. They paid the deposit and signed the agreement. The next stage of the transaction was to return a month later with a larger payment. The house was due to be completed by summer of 2005. Golly and Carol retuned in December of 2004 with a substantial amount of cash which was to be their next instalment of the purchase. At this time they had not yet opened a Spanish bank account, hence the cash. It was a late flight so they took a taxi to their hotel. The next morning they returned to the Airport to pick up a rental car, leaving the money in the hotel safe.

Having picked up a hire car they drove out of the airport and headed back to the hotel. As they made the journey with Carol driving, they hit a bit of heavy traffic. A car pulled alongside of their vehicle and the driver was gesticulating and making hand signals to Golly. He wound his window down and the driver of the other car said to him, in broken English, "Your tyre." Looking back as he leaned out of the window Golly could see the back tyre on their car was going down. Carol pulled over and stopped at the first convenient place. And they both got out of the car.

The back tyre was completely flat, Golly opened the boot, got the jack out and tried to figure out how it opened, he had never seen one like it before. The next thing was that a young lad who was walking past stopped and spoke to them because he could see they were both getting stressed with the situation. He asked them, "Do you need any help changing the wheel?" He too was speaking in broken English. He took the jack from Golly, opened it up, found the jacking place and started to lift the car. "Can you manage now?" He asked Golly, "Yes and thank you so much," Golly replied. As he walked away Carol said, "What a grand lad, you should have offered him some money." Golly changed the wheel and then he and Carol got back in to the car to continue their journey back to the hotel.

At this point, Carol asked Golly "Have you seen my handbag?" They looked in the back and in the boot. It was gone! They'd been set-up. The whole thing had been a scam, the driver of the other car pulled them over, the second lad offers to help, therefore distracting them, then while this is going on a third lad takes Carol's handbag from the back seat of the car. Golly and Carol had been well and truly robbed. They drove to the Police Station in Torremolinos, where they had to fill in various statements. Everything they needed (almost) was in Carol's bag. Passports, credit cards, phone, flight tickets, camera and a small amount of cash.

They had to spend a few hours in the police station and during that time, the police told them that there was a gang operating up and down the coast and that they were not alone in their predicament. They were just two of many victims. As Golly and Carol were leaving the Police Station another English couple just happened to walking in, the same thing had happened to them. It seems that the gangs target cars with

A House in Spain

rental stickers on the back. How did they puncture the tyre? Golly doesn't know. Although the police did suggest that it could be done with a pellet or dart fired from an air pistol.

Their next job was to cancel the credit cards, Carol was told that the thieves had been trying to use them all afternoon, but they had been unsuccessful. The phone had been in continuous use, calling numbers in the Middle East. Then it was back to the airport to try and sort out their return tickets. They were due to fly back few days later. 'Monarch Airlines' told them. "In circumstances like this, your flight home will not be affected, because you have the right paperwork from the police."

The luckiest thing was that there was no real amount of money in the handbag. Golly confesses that if ever they need cash for any transaction he always dumps it on Carol. "Here stick this lot in your bag" he would say. On this occasion, by sheer luck, he hadn't. He had taken it straight out of his pockets and put it in the hotel safe. If they hadn't had a late flight the previous night, they would, as per usual have picked up their rental car as soon as they got off the plane. The awful experience of being robbed on the highway in broad daylight had well and truly shaken them up. The obvious question that crossed their minds now was, "Do we really want to be here" Golly said to Carol, "We can't let a thing like this, spoil it for us." That night, they went to a nice restaurant for dinner, as they ate and were chatting away, Carol said, "Well at least we won't need our passports for a while." Golly replied, "Oh but we do." "Why?"asked Carol. Unbeknown to Carol, Carol-Anne had booked a surprise trip to 'Centre Parks' in Holland. It had been intended as Carol's 60th birthday present. Never one to allow reversals of fortunes to effect her, Carol-Anne managed to swap the 'Dutch Centre Parks' holiday for another 'Centre Parks' in the South of England.

Even so, what a terrible experience to have suffered, sadly, not an uncommon one. Since the event they've spoken to other people about it and several people have been through similar things. For example, walking back to the car from the supermarket and discover they have a puncture. Next thing of course is the offer of help. When the gang

289

hear the reply, "No thank you, we don't need any help." they quickly move on. Early the following year this gang made the front page of the newspapers, they had been finally caught and jailed for their activities.

Golly and Carol haven't heard much about this type of crime for a few years now, but you can bet they will be operating somewhere. Golly and Carol received 100% compensation from their insurance company. They didn't jack up the claim like many people do and they easily could have done. As Golly says, "I don't want anything more than what I am entitled to, I only want what's mine." Their house was completed in August 2005 and they brought a container of furniture etc. from the U.K. Golly and Carol now have a busy social life when in the 'Costa-Del-Sol'. They have many good friends and neighbours around them. Up to press they have had close to 100 good holidays out there, so you can see the place gets very well used. Golly says "If you have a holiday home and don't use it, you might as well not have one."

CHAPTER 39

DEREK 'THUNDER'JACKSON AND GOLLY'S RETURN TO THE MUSIC SCENE

We haven't touched on Golly and the music scene for a while now and he thinks it is time we got back to it. Derek 'Thunder' Jackson who Golly rates very highly, came back to live in the Lancaster area. If you recall, Derek had left town many years ago after having had quite a lot of success with Golly in 'Citizens Band'. Golly had always hoped that Derek would return and he finally did, around 2008. Derek approached Golly in the hope that they could take up where they had left off, thirty odd years previously. Golly was delighted to receive the call from Derek in which the offer was made for him to play with his favourite Group once again.

Re-formed Citizens Band

So 'Citizens Band' was reborn with its original line up of Mick Bannon on Bass, Eric Broadbent on Drums. Eric has been credited several times in this book and he is one of Golly's old hero's. Golly on lead guitar and of course Derek on Vocals and Blues Harmonica. They were a great little Band and they soon started to get busy again. Filled with enthusiasm they bought a brand new PA system and recorded another CD. It was all going really well and with history repeating itself. The same thing happened again. Derek got fed up and things started to fall apart. Golly still works with Derek from time to time, but he would never get involved in anything serious with him again. He knows Derek, whether he intended to or not, would let him down. Really it is a great shame, because Derek is an excellent performer and as Golly says "The Best in The Business."

Just a few weeks after the group broke up, Paul Hayes phoned Golly with an invitation to his '40th Birthday Party'. He was having a Hawaiian themed party at his home. As you know Golly has known Paul for many years, in fact Golly knows the family very well. So on August the 4th 2010. Golly and Carol attended and it was a really good night and went on fairly late. Paul's brother Sean had a Karaoke System rigged up and various people, including Paul, got up to do a bit of singing. Paul sang a few Elvis numbers and was clearly enjoying himself.

Afterwards, Golly said to Paul. "I didn't know that you were into that stuff". Paul replied, "I love all that vintage Rock and Roll music." Up until then and especially after all the years he'd known him, Golly had no idea that Paul was a music freak. Co-incidentally on the same road as Paul's house, Gary Pugh, Golly's long time friend and Bass player was the Landlord of 'The Park Hotel' which was situated on the corner and Golly was due to play there the following Friday. He'd put a scratch Band together with Garry, Derek and Eric. They were just doing it for the fun of it. So, he said to Paul, "Why don't you nip down and check us out. Now just as Golly had no idea that Paul was into vintage music, Paul had no idea that Golly was too. He knew that he played guitar, but he had never realised that he was a serious musician. After all, they'd only ever talked about Antiques.

Sure enough on the Friday night, Paul came in to watch the Band. He thought it was amazing and was completely in awe of them. He said to Golly, "I never realised that you could play like that." Golly replied, "I'm OK." After a bit of chit chat, Paul told Golly that he'd always dreamed of being a 'Rock n Roll' singer. "Come down to our place sometime, you can have a jam with us," Golly said. Paul took him up on the offer and came down a week later and they had a session together. He could sing in key and his timing was spot on. Golly and the other guys thought, "This lad might have something." One thing led to another and they formed a little Group.

Because Garry had the Park Hotel, they weren't short of a place to play. So after a few months of rehearsal, they did their first booking. The place was heaving. With Paul being a TV celebrity, everybody was keen to see him perform, he did so and he made a pretty good job of it.

Now when it comes to being on stage, as we all know, Paul is a natural. So it was decided to go ahead and form a serious outfit. A name was needed and Golly came up with 'Paul Hayes and The Cats from the Attic'. A good, catchy name, although a play on words from 'Cash in the attic'.

The group was now up and running and the work came pouring in. Paul was constantly away filming but his weekends were virtually free. The one thing that he was always concerned about was the name of the Band, so he had a word with one of the producers at the BBC. She told him that it was OK right now but it is possible that that at some stage the BBC could change their mind and say it sounds too much like 'Cash in the Attic'. If they did there could be legal implications. Consequently there was a change of name about to happen.

Paul being the constant worrier, he let the boys in the Band know his thoughts and what had been said to him. He also revealed how he felt about it. The lads all agreed, although they knew he was over-reacting and making an issue out of something that was never likely to happen, they should come up with an alternative Band name. Garry thought of 'The Paul Hayes Collection' and that's what they decided on. That name took the Group to some of the better bookings. There have been many good spots where Golly has performed, not necessarily Theatres, but Ballrooms, Clubs and even Pubs. As Golly says, "Sometimes you can have better night performing in a friendly Pub than you can in one of the top Clubs."

One of the highlights of Golly's career was being introduced to 'James Burton'. Golly even knew all about 'James Burton' when he was at school and he left in 1962. James had been 'Ricky Nelson's' guitarist. When listening to a record, almost everyone listens to the singer and the lyrics, not Mr G, he is really only interested in the backing. "Does anyone think this is a bit unusual ? I think it could be."

An example of this is. When Golly first saw 'Lonnie Donegan' at 'The Winter Gardens Theatre' in Morecambe, he was about ten or eleven years old, he couldn't take his eyes off Lonnie's lead guitarist 'Les Bennetts'. He was in awe of his playing and his electric guitar. It has been the same all his life, always interested in the backing musicians.

Returning to 'James Burton.' People of today recognise him as being 'Elvis's' guitarist. James started playing for 'Elvis' in 1968. Why as late as 1968? The reason being, James was in such high demand and contracted to play 'here, there and every-

The very first James Burton / Albert Lee tour

where'. 'Elvis tried to pull him a few years previous, but he was under strict contract to 'Frank Sinatra'. James was 'Elvis's' Guitarist, right up to his passing which was the 16th August 1977. How about this? Early one evening 'The Paul Hayes Collection' were rehearsing at Golly's place, when Paul received a phone call from a promoter in Liverpool. He asked if the Group wanted to be backing Band for 'James Burton'. James was booked to do some Summer Shows around the North of England. This promoter had previously seen the Group perform and knew their capabilities. Paul asked Golly, "Do we want to do it?" Golly was stunned to be asked, but he replied without hesitation, "Bloody right we do." Looking back, Golly thinks that Paul and their drummer Eric were nervous about the gigs, Golly and Garry were not, they definitely wanted to do it.

Golly, James, Sue and Albert

Golly was still having difficulty believing that these gigs would actually happen and he said to the other lads. "Whether this happens or not, just the mere fact that we have been asked is enough and an honour." Well of course it did happen, a few weeks went by and the Group started to receive lists of numbers that needed learning. The first list included about thirty numbers and that soon increased to fifty. Most of these numbers were fresh to the Band, because they were all based on 'Elvis's' Vegas Years. The others were from the famous 'Aloha' Concert' 'Elvis' in Hawaii. Any musician will tell you that these songs aren't straight forward, the arrangements are so intricate. "Bloody Tricky" as our man puts it. When 'Elvis' performed in these Shows, he had 20 to 30 musicians on stage, plus male and female backing vocalists. There were only 4 of these lads and Golly knew they'd be OK. Why? "I've always played in small Bands. We just get on with it and make the most of what we've got" Golly says.

So they set about learning all this new material. By the way Paul was not included in this, he would be appearing with 'The Collection' as support act, which also meant Golly's lot would be on stage all night and that takes a bit of doing. So Golly, Garry and Eric were rehearsing without a singer. Then a week before the shows, Eric walked out, he had the notion that the group wanted to replace him. Golly quotes the reaction, "This was pure Bullshit, God Strike Me Dead, there was never any mention of such a thing, I swear." Now the group, what Group? Needed a drummer, capable of doing the job, fast!!

Garry had worked with a drummer called Frank a few years ago, so they asked him and luckily he agreed to do the gig. Frank is very good drummer with a lot of experience and he came in with confidence. So after all those months of rehearsals they had to go over it all again with Frank. They rehearsed with him for three solid days and nights. It was as good as they could get it.

'James Burton' was due to fly in on Thursday morning and perform concerts on, Friday, Saturday and Sunday nights. So on the Wednesday morning, Golly, Garry and Frank went to Liverpool and met up with keyboard player Sue Hedges. An Elvis style singer, Chris Clayton was recruited as vocalist. They rehearsed together all Wednesday afternoon and evening finishing well after midnight. Thursday morning was the same, then in the afternoon 'James Burton' arrived, ready to sit in.

Golly went to shake James's hand. He remembers exactly what he said to him. "Mr Burton, it is an honour to meet you. I've been your biggest fan for over fifty years." James responded, "It is a pleasure to meet you too Golly." That was it, friends to this day.

So the rehearsals started, Golly says, "I can tell you it wasn't easy." Sue had worked with James on many previous occasions and she knew the stuff inside out. Chris Clayton is an Elvis freak so he was OK. Golly was only playing rhythm guitar so he didn't have much responsibility. Garry and Frank were the engine room as the saying goes and they did fine. Once again they rehearsed well into the early hours of Friday morning, then again Friday afternoon. The show started at 7.45pm 'The Paul Hayes Collection' opened up with a forty five minute spot. 'James Burton' came on stage at 8.45pm and did the first half. Everything went well. Maybe a bit raggy in places, but no one in the audience knew. The second half opened up with Paul again and then James was back on stage for the final set. Paul joined them all on stage for the last three or four numbers.

The Saturday show was much the same but a little more polished and the Sunday show was spot on. As Golly says, "By the end of the Sunday show we were ready to go anywhere." They did, it was back to Morecambe for the group and James went back to Louisiana. Sue actually stayed with the Paul Hayes Collection for another year or so. It was a really busy year, they were playing Theatres, Festivals, Clubs etc. One particular gig that they class as a real achievement was 'The Royal Festival Hall', South Bank, London. How many Bands can say that they have performed there? Other highlights from that time, playing at 'The Cavern Club' Liverpool, classed as the most famous club in the world. Loads of work and some really good gigs.

Then another phone call from the promoter, to tell Golly, "James is coming over again and I am putting on a short tour of Theatres in different parts of the Country are you interested?"

"Bloody Hell", said Golly, "Here we go again."

This time 'Albert Lee' was to be included, how about that? 'Albert Lee' and 'James Burton' on stage together in the U.K. for the first time ever. This tour was to make history. Golly's Band would not only be supporting them in their own right, but backing them also. At this point as the author, I need to tell you that Albert Lee is classed by Golly as the best guitarist in the world. He has been a big fan of Albert's for many years. Albert Lee had been appearing with the 'Everly Brothers' for seventeen years. Golly, Carol, the author and his wife were at the 'Everly's Reunion Concert' at the 'Albert Hall' in 1983. Now Golly was going on tour with James, Albert and 'Vince Eager', who was the support artist.

When James comes over to the U.K. he never brings a guitar with him. He always manages to borrow or hire a Fender Telecaster. Fast thinking Golly thought there is an opportunity here. What if the guitar that 'James Burton' plays on his tour of England, belonged to Golly? So he ordered a 'James Burton' Fender Telecaster from his local music shop, Promenade Music. It had to be imported from the U.S.A. Golly also knew that James always insisted on playing through two Fender Twin Re-verb Amplifiers, (Photo) these are now classed as collectables and not easy to come by. Anyway Golly scoured the Country and bought four of them, two for James and two for Albert. These turned out to be one Hell of an investment.

This time the preparation was pretty much the same story as the last. Plenty of rehearsals etc, but more so, they had to learn Albert's stuff as well. Golly spoke with Albert about half a dozen times and Albert sent Golly a couple of CD's of his chosen numbers. Albert's big number is 'Country Boy' and in Golly's own words, "It is a bastard!" You have be a lot better than an average player to tackle that one.

By now Frank opted out of the Band once he'd learned about the forthcoming tour. He confessed that he'd been a bundle of nerves backing James, first time round. So a first class drummer was required. Golly had heard of a great drummer who had been doing a bit of playing with 'Derek "Thunder" Jackson', by the name of Pip Mailing.

Pip is only a young lad but he is an out and out pro, who was more than capable of playing anything that was required. So Golly had no hesitation in hiring him to do the tour. They did the tour it was a huge success and history was made. 'James Burton' and 'Albert Lee' on stage together in the U.K. for the first time ever. Golly still has the guitar and amps used by James and Albert during the tour. What does Golly think they are worth now? He says, "I don't know" I didn't do it for monetary value, I just wanted them for my own personal collection."

Some time down the road when Golly is no longer around, 'The Hard Rock Cafe' or somewhere similar will want to buy them, They are very special, because only one man in the world has ever played that Telecaster and that is the man himself, 'James Burton'. Also, Golly has tons of provenance to prove everything, Photo's, Posters, Footage, the lot. To Golly these things are priceless. James knows that he will never sell them. Incidentally James will not sign any guitars or music related items, not that Golly wanted anything signing, but he knows why. James told him that a few years ago, he signed a guitar for a so called fan then saw it was for sale on ebay a few weeks later. Golly spotted Vince Eager asking James to sign a guitar for him one time, James refused. Golly says, "Good on you James, I don't blame you."

Of course Golly does have plenty of signed photos, letters, posters and messages from James. One example James wrote, "Golly, when you get down to play, you really give it to them!" 'James Burton' does not give complements lightly, he talks plain and he means what he says. Golly is one of the few people who has all of James's phone numbers, business, home and cell phone. His words to Golly, "Ring me anytime, night or day, I will always be delighted to hear from you." When he told Golly that, Golly says, "I was stunned and delighted."

A couple of years ago James was topping the bill at 'The Strictly Elvis Festival' in Great Yarmouth. Golly and Paul went down to see him. When they arrived he was in the middle of a photo signing session, the queue was a mile long. He spotted Golly, who wasn't in the queue by the way and he immediately dropped everything, walked over to Golly and gave him a great big hug. Golly says, "Imagine how I felt, it was like being a rock star." Authors note: "In my opinion this is a fine example of the respect that exists between two exceptional musicians".

Incidentally Golly himself has played 'The Strictly Elvis Festival' on three occasions and has been booked to return. Returning to James. On another occasion Paul and Golly went to see him at 'The London Palladium' he was Guest Guitarist on 'The Jerry Lee Lewis Final Tour' Once again they were invited back stage and naturally there were hugs all round.

CHAPTER 40

BRIGHT-MORE PROMOTIONS LTD

Around about 2012 Golly formed 'Bright-More Promotions Ltd'. It was something he had fancied doing for many years. The idea being, that he would arrange and promote his own Shows and in so doing bring people back to the Morecambe area, where they hadn't been for decades. Just to name a few of artistes that have been included in his shows, Billie Davis, Charlie Gracie, Ricky Valance, Wee Willie Harris, Dave Berry, Herman's Hermits, The Merseybeats, The Swinging Blue Jeans, The Fourmost, The Bachelors, The Grumbleweeds, The Mindbenders, plus may others. Golly would like to thank Dave Lodge, the author of this book for putting him in touch with some of these artistes. Golly already has plans in the pipeline for many more Shows.

The venues that Golly has at his disposal include Hotels and all his Shows are ticketed events which always include a hot supper. The largest venue in Morecambe these days is 'The Platform' which is limited to two

hundred and sixty people seated at tables. This arrangement is described as cabaret style. Because of the relatively small number of people that are accommodated in this venue Golly is reluctant to bring in some of the bigger names. As he points out the ticket prices would need to be fairly high and they may not sell. It's a gamble but Golly still fancies giving it a go. "Watch this space". Golly also puts on a two day yearly event titled 'Rock Back the Clock' which is held at 'The Platform' every July. He remembers the 2014 year being the best one because it was based on 'MerseyBeat', which featured 'The Mojos' and 'The Undertakers'. Two Liverpool Groups that Golly has always admired, due to their 'Gutsy, Driving' style of playing.

2017 he has 'The Fourmost' making a welcome return appearance and 'The Tornados'. The latter, being one of Joe Meek's groups. Joe wrote their massive hit 'Telstar' in 1962 which was the first and only British instrumental to hit the number one spot in the American Charts and at the same time holding the number 1 slot here in the U.K. Golly has been a member of 'The Joe Meek Society' for many years and he knows plenty about him and all the great Musicians and Artists he recorded at his studio in Holloway Road, London, as does the author of this book.

It is a story with a tragic ending, because history tells us that in 1967 Joe shot his landlady and himself with a shotgun left at the flat by 'Heinz'.

Golly describes himself as a 'Meek Freak' and he is a great admirer of the man and his recording. Anyone who hasn't read 'The Joe Meek Story', 'The Telstar Man' by John Repsch, should definitely watch the movie made about Meek's life, 'Telstar'. Golly would be keen to put on a show that includes many of Joe Meek's artistes, for example 'John Leyton', 'The Honeycombs' and many more. Authors note, I have known John for a few years having close contact' but in recent times I have had to rely on his personal manager Steve for news. Steve has told me that John is not likely to be doing gigs in the foreseeable future. We all miss John and wish him well and hope to see him again, he is a great talent and a lovely man.

'The Paul Hayes Collection' has also done quite a bit of recording and apart from their general CD's there have been a couple of gems. Paul is known by the general public as "Mr Morecambe" and he loves the Song 'Bring me Sunshine'. Golly says, "I bet many of the readers of this book associate this song with Morecambe and Wise" people would be right to do so because they made the song famous in the 1970's due to using it as the signature tune to their popular TV shows. Well people will, I am sure be interested to know, that in fact the song was recorded in the 1960's by 'Brenda Lee'. It was also covered by 'Willie Nelson'. The author says, few people can rival Golly's knowledge of music in his era. I recommend, that if you get the chance, buy the CD and have a listen to Golly's arrangement and recording of this memorable song. It is reminiscent of 'The Hot Club of Paris' played with a jazzy/type style arrangement. It is as we say, 'A Real Gem'.

When Paul was a boy his Dad, Pete used to sing him a little song about a cowboy. He had made up. Pete was a bit like Golly in as much that he was a Dealer/Musician, piano being his instrument. This little tune had always played on Paul's mind and around 2013 he sang it to Golly saying "I would like to do something with this tune and I have an idea for a song." Golly asked him about it and Paul went on to say,

"I've written down some words, can you do anything with them"? I'd like to call it 'Credit Card Christmas'. It's based on people who buy all the Christmas stuff, using their credit cards, then, paying them off over the next twelve months. And then they go and do exactly the same thing again the following year."

Paul wrote out some words and Golly played around with them for a while and he had arranged it as a driving 'Rock and Roll' number. This really appealed to Paul. So Golly took the idea off to Spain with him, (this is where he tends to do most of his musical arrangements) and he came back with the finished product. Garry and Rod were pulled into the studio and they made the first cut of 'Credit Card Christmas'. That was the bones of the number done. Later in the week Paul and Golly returned to the studio to tidy it up. Paul needed to change a few of the lyrics and the phrasing. Then Golly created and recorded all the vocal backings and harmonies, for Garry to learn. Mick Armistead the Recording Manager added some sleigh bells and then Golly's grandchildren, Millie, Teddy, Wilsy and Jonny added a bit of chit chat. The kids were all excitedly talking at once, about what they'd like for Christmas presents. I'm sure you get the picture. This was used on the Intro and Coda and the finished product came out great.

The CD was always intended to be a fund raiser. The Group had already done a bit of fund raising throughout the year for the local 'St John's Hospice'. Vilma a good friend of Golly's, created the artwork for the cover and 1,000 CDs were ordered, just prior to Christmas. Within three weeks every copy had been sold, they didn't even manage to keep one for themselves. Mick obviously had the master recording. So they had a few more copies made. Golly still has a few for keepsakes. Garry is convinced that if it was released again it would be a success. It is a very good song and with the right plugging and promotion who knows? In any event it would only ever be released as a charity fund raiser.

We are heading towards the end of this chapter of the 'Golly Goulding' story. Paul left the band at late 2015, but there were still several outstanding contracts for 'The Paul Hayes Collection' which had to be honoured and he has been happy to do them. The final one being August 2016. Paul is now concentrating solely on his career as an 'Antiques Consultant' for a major London Pawnbrokers plus five days a week at 'The Swan' in Oxfordshire, researching specialist Antiques that are being entered for Auction. He's also just finished filming another series of 'Put your money where your mouth is' for the B.B.C. He dearly, indeed clearly, misses performing with the Band, but with so little time back home in Morecambe, he needs to spend it with his wife and family.

The Group is still going strong. They now have a new front man 'Andy Fox'. Andy is a very talented singer and he too has done a bit of telly and film work plus Theatre appearances and voiceovers. Andy has never fronted a Band before so he still has a bit to learn. It's early days yet and the Band are still working on polishing up the act. The name they chose was 'Rock-Ola', which was the name of a Band that Golly once had connections to, but after a bit of thought they extended it to 'Golly's Rock-Ola'. It is a proven fact that certain people come along to gigs just to see Golly perform. Golly himself is a bit shy about putting his name in front of 'Rock-Ola' but all the members of the band agree that Golly's name really is a bit of a draw. The name 'Golly's Rock-Ola' seems to carry a bit of weight. "So do I" says Golly. "What?" asked Dave. Golly laughing says, "Carry a bit of weight." "You are not alone" replied Dave.

On the Antique side Golly is still as busy as ever or as he says, "As busy as I want to be". He's still buying loads of stuff which he ships out to Japan, China and the U.S.A. plus several European Countries. Basically he does what he wants, when he wants. Yes he could have retired and lived comfortable life early on in his career. If he had wanted to, that is. But he didn't. Dave asked him "Do you want to now? "No" He replied, "I don't think I do, I please myself as I have done throughout most of my life. I have never answered to anybody since I left school in 1962". How many people can say that?

Carol quit her day job forty odd years ago and she has never had to go back to work. Golly says, "I have always managed to earn enough to keep the family going and they have all prospered, touch wood. None of our family are spendthrifts, but on the other hand we've never been afraid to spend money on home comforts." Golly says, "Basically we are reaping back what we have sown over the last fifty years." Golly also quotes. "It's not been easy, but as I've always said "In this life you don't get owt for nowt!"

Golly and Carol are over at their beautiful house in Spain, where he will be putting the finishing touches to this book. He says, "We have so much to be thankful for and we never, ever take anything for granted." Golly's Dad used to say, "Health is Wealth". Truer words have never been spoken.

Authors note: It has been an absolute pleasure to have been involved in putting this book together. Golly Goulding is a force of nature and is still driving forward, with many more achievements to come in his life. It has been a privilege to be allowed an insight into this remarkable man's life. My own life and that of my wife Margaret has been enriched by the time we have spent in the company of Golly and his lovely and exceptional wife Carol.

This you might think is the end, you would be wrong. This is the starting point for the many more achievements that are in store for the hard working and talented Golly Goulding, both in Business and Musically. Golly is a good friend, a man of integrity and as we used to say in my youth, "A good man to ride the river with." As I conclude my part in this I can only say that I have discovered that Golly and his wife Carol are everything that all human beings should strive to be. Thank you so much for this opportunity Golly, it has been a blast, here's to the next twenty five or more years.

Dave Lodge.

Lightning Source UK Ltd.
Milton Keynes UK
UKHW021443061219
354821UK00005B/47/P

9 781527 211353